HIKING WYOMING'S CLOUD PEAK WILDERNESS

A GUIDE TO THE AREA'S BEST HIKING ADVENTURES

SECOND EDITION

Erik Molvar

FALCONGUIDES

GUILFORD, CONNECTICUT

FALCONGUIDES®

An imprint of The Rowman & Littlefield Publishing Group, Inc.
4501 Forbes Blvd., Ste. 200
Lanham, MD 20706
www.rowman.com

Falcon and FalconGuides are registered trademarks and Make Adventure Your Story is a
trademark of The Rowman & Littlefield Publishing Group, Inc.

Distributed by NATIONAL BOOK NETWORK

Copyright © 2021 The Rowman & Littlefield Publishing Group, Inc.

Photos by Erik Molvar
Maps by Melissa Baker

British Library Cataloguing in Publication Information available

Library of Congress Cataloging-in-Publication Data available

ISBN 978-1-4930-4434-4 (paper : alk. paper)
ISBN 978-1-4930-4435-1 (electronic)

♾™ The paper used in this publication meets the minimum requirements of American National
Standard for Information Sciences—Permanence of Paper for Printed Library Materials, ANSI/
NISO Z39.48-1992.

CONTENTS

THE HIKES

This book is dedicated to the Backcountry Horsemen of Wyoming, in recognition of their efforts to maintain and improve trails in the Bighorn Mountains.

ACKNOWLEDGMENTS

Thanks first to Craig Cope and Glenn Hare of the Bighorn National Forest for providing trail information, identifying off-trail areas, and reviewing the material presented in this book. Dave Malutich, Silas Davidson, and Justin Reimer were helpful with revision information. David Baker of the Bureau of Land Management's Worland office was a wellspring of information concerning hikes in the lowlands to the west of the range. Many thanks for identifying the off-trail hiking routes in the spectacular canyon country of the western Bighorns and for reviewing the book.

Thanks to Bill Brazelton and Gene Little of the Backcountry Horsemen's Association for identifying new trails in the Battle Park area and to Lonnie Gibson of Eaton's Guest Ranch for sharing information on the Wolf Creek area. Thanks to Liz Howell of Story, Wyoming, for providing information on some of the non–wilderness areas of the Bighorn National Forest. Adeline White Wolf provided interpretive information concerning the Medicine Wheel National Historic Landmark. A special thanks to the ranger staff of the Medicine Lodge Archaeological Site, who got me to the hospital after a snakebite.

I gathered background materials at the libraries of the University of Montana and the University of Idaho. Thanks to the map collections of these universities and the Worland office of the Forest Service for providing access to topographic maps. One final note of appreciation to the crews of the *Mary Gail* and the *Sara Brix* for allowing me to use their galleys as an office when this book was transformed into its final form.

TOPOGRAPHIC MAP INDEX

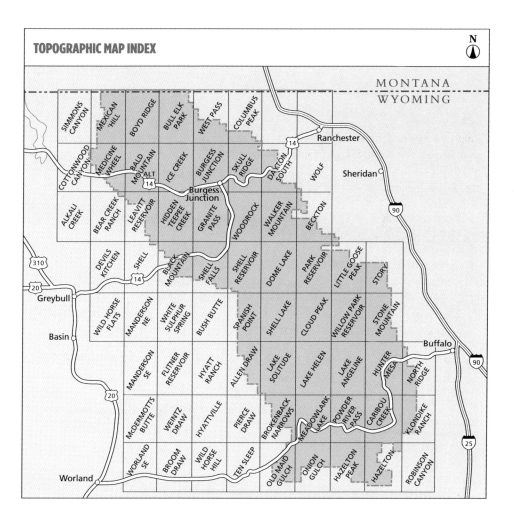

MAP LEGEND

Municipal

≡(90)≡ Interstate Highway

≡(14)≡ US Highway

≡(434)≡ State Highway

≡[27]≡ Forest Service Road

==== Gravel Road

==== Unimproved Road

······· State Border

Trails

------ Featured Trail

------ Trail

··········· Featured Cross-Country Trail

··········· Cross-Country Trail

Water Features

⬭ Body of Water

🌿 Marsh

〰 River/Creek

〰 Intermittent Stream

⫶ Waterfall

⟃ Spring

Land Features

⊓⊓⊓⊓ Cliffs

⬭ Glacier

〜9400〜 Elevation Contour

Symbols

▲ Automobile Camping

≍ Bridge

■ Building/Cabin/Point of Interest

∧ Cave

× Elevation

① Featured Trailhead

×— —×· Fence

⫮ Gate

⚒ Mine Site

≍ Pass

▲ Peak/Elevation

🎋 Picnic Area

•·•·• Power Line

🏠 Ranger Station

Ⓡ Registration Box

∴ Ruins

🏔 Scenic View

🌲 Small Park

○ Town

Land Management

▬▬▬ National Forest

------- Wilderness

▨▨▨ Private Land

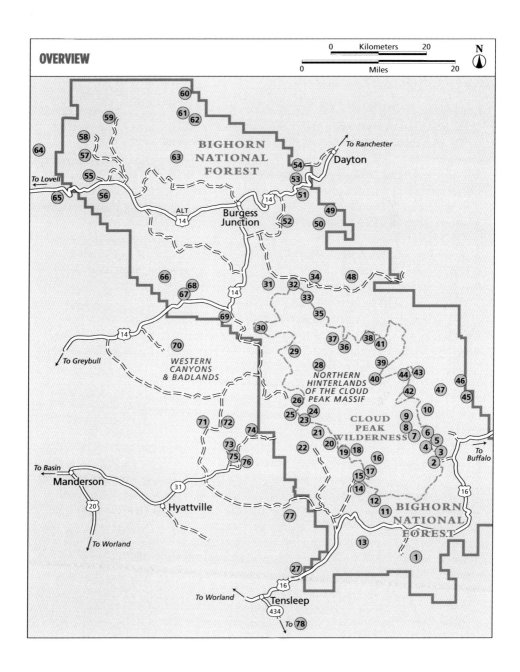

OVERVIEW

0　　Kilometers　　20

0　　Miles　　20

N

BIGHORN
NATIONAL
FOREST

To Ranchester

Dayton

To Lovell

Burgess
Junction

ALT
14

14

14

To Greybull

WESTERN
CANYONS
& BADLANDS

NORTHERN
HINTERLANDS
OF THE CLOUD
PEAK MASSIF

CLOUD
PEAK
WILDERNESS

To
Buffalo

To Basin

Manderson

Hyattville

31

20

To Worland

BIGHORN
NATIONAL
FOREST

16

To Worland

Tensleep

16

434

To 78

INTRODUCTION

Over 170 miles long from end to end, the Bighorn Mountains rise from the High Plains like a great swell on the surface of the sea. The northern half of the range has been preserved for public use within the Bighorn National Forest. The southern half has been carved up into private timber holdings and ranches. This is a landscape of deep canyons and high mountain meadows stretching for miles. Crowning it all is the Cloud Peak Wilderness, where the cliff-girt massif of granite rises over 13,000 feet above sea level. This wilderness is a wonderland of alpine lakes, sheer cliff walls, and half domes; it is the Yosemite of the Rocky Mountains.

The Bighorn Mountains represent one of the prime backpacking areas in the state of Wyoming. The range lies 120 miles east of Yellowstone National Park. Visitors who approach it from the east will find it at the crossroads of Interstate 25 and Interstate 90. Three major highways climb over the crest of the range and each has been designated a scenic byway and has overlooks and interpretive displays along the way. US Highway 16, the Cloud Peak Skyway, links Worland with Buffalo via Tensleep Canyon. It offers excellent views of the Cloud Peak massif and access to the southern half of the wilderness. The Bighorn Scenic Byway (US Highway 14) runs from Greybull up scenic Shell Canyon to Burgess Junction, then descends past Steamboat Point to reach Dayton and Ranchester. The Medicine Wheel Passage (US Alternate 14) runs from Lovell to the crest of the range. It passes through vast mountain meadows, offering access to the Medicine Wheel archaeological site and the historic ghost town of Bald Mountain City en route to Burgess Junction.

Hiking opportunities in the Bighorn Mountains are varied and extensive. The Cloud Peak Wilderness covers 189,000 acres of high alpine country, encompassing spectacular peaks, countless alpine lakes, and picturesque meadows. The eastern front of the Bighorns is typified by short, rugged canyons leading to vast grasslands that are guarded by reefs of sedimentary rock. The northern end of the range is crowned with rolling alpine meadows that stretch for miles. Along the arid western edge of the Bighorns, you can explore deep canyons and trackless badlands that remain accessible in spring and fall when the rest of the range is locked in snow. This guidebook is designed to present a comprehensive account of hiking opportunities in the Bighorn Mountains. Some visitors will be drawn to the alpine scenery of the Cloud Peak Wilderness, others to the rugged grandeur of the western canyons, and still others to the blue-ribbon trout fishing to be found in the remote corners of the range. Regardless of the trail you choose, walk softly and respect the original inhabitants of our western mountains—the wild animals that make their homes in this bastion of wild country.

THE ORIGINAL INHABITANTS

The lowlands bordering the Bighorn Mountains were occupied by nomadic hunter-gatherers as early as 12,000 years ago. These earliest explorers are thought to have wintered in the sandstone canyons at the edges of the mountains. They are believed to have made forays into the uplands during the summer months to hunt, gather the bulbs of bitterroot and sego lily, and collect chert and quartzite for making stone tools and points. They spent their autumns hunting bison in the grassy lowlands. Early inhabitants hunted bison on foot by driving them over the edges of steep bluffs and low cliffs. The animals would be funneled toward the edge by sentries stationed at regular intervals. Once the lead buffalo jumped off, the rest would follow out of herd instinct. The survivors landed in a brush corral, where they were easily dispatched by spear-wielding hunters. A kill site on Hunt Mountain in the northern Bighorns contained bison, elk, and bighorn sheep bones dating from 3,000 B.C.

Anthropologists believe that the horse was introduced to the Plains Indians during the 1700s. The horse revolutionized the way of life for the indigenous people. Hunters then could travel great distances to reach buffalo herds, and their success increased markedly. This left hunters with more time on their hands. At the same time, the horse gave tribal people a measurable form of wealth and an object of plunder worth the risk of stealing. As a result of these changes, intertribal warfare increased as tribes sent raiding parties to plunder the villages of their rivals. During this period, the Bighorn Mountains continued to draw indigenous people, who used the barren peaks as sites for vision quests and religious ceremonies. Several Indian trails from this period follow the mountain crest through the northern marches of the range. The Shoshone and Flathead peoples occupied the Bighorn Basin while the Crow, Cheyenne, and Arapaho tribes ruled the plains to the east of the mountains.

With the arrival of white explorers, the native way of life came under siege. The earliest visitors traded peacefully or trapped for fur. However, they brought with them diseases like smallpox and tuberculosis to which the native people had no immunity. Periodic outbreaks of infectious diseases wracked the Plains tribes during the 1800s, reducing their population to a tenth of its former strength. In 1861, a gold rush in the neighboring Montana Territory sparked an influx of whites into the region. The insidious invasion occurred almost imperceptibly. At first, it was only a trickle of whites who didn't stay for long. Over time, the Bozeman Trail became established to the east of the mountains and the US Army built posts on tribal lands to protect the trail.

As the numbers of white immigrants increased, the tribes began to realize that the interlopers posed a threat to their traditional way of life. Intermittent warfare broke out to the east of the Bighorns between the Indians and the white invaders and dragged on through the 1860s and 1870s. The US Army could only field a rather pitiful contingent of troops: Cavalry that had to dismount to fight and infantry totally unfit for fighting skilled horsemen on the open plains. The tribes tended to carry the day when engaging the Army in the open. The Sioux won several major victories over the US Army during this time. They wiped out a force of 81 mounted men at the Fetterman Massacre near Story, Wyoming, in 1861. In 1876, just north of the modern Montana border, a confederated force of Sioux and Cheyenne annihilated General George Custer's 7th Cavalry at the Battle of the Little Bighorn.

However, the Indians were totally unprepared for siege-style warfare and were rarely successful at dislodging Army units from fortified posts. All in all, the Plains tribes won more battles than they lost, but the US government had the advantages of better weapons technology and an almost unlimited supply of manpower. With the help of President Grant's policy of exterminating the bison to starve out the Plains Indians, the US Army was ultimately able to convince the tribes that war was a losing proposition. The tribes signed a series of treaties in which they ceded parts of their lands to the United States in return for trading goods and rations. Over time, Indian lands shrank as the United States renegotiated the treaties to squeeze the indigenous people off lands coveted by white settlers. By the time the plains buffalo disappeared in the 1880s, the Indians found themselves restricted to reservations and dependent on government aid for their survival.

EARLY HISTORY

The first white men to visit the Bighorn Mountains were fur trappers in the employ of fur baron John Jacob Astor. These independent mountain men trapped through the Bighorns and moved on, leaving few traces of their existence. With the 1860s came the first wave of settlers, mostly traders, woodcutters, and craftsmen who attached themselves to the Army posts along the Bozeman Trail to the east of the mountains. As the Sioux, Crow, Cheyenne, and Arapaho were pushed out of the Powder River Basin, large herds of cattle backed by English financial interests were driven into the country and large ranches were soon established. The cattle barons and small ranchers fought wars over dubious claims to the public domain, and hired gunmen were brought in to burn out homesteaders and eliminate any opposition through trumped-up charges of cattle rustling. Stockmen soon discovered the lush grasslands high in the Bighorn Mountains and began to drive their herds to the higher elevations for summer grazing.

As the railroads pushed their way across the continent, lumbering became a thriving industry in the Bighorn Mountains. Loggers known as "tie hacks" worked the high forests, using heavy broadaxes to rough out railroad ties. The ties were transported down from the mountains via an elaborate waterworks of splash dams and flumes. Around the turn of the century, one such aqueduct extended from the headwaters of the South Tongue River to the mouth of Tongue Canyon, a distance of over 15 miles. During the 1890s, a brief flurry of gold prospecting took place in the northern Bighorns. At one time, the boomtown of Bald Mountain City boasted 20 cabins. But the gold was never present in paying quantities and it played out quickly, so the mountains soon reverted to cattle and sheep ranges.

GEOLOGY OF THE BIGHORN UPLIFT

The Bighorn Mountains provide a textbook example of an *anticline,* a massive upward bulge of the earth's crust. As continents collided, the forces of the impact caused the bedrock to fold upward like the pleats of an accordion. Over the eons, streams coursing down the flanks of the swell cut down through the sedimentary strata, eventually forming deep canyons along the edge of the range. Erosion began as soon as the landscape began to rise. It ultimately washed away the sedimentary layers at the crest of the mountains, laying bare a core of ancient granite. Between 50,000 and 8,000 years ago (just an eye-blink in geologic time), the ice ages produced a colder climate here and mantled the highest summits in a deep layer of ice. The grinding actions of the glaciers sculpted the half-domes, sheer cliffs, and deep lake basins that have become the hallmark of the Cloud Peak Wilderness.

Bedrock Origins. The oldest rock in the Bighorn Mountains is the Precambrian granite found at the core of the range. This granite takes the form of a *batholith*, which means "sea of stone" in Greek. Over 1 billion years ago, a great body of magma, or molten rock, welled up from the superheated core of the planet. It formed a great subterranean pool of liquid rock below the Earth's surface and crystallized to form granite as it cooled.

As the cooling rock contracted, cracks formed around the edges of the batholith. Much later, major faults appeared. Many of the large faults were later filled with an igneous rock called *dolerite*, which forms dikes in the granite in the northern part of the range and accounts for the dark summit of Black Tooth Mountain. Superheated water coursed through the minor cracks, depositing minerals and trace quantities of precious metals. These minerals hardened to become the quartz veins that tantalized gold prospectors with false hopes of riches during the late 1800s.

With the dawn of the Cambrian Era 800 million years ago, the granite batholith that became the Bighorn Mountains rose as a chain of islands in the shallow sea that covered much of the central United States at that time. Sediments deposited in this sea piled up to a thickness of 1,150 feet in some places. These sediments hardened into rock over time, forming an assemblage of limestones, shales, and sandstones geologists now call the Deadwood formation. Relatively weak and brittle rock, forming slopes rather than cliffs, typify this formation. The rounded summits of Bald and Cone Mountains are composed of Deadwood sediments. These rocks form the lower slopes of Tongue Canyon.

Around 450 million years ago, during the Ordovician period, massive beds of limestone were deposited as the batholith subsided into the sea. This rock is composed of the calcium-rich outer skeletons of marine invertebrates such as corals and mollusks. This was a time of rich diversity of primitive sea life, when such exotic creatures as trilobites swam the seas. Occasionally, their calcareous bodies are found today as fossils. Over the millennia, the ocean sediments solidified into a hard form of limestone called *dolomite*, and geologists call this *stratum* (or layer) the Bighorn formation. Its castellated cliffs figure prominently in most of the major canyons on both sides of the range. It also forms a caprock over the weaker Deadwood formation, cropping up on the summits of Sheep and Medicine mountains where erosion has whittled it into strange pillars.

During the Carboniferous period, vast swamps and shallow seas covered much of the planet. During this time, many insects evolved into forms that would be recognized today. This period saw the Bighorn batholith recede into the ocean a number of times, producing a suite of sedimentary strata. Oldest is the Madison formation, a thick layer of limestone that is found in the upper cliffs of some of the western canyons. The prevalence of limestone is an indication that the surrounding land was low-lying with sluggish streams too weak to move much sand and silt into the sea. As a result, the sediments are composed mainly of particles that settled out of the seawater. The Amsden shales and limestones lie atop the Madison formation in a relatively thin and inconspicuous layer.

The Tensleep sandstone forms the upper rims of such western canyons as Tensleep and Alkali as well as the slickrock badlands found in Salt Trough and Meyers Spring Draw. On the eastern side of the range, it forms the caprock of reefs like Steamboat Point and Walker Mountain. This cross-bedded sandstone is said to be *massive*, forming a single, thick layer of great structural integrity rather than taking the form of many thin layers. Geologists believe this rock was laid down in the ocean when strong currents deposited an extensive sheet of sand over the seafloor. The youngest rock from the Carboniferous period is the Embar limestone, a weak rock that forms rounded slopes along the edges of the range.

Younger rocks crop up in the Bighorn Basin just west of the mountains. The bright crimson sandstone of the Chugwater formation is thought to have been deposited during the Triassic period when dinosaurs roamed the earth. These rocks derive their red tint from the oxidation of iron within sediments deposited on dry land following the retreat of the seas. The Colorado formation contains weak, coal-bearing strata that form badlands to the west of the range. It is underlain by the Cloverly formation, which forms the painted desert layers of Rainbow Canyon.

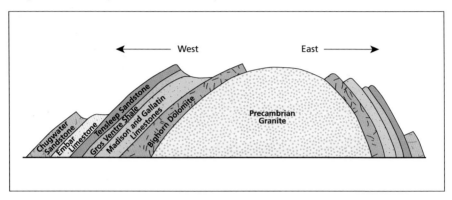

Uplifts and Mountain Building. The modern Bighorn Mountains are only the latest in a long series of geologic upheavals of the Bighorn batholith. The earliest known uplifts occurred over 800 million years ago during the Cambrian period, when the Bighorns were islands off the coast of a vast upland that roughly followed the present location of the Rocky Mountain front. The uplift continued late into the Cambrian period until, finally, a continuous landmass stretched from the Bighorn Mountains southward to the Laramie Mountains. The Ordovician period saw several uplifts and submergences. Then the batholith sank beneath the sea for most of the Carboniferous period.

The latest uplift's origins may have been in the late Carboniferous, when the landmass that became the Bighorns rose into the ocean shallows and the Tensleep sandstone was deposited. A more widespread uplift followed as the seas drained away from the North American continent. During this time, the Bighorn batholith occupied an arid region where beds of gypsum and bentonite were deposited in low-lying *playas*, the dry beds of alkali lakes. The seas returned for brief periods during the Jurassic and Cretaceous periods, as dinosaurs gave way to mammals as inheritors of the Earth.

The modern uplift that formed the Bighorn Mountain anticline began 75 million years ago during the clash of continents that created the Rocky Mountains. When comparing exposed rock at the top of the range with the same strata in the neighboring basins, the total height of the uplift is over 25,000 feet. In other words, strata found at the surface along the crest of the Bighorns are buried over 10,000 feet deep in the neighboring lowlands!

Glacial History. During the Pleistocene epoch, as woolly mammoths and saber-toothed cats wandered across the Bering land bridge and into North America, the central core of the Bighorn Mountains was locked in a deep layer of glacial ice. Seventeen major glaciers crept down from the center of the batholith and Cloud Peak rose from the ice as a *nunatak*, a mountain surrounded on all sides by glacial ice. The glaciers became the major forces in sculpting the modern landforms of the Cloud Peak Wilderness. In later centuries, the ice retreated. Today only one small glacier remains in the range, occupying

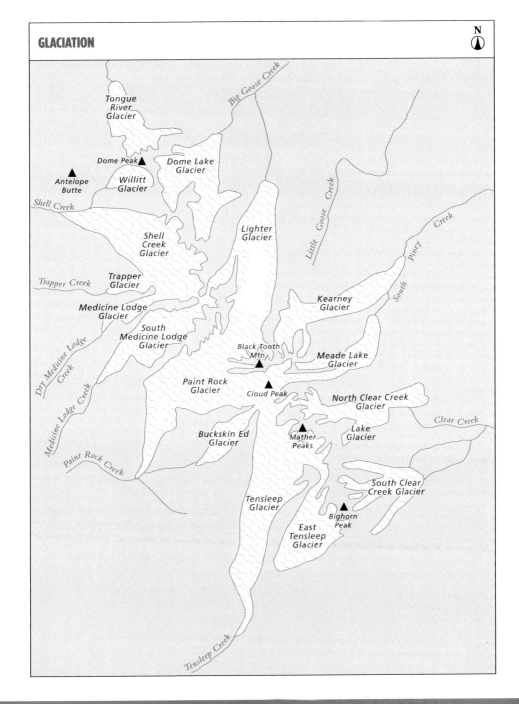

a remote basin to the east of Cloud Peak. But the vast glaciers of the Pleistocene left behind a legacy of deep lake basins and sheer cliffs to mark their passage.

Glaciers form in spots where winter snowfall is greater than snowmelt in summer. Over the course of decades, accumulating snow packs down and is compressed into ice. The ice will eventually creep downhill under its own weight. At this point, it becomes a glacier. As glaciers move, they pluck and scour at the bedrock below them. Small mountain glaciers carve out small basins called *cirques* on the mountainsides. Larger glaciers might fill entire valleys, deepening them into a characteristic U-shaped cross section. As the ice grinds away at the rock along the sides of the glacier, it carves sheer cliffs that grow in height as the glacier cuts deeper and deeper into the bedrock.

As they move, glaciers deposit ridges of rocky debris along their edges. These ridges are called *lateral moraines* and they remain behind long after the ice has receded. Bald Ridge is a lateral moraine, and the Ant Hill Trail crosses several identifiable lateral moraines. Glaciers also deposit ridges of debris at their toes, or melting points. Called *terminal moraines*, these ridges of gravel often are laid down repeatedly as the glacier surges and then melts back again. Streams of icy water typically run through tunnels beneath glaciers where friction with the bedrock causes the ice to melt. They build up sinuous little ridges of gravel in their courses, which become *eskers* when the stagnant glacier melts. These streams deposit finer sediments in a level outwash plain below the foot of the glacier.

Glaciers are responsible for creating most of the lakes in the Cloud Peak Wilderness. Some of the higher lakes occupy rock basins, where the glacier scooped out a depression in the bedrock. Other lakes occupy valleys dammed by terminal moraines and filled with water after the ice retreated. East Tensleep Lake and Lake Geneva are good examples. Still other lakes, like Elk Lake and Lake Winnie, occupy side drainages dammed by lateral moraines. The northern two of the Seven Brothers Lakes formed this way, while the remaining lakes are dammed by terminal moraines. Cirque lakes, like Lake Angeline, were scooped out later by small mountain glaciers at the heads of the valleys.

There are a number of spots in the Bighorn Mountains where stagnant glaciers buried large chunks of ice in their outwash plains. As the climate warmed, these ice chunks melted and the sediment collapsed around the edge of the resulting hole. The result was a circular depression that soon filled with water, forming a *kettle pond*. Scores of these ponds can be found in old outwash plains in several locations, most notably the Sherd Lake area of South Clear Creek and the forest north of Soldier Park.

Glaciers also had a hand in creating some of the meadows that dot the landscape of the Cloud Peak Wilderness. Many of the glacial lakes occupying shallow basins soon filled in with silt. Sedges and other marsh plants colonized these former lakes, forming wet meadows. Over time, enough silt and humus were deposited to raise the topsoil above the water table, creating dry meadows. In these diverse ways, the artistry of glacial ice sculpting the ancient granite resulted in the masterpiece of landscape art that has become known as the Cloud Peak Wilderness.

THE FORESTS OF THE BIG HORN MOUNTAINS

In the Big Horn Mountains, coniferous forest occurs wherever there is ample moisture in the soil to sustain trees. This occurs throughout the middle and higher elevations, ending at the timberline, which here is about 9,500 feet above sea level. On the arid slopes of the western foothills, conifers are generally found on north-facing slopes, which receive less sunlight (and thus lose less moisture to evaporation) during the summer months. Grasslands occupy the more arid slopes as well as limestone soils where groundwater seeps away through the porous bedrock.

The types of trees found in any given location are closely tied to the microclimate of the local area. Ponderosa pine prefers warm, semi-arid sites with good soil development and lots of sunlight. These conditions are found in some parts of the eastern foothills. Douglas fir occupies drier slopes and is fairly shade tolerant. Subalpine fir can be found near the timberline, where its conical shape makes it well adapted to deep snows. Englemann spruce requires cool sites with ample groundwater, in spots that remain free from fire for long periods. Aspen also prefers damp soils, but grows best in open sunlight. Cottonwood grows in warm sites with completely saturated soils. This tree

Mountain aster, harebells, and sego lilies are typical of mid-elevation meadows.

requires the bare gravels found after floods to become established. Finally, lodgepole pine thrives in a broad range of conditions, but its seedlings require direct sunlight and it specializes in colonizing after forest fires.

Fire is a natural and integral agent of change in the forests of the Bighorn Mountains; it is the single most important factor accounting for the forest distributions we see today. Lightning storms are a frequent occurrence in late summer. Small wildfires will often result if the weather has been hot and dry. Before the arrival of Europeans, natural fires were commonplace in the Bighorn Mountains and the native peoples may have even set fires deliberately to improve the range conditions for game animals. Much later, white cattlemen and sheep drovers set fires for much the same reason. It is only within the last century that forest fires have been suppressed systematically.

In the absence of human interference, wildfires burned small areas, creating a mosaic of conifer stands of differing ages and species. Old stands burn readily since they contain lots of downed wood and deep layers of dry needles. Young stands are virtually fire-proof through their lack of dry fuel, and they form natural firebreaks. Wildfires occurred in a self-regulating cycle, burning out the old stands and stopping at the edges of young ones. With modern fire suppression, however, all of the stands have been allowed to reach maturity. As a result, any fire started during the dry season spreads quickly and has a good chance to reach catastrophic proportions.

GLOSSARY OF SPECIALIZED TERMS

The following specialized terms relating to the natural world appear occasionally in *Hiking Wyoming's Cloud Peak Wilderness*. Rather than replace them with more common terms, we offer this brief glossary.

bald *n.* An open, rounded height of land.

blowdown *n.* Tree or trees blown down by high wind.

karst *adj.* Of or pertaining to glacial activity.

klippes *n.* Erosional remnants of a rock strata isolated at high elevations.

mead *n.* Meadow.

mere *n.* Pool of water, pond, lake.

rill *n.* Small brook.

scarp *n.* Bluff or escarpment.

tarn *n.* Alpine lake.

tor *n.* German for "tower"; refers to pillar of rock.

wind throw *n.* Tree or trees blown down by high winds.

Old tie flume.

PLANNING YOUR TRIP

It is important to gather as much current information as possible before starting out on a wilderness expedition. Self-registration permits are required for both day hikes and overnight trips in the Cloud Peak Wilderness. Self-registration stations are located at several major trailheads and these stations are marked on the maps in this book with a ★★★ symbol. In addition, Greybull, Buffalo, and Sheridan, Wyoming, have ranger stations capable of issuing backcountry permits. For further information, the Appendix at the back of this book lists addresses and phone numbers for these ranger stations. Permits are not required for routes that stay out of the Cloud Peak Wilderness, but special regulations often apply to these areas as well (see page xxxv).

The key to a quality hiking experience is good planning. Hikers who underestimate the distance or time required to complete a trip may find themselves hiking in the dark, a dangerous proposition at best. An experienced hiker traveling at a fast clip without rest stops can generally make 3 miles per hour on any terrain and perhaps more if the distance is all downhill. Hikers in less than peak physical condition or who are new to the sport have a maximum speed of 2.5 miles per hour. Note that these rates do not include stops for rest and refreshment, which add tremendously to the hiker's enjoyment and appreciation of the surroundings. Eight miles a day is a good goal for travelers new to backpacking, while old hands can generally cover at least 12 miles comfortably. We recommend traveling below top speed in order to focus more attention on the surrounding natural beauty and less on the exercise of hiking. Be sure to read the section on altitude sickness in A Few Words of Caution (see page xxv).

CROSS-COUNTRY TRAVEL

The Cloud Peak Wilderness is eminently suited to cross-country hiking. Much of the area around the skirts of the mountains is covered in open meadows and alpine tundra, a pleasant (but fragile) walking surface. Groups should spread out in a broad fan rather than hiking in single file to avoid creating new trails in pristine areas. The domes at the crest of the range are covered in frost-shattered granite, which makes hiking a slow and painstaking process. Once you navigate around the sheer cliffs, the tops of the domes offer a fairly safe traveling surface.

Cross-country travel at lower elevations is a more daunting proposition. Closed-canopy stands of lodgepole pine cover vast expanses of the foothills, and the rolling benches offer no landmarks to aid your navigation efforts. Map-and-compass navigation will be a must in such areas. Long scarps of sedimentary cliffs are also a common obstacle in the foothills and it may be nearly impossible to find a break in the ramparts to pass through.

Cross-country travelers must be constantly prepared to change their planned route or turn back when confronted with such obstacles as sheer cliffs and flood-swollen streams.

Common sense is a must in off-trail areas, where rescue is generally a do-it-yourself proposition.

DRIVING TIPS FOR THE BIGHORN MOUNTAINS

Although some of the hikes in this book can be accessed from paved highways, most of the trailheads lie at the end of gravel trunk roads or primitive jeep tracks. As a rule, *all* primitive roads (designated on maps with dashed lines) and many trunk roads turn into deep, soft mud when it rains. Folks who think they can go anywhere in a four-wheel drive have never driven the back roads of the Bighorns in a rainstorm. Some of the locals chain up all four tires on their four-wheel-drive rigs when the rain starts falling. This will get you about 100 yards down the road before the mud builds up on the chains or you dig yourself in up to your axles. If the weather is wet and you find yourself on a road that is liquefying, turn off the ignition and wait out the storm. Inconsiderate drivers who tear up the road in a futile attempt to get to pavement cause severe erosion and road damage that may lead to road closures.

The trailhead descriptions for each hike contain detailed information about specific road conditions. Watch for key words: a *trunk* road usually receives routine grading and should be passable for all vehicles in dry weather. A *fair weather* road will become an impassable mire if it rains, while a *primitive* or *four-wheel-drive* road will usually have lots of boulders or other obstacles requiring high clearance. As a result of federal funding cuts, road maintenance budgets are stretched thin, and many roadways in the Bighorn National Forest are slipping into neglect. Wise travelers ask for current road conditions before they hit the trail.

A few of the trailheads require vehicle fords on the access roads. Do not attempt these fords during spring runoff or high water that results from rainstorms. If you do attempt a ford, follow the following procedure: First, check under the hood to identify the engine's air intake (it enters the air filter compartment on most vehicles). You cannot drive across a ford where the water is deeper than this intake. Engage your four-wheel drive if you have the option. Put your vehicle in the lowest gear. Hit the water at a moderate speed, then slow down slightly to follow the low trough behind the bow wave that your car has created. Drive steadily through the water—never shift gears or engage the clutch on the way across, because this will cause water to be sucked into your engine via the exhaust pipe. Above all, use your judgment—if you have any doubts at all, you can always turn back.

HOW TO USE THIS GUIDE

The primary intents of this guide are to provide information that will help hikers choose backpacking trips according to their desires and abilities and to provide a detailed description of the trail system for interpretation of the natural features found along the way. This guide should be used in conjunction with topographic maps, which can be purchased at ranger stations, in local gift and sporting goods stores, or through the US Geological Survey (USGS).

Each trail description begins with a statistical section that gives the physical characteristics of the trail for quick and easy reference. The **General description** lists overall distance in miles and describes the hike type: day hike, backpack, extended trip, or wilderness route. *Extended* trips cannot be reached by road, while *wilderness routes* represent abandoned trails and cross-country routes, where the only indication of a trail may be an occasional cairn.

A **Difficulty rating** comes next. The difficulty rating can be interpreted as follows: *Easy* trails can be completed without difficulty by hikers of all abilities; hikes rated *Moderate* will challenge novices; *Moderately strenuous* hikes will tax even experienced travelers, and *Strenuous* trails will push the physical limits of the most Herculean hiker.

The **Route finding** entry is a measure of how obvious the trail is, and whether there are any spots where cross-country navigation will be required. Trails are rated as *No problem* if you should have no difficulty finding the route. In these cases, you can assume that trail junctions are well marked and that there is an obvious trail tread along the entire length of the route. Trails rated as having *Some challenges* are likely to have spots where the trail disappears and you may have to follow cairns or guideposts to stay on the route. Experienced hikers will be able to follow the trail, but neophytes may need to consult their topographic map frequently to avoid losing their way. Treks that follow trailless canyons also fall under this category when the route of the hike is fairly obvious. Routes that rate a *Map and compass* level of difficulty demand well-honed wilderness skills and aptitude at following topographic maps. Such routes include trails that have been abandoned for many years as well as off-trail hikes where it is necessary to navigate with the help of natural landmarks.

The **Best season** provides an index of when the trail will be passable without special aids like crampons, ice axes, or skis. It does not necessarily reflect a schedule of trail maintenance, which varies unpredictably from year to year. This is a relative measure, and late snowstorms may delay the opening of a trail beyond the time published here. Use this guidebook to get a general feel for the dates when the trail is usually open, and check with local authorities before your trip to get the latest trail conditions.

The **Visitation** entry is a measure of a trail's popularity. Trails with *Very heavy* use are often crowded. On any given day, chances are that you will meet numerous parties on trails with *Heavy* visitation. On Moderate trails, you are likely to meet a party or two, while on *Light* trails, chances are about 50-50 that you will run into one other party. On *Very light* trails, the chances of meeting other hikers are quite low.

Elevation gains and **Elevation losses** are calculated as a sum of all grades over the course of the entire hike. The **Maximum elevation** represents the highest point on the trail.

Topo maps refers to a list of topographic quadrangles that cover the trail. The US Geological Survey quads tend to be outdated, and the *Trails Illustrated*® map that covers the region incorporates the USGS errors. The appropriate quadrangle maps (several are usually required) are listed for each featured hike in this guidebook, and the *Trails Illustrated* map appears in italics if it covers the hike in question.

The **Jurisdiction** entry lists the agency that is in charge of managing the area covered by the trail in question. Direct your inquiries to this office when you seek out current trail conditions. Bear in mind that all hikes that fall within the boundaries of the Cloud Peak Wilderness require a special registration form and are subject to special regulations (see page xxxv).

The section entitled **Finding the trailhead** provides detailed directions for getting to the starting point of the hike. This section describes roads according to their ease of travel by different kinds of vehicles, and it notes weather-related difficulties.

Following this at-a-glance statistical section is **the hike,** which offers a detailed interpretive description of the route, including geologic and ecological features, fishing opportunities, campsites, and other important information. Photographs give the reader a visual preview of some of the prominent features seen along the trail, while an elevation profile accompanies each trail description and provides a schematic look at the major elevation gains and losses incurred during the course of the trip.

Next are the **Miles and Directions**, a mile-by-mile listing of landmarks, trail junctions, and gradient changes. We have used official mileage for all trails that had them. In the absence of official mileage, distances were measured by planimeter on 1:24,000 scale topographic maps.

Each featured hike has a corresponding map that clearly shows the hike route and the prominent landmarks along the way. It is not intended to be a substitute for the appropriate topographic map or maps.

A FEW WORDS OF CAUTION

Weather patterns in the Bighorn Mountains can change frequently and without warning. Cold temperatures can occur even during the height of summer, and nighttime temperatures routinely dip into the 40s and even 30s on clear nights. Thunderstorms may suddenly change cloudless days into drenching downpours, so carry appropriate rain gear at all times. Ponchos are generally sufficient for day hikes, but backpackers should carry full rain suits. Snowfall is always a distinct possibility in the high country, and backpackers should carry clothing and gear with this possibility in mind.

In most years, snow lingers in the high country into early June. Hikers who head for the high country in early summer should check with local rangers for current trail conditions. In extreme cases, ice axes and crampons may be required, especially on high passes within the Cloud Peak Wilderness. The first snow squalls typically visit the high country in early September, and by mid-October a deep blanket of snow may cover the passes.

Drinking water from the pristine streams and lakes of the Bighorn Mountains is quite refreshing, but all such sources may contain a microorganism called *Giardia lamblia*. Giardia is readily spread to surface water supplies through the feces of mammals (especially beaver) and infected humans, causing severe diarrhea and dehydration when ingested by humans. Water can be rendered safe for drinking by boiling it for at least 5 minutes or by passing it through a filter system with a mesh no larger than 2 microns. Iodine tablets and other purification additives are not considered 100% effective against giardia. No natural water source is safe, and a single sip of untreated water can transmit the illness. Symptoms (gas, cramps, nausea, and diarrhea) usually appear within three weeks and demand medical attention.

Altitude Sickness. Much of the terrain of the Cloud Peak Wilderness is at or above 10,000 feet. If you live at low elevations, you should plan to spend a day or two in leisurely activities at the high altitude before exerting yourself. Visitors who fail to acclimate themselves to the thin air may develop a medical condition known as *altitude sickness*, in which the victim becomes dizzy and nauseous and may experience headaches or a lack of appetite. If one of your party suffers from this condition, get them to a low elevation *immediately* and rehydrate them with plenty of water or juice (not alcohol, which will make their condition worse). Bottled oxygen helps, but it is rarely available when you need it. Altitude sickness is debilitating and potentially fatal in extreme cases, particularly if the victim suffers from other health problems.

Many of the wild animals in the Bighorn Mountains present a potential hazard to backcountry visitors. **Black bears** are particularly troublesome in their quest for human food. Although there have been few problems with bears up to this point, campers should hang their food in a tree to be completely safe. In camp, hang all cosmetics and food-scented items well out of a bear's reach. The food should be at least 10 feet above the ground and 6 feet away from the tree trunk. These bears are able climbers and will raid food containers that are hung too close to the trunk. At the time this book was written, there were no recent sightings of grizzly bears in the Bighorn Mountains.

Mountain lions are scattered sparsely throughout the Bighorn Mountains, although their numbers may be on the increase. Because of their reclusive habits, hikers rarely see them. However, they can present a real threat if encountered at close range. The current wisdom is that hikers encountering a cougar should behave aggressively in order to scare it off. Remain standing and never turn your back on a cougar or attempt to run away. Such behavior may incite an attack. Report all sightings at the nearest ranger station.

Rattlesnakes are rarely seen above 8,000 feet in the Bighorn Mountains, but they are common at the lower elevations. The species that is present here is the northern prairie rattler, smaller than a diamondback and with less-potent venom. The bites are painful but rarely life-threatening; seek medical attention if you are bitten.

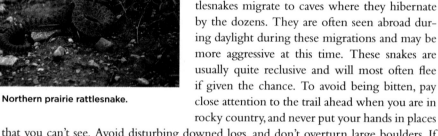

Northern prairie rattlesnakes are nocturnal during the summer months, but may be encountered on rock ledges during the morning and evening hours. During spring and autumn, rattlesnakes migrate to caves where they hibernate by the dozens. They are often seen abroad during daylight during these migrations and may be more aggressive at this time. These snakes are usually quite reclusive and will most often flee if given the chance. To avoid being bitten, pay close attention to the trail ahead when you are in rocky country, and never put your hands in places that you can't see. Avoid disturbing downed logs, and don't overturn large boulders. If you encounter a rattlesnake, hold still for a few minutes and allow the snake to retreat to a place of safety.

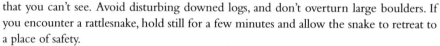

Northern prairie rattlesnake.

Other animals are more of a nuisance than a danger. Deer may hang around campsites and try to steal sweat-soaked clothing and saddle tack. At higher elevations, rodents dwelling in rockslides may chew their way into a pack in search of food or salt.

HOW TO FOLLOW A FAINT TRAIL

Some of the trails that appear on maps of the Bighorn National Forest are quite faint and difficult to follow. Visitors should have a few elementary trail-finding skills in their bag of tricks, in case a trail peters out or a snowfall covers the pathway. A topographic map and compass—and the ability to use them—are essential insurance against disaster when a trail takes a wrong turn or disappears completely. There are also a few tricks that may aid a traveler in such a time of need.

Maintained trails in the Bighorn Mountains are marked in a variety of ways. Signs bearing the name of the trail are present at some trail junctions. The trail signs are usually fashioned of plain wood, with the script carved into them. They sometimes blend in well with the surrounding forest and may go unnoticed at junctions where a major trail meets a lightly traveled one. These signs may contain mileage information, but this information is often inaccurate.

Along the trail, several kinds of markers indicate the location of maintained trails. In forested areas, old blazes cut into the bark of trees may mark the path. In spots where a trail crosses a gravel streambed or rock outcrop, piles of rocks called *cairns* may mark the route. Cairns are also used in windswept alpine areas. These cairns are typically constructed of three or more stones stacked one on top of the other, a formation that almost never occurs naturally. In open meadows, guideposts mark the route where a trail is overgrown by the grasses. Guideposts can take the form of large cairns with fence posts sticking up, or may be plastic composite strips with "Trail" decals on them

In the case of a long-abandoned trail, markings of any kind may be impossible to find. On such a trail, the techniques used to build the trail may serve as clues to its location. Well-constructed trails have rather wide, flat beds. Let your feet seek level spots when traveling across a hillside, and you will almost always find yourself on the trail. Old sawed logs from previous trail maintenance can be used to navigate in

Cairn posts mark the spots where trails cross grassy meadows.

spots where the trail bed is obscured; if you find a sawed log, then you must be on a trail that was maintained at some point. Switchbacks are also a sure sign of an official trail; wild animals travel in straight lines and rarely zigzag across hillsides.

Trail specifications often call for the clearing of all trees and branches for several feet on each side of a trail. In a forest situation, this results in a distinct "hall of trees" effect, where a corridor of cleared vegetation extends continuously through the woods. Trees grow randomly in a natural situation, so a long, thin clearing bordered by tree trunks usually indicates an old trail bed. On more open ground, look for trees that have lost all of their lower branches on only one side. Such trees often indicate a spot where the old trail once passed close to a lone tree.

When attempting to find a trail that has disappeared, ask yourself where the most logical place would be to build a trail, given its source and destination. Trail builders tend to seek level ground where it is available and often follow the natural contours of streamcourses and ridgelines. Bear in mind that most trails avoid up-and-down motion in favor of long, sustained grades culminating in major passes or hilltops. Old trail beds can sometimes be spotted from a distance as they cut across hillsides at a constant angle.

Many areas within the Cloud Peak Wilderness are managed in a trail-free and pristine state. In general, cross-country travel is possible above timberline, both below the peaks and atop the domes, limited only by the sheer cliffs (which are easy to identify on a topographic map). The traveling is slow, however, since the landscape is often covered with loose, frost-shattered granite that forces the traveler to hop from boulder to boulder. A maximum speed of 1 mile per hour is a good rule of thumb. When traveling off-trail, **do**

not build cairns, blaze trees, or hang flagging; such actions mar the pristine quality of the area and interfere with the wilderness experience of other visitors.

FORDING STREAMS AND RIVERS

There are only a few places in the Bighorn Mountains where trails cross substantial streams without the benefit of a bridge. Bear in mind, however, that footlogs and bridges can be washed out during floods. Unbridged stream crossings are labeled as fords on the maps provided in this book. Streams are typically highest in early summer, when snowmelt swells the watercourses with silty discharge. Water levels also rise following rainstorms. Stream crossings should always be approached with caution; even a shallow stream can harbor slippery stones that can cause a sprained ankle, or worse. However, wilderness travelers can almost always make safe crossings by exercising good judgment and employing a few simple techniques.

When you get to the water's edge, the first thing you'll probably think is, "This is going to be really cold!" It will be even colder if you try to cross barefooted. Since most folks don't like to hike around in wet boots all day, we recommend bringing a pair of lightweight canvas sneakers or river sandals specifically for the purpose of fording streams. Wearing something on your feet will prevent heat from being conducted from your feet to the stream cobbles and will give you superior traction for a safer crossing. Walking staffs add additional stability when wading streams. Some manufacturers make special staffs for wading with metal tips, and some staffs even telescope down to manageable proportions. If you use one of these, remember not to lean too hard on it; your legs should always bear most of the burden.

Before entering the stream, unclip your hip belt and other restrictive straps; this can save you from drowning if you fall in. Water up to knee-depth can usually be forded without much difficulty; mid-thigh is the greatest safe depth for crossing unless the water is barely moving. Once you get in up to your crotch, your body starts giving the current a broad profile to push against, and you can bet that it won't be long before you are swimming.

When wading, discipline yourself to take tiny steps. The water will be cold, and your first impulse will be to rush across and get warm again, but this kind of carelessness frequently results in a dunking. While inching your way across, your feet should seek the lowest possible footing, so that it is impossible to slip downward any farther. Use boulders sticking out of the streambed as braces for your feet. These boulders will have tiny underwater eddies on their upstream and downstream sides, and thus the force of the current against you will be reduced by a fraction. When emerging from the water, towel off as quickly as possible with an absorbent piece

A Forest Service blaze.

of clothing. If you let the water evaporate from your body, it will take with it additional heat that you could have used to warm up.

Some streams will be narrow, with boulders sticking up from the water beckoning you to hopscotch across without getting your feet wet. Be careful, because you are in prime ankle-spraining country. Rocks that are damp at all may have a film of slippery algae on them, and even dry rocks may be unstable and roll out from underfoot. To avoid calamity, step only on boulders that are completely dry, and do not jump onto an untested boulder, since it may give way. The best policy is to keep one foot on the rocks at all times, so that you have firm footing to fall back on in case a foothold proves to be unstable.

SHARING THE TRAIL

A wide variety of different user groups seek out the Bighorn Mountains as a setting for outdoor recreation. The Bighorn backcountry is a magnet for hunters, anglers, and solitude seekers of all descriptions. In the interest of a safe and pleasant outdoor experience for all, follow established regulations and exercise consideration and good manners when meeting other parties on the trail. Respect for others is the cornerstone of the traditional western ethic, a code that remains in force throughout Wyoming. A few commonsense guidelines will help you avoid bad experiences when encountering other backcountry visitors.

Motorized vehicles are allowed in many parts of the Bighorn National Forest, although they are prohibited within the Cloud Peak Wilderness and on certain other trails. Knowing the current regulations is the responsibility of the forest visitor here: ATVs may be allowed off-trail in some parts of the forest, on established trails only in other areas, while some trails are closed to all motorized recreation. On BLM land, ATVs are never allowed off established roads and trails and may be excluded from some trails entirely. Non-motorized users should expect to encounter ATVs in areas where they are allowed. It has been my experience that most ATV users in the Bighorn Mountains are courteous and thoughtful visitors who try to minimize their impacts just as other backcountry users do.

When several parties meet on the trail, the following order of priority is observed: Hikers should yield to livestock parties, traveling well off the trail and talking softly to the animals so they don't spook. Mountain bikers and motorized users should yield to both horse and foot parties. When two horse parties meet, generally it is the smaller party that should pull to the side.

LEAVE NO TRACE

One of the aims of this book is to encourage people to heft a pack and strike out on one of the trails in the wildest corners of the Bighorn Mountains. But many of these same trails already receive moderate to heavy use, and they are showing signs of wear. Erosion is a problem where an army of boots and hooves has short-cut switchbacks. Litter seems to beget more litter, especially near trailheads and at backcountry campsites. Unofficial trails have proliferated across some high alpine meadows, marring the otherwise pristine environment. Fortunately, all of these problems are avoidable—as are most impacts caused by backcountry visitors—if a few simple guidelines are heeded. Remember: the goal is to *leave no trace* of your passing.

ADVANCE PLANNING TO MINIMIZE IMPACTS

Careful planning before the trip could reduce much of the wear and tear that occurs in the Bighorn Mountains. Visitors should contact local authorities (see Appendix) to find out about areas that are particularly sensitive to disturbance or receive heavy use. The avoidance of the most popular sites can only enhance your wilderness experience since the goal of most wilderness travelers is to visit pristine and untrammeled areas.

We encourage travelers to plan their routes using established trails whenever possible, as these travel corridors are least susceptible to damage. Alpine habitats above the timberline are particularly fragile. Travelers who lack thorough training in minimum impact techniques should cross them only on designated trails. Backcountry visitors can also travel more lightly by moving about in small groups. Small groups stress the landscape to a lesser degree than do large groups, especially around campsites, and they also lend themselves to greater flexibility in route choice and on-the-spot problem solving. Groups of two to six are optimal, while groups larger than ten hikers have a greater potential for environmental damage and should be split up into smaller components.

The proper equipment can also help visitors reduce their visual presence and trampling effects in the wilderness. Dark-hued or muted clothing, tents, and packs help make you less conspicuous to other travelers. One bright-yellow or orange shirt can be carried to attract attention in an emergency. Hiking shoes with a shallow tread design are gentler on plants and soils and won't clog with mud. Backpackers can also carry a pair of smooth-soled camp shoes—sport sandals, boat shoes, or moccasins. These feel terrific after a day on the trail and they greatly reduce wear and tear on the plants and soils around camp.

ON THE TRAIL

Please stay on established trails. Cutting switchbacks or crossing previously untracked ground leaves behind footprints and trampled plants—signs that may invite the next person to follow in your footsteps. Eventually, enough footsteps lead to damaged plants and soils, erosion, and unwanted "social" trails.

If you must travel off trail, look for trample-resistant surfaces: rock, gravel, snow (if it's not too steep), or a streambed below the high-water mark. Parties traveling cross-country should spread out in a line abreast rather than traveling single file. This reduces the potential for creating new and unwanted trails and erosion in pristine areas. Leave your route unmarked—no blazes, cairns, flagging, or arrows scratched in the dirt.

As you hike along, always be conscious to reduce short- and long-term disturbances in the environment. Making loud noises can be helpful in avoiding encounters with bears and mountain lions where visibility is limited, but it disturbs the less dangerous wildlife as well as other travelers. If you do spot wildlife along the trail, be careful to respect the animal's comfort zone. If an animal changes behavior as a result of your presence, you are too close. You may also chance upon sites of historical or archaeological significance as you travel in the Bighorns. These sites are an irreplaceable treasure of national importance and are protected by federal law. Enjoy them without rendering any changes to the site.

SELECTING A CAMPSITE

On Forest Service lands, established campsites will not be marked. If you cannot locate such a site, you will need to choose an impact-resistant spot to pitch your camp. Shorelines of lakes and stream banks are particularly sensitive to disturbance. Keep all campsites at least 200 feet from the nearest lake or stream. Alpine meadows are also very fragile and should be avoided by campers, particularly wet meadows. Also, camp well away from travel corridors—this will increase your own seclusion and help other parties preserve their wilderness experience.

When leaving any campsite, be sure the area is returned to its natural state. Make an extra check around the area to be sure you don't leave any belongings or litter. Leaves, duff, and twigs should be scattered about to camouflage your tent site and any high foot-traffic areas.

CAMPFIRES

In the Cloud Peak Wilderness, campfires are prohibited within 300 feet of trails, streams, or lakes in order to protect the fragile riparian zones. Fires are also prohibited above 9,200 feet in the Cloud Peak Wilderness. Many of the high lake basins do not have any legal sites at which to build a fire, and there tends to be a lack of firewood at and near the timberline. Even where campfires are allowed, consider doing without one. A lightweight stove is a far superior alternative for cooking, and a flashlight or candle lantern can supply light.

If you build a fire, do so only where downed, dead wood is abundant. Use sticks small enough to be broken by hand and gather only as much as you need. Keep the fire small and brief. All fire rings must be dismantled and the fire site completely restored to a natural appearance before you leave the site. The backcountry of the Bighorn Mountains is managed as a pristine environment. If you find a fire ring left by less considerate visitors during your travels, dismantle it, scatter the ashes and camouflage the site. A fire should never be left unattended. Once it is out, make sure the ashes are cold. Pack out any remaining unburned trash after the fire is doused.

HUMAN WASTE DISPOSAL

Many people are surprised to learn that human waste, even when properly buried in a "cat hole" under ideal conditions, requires a year or more to decompose naturally. Any fecal bacteria present will remain viable (that is, infectious) for this length of time. The decomposition process is slowed even more when waste is concentrated (as in a group latrine) or deposited in excessively dry, wet, or cold conditions.

Once the traveler understands these facts, it is easy to see that natural composting cannot always keep pace with the amount of human waste, particularly at heavily used backcountry campsites. The problem is compounded when the site is near a lake or stream (as are many popular campsites) because runoff or groundwater can easily carry fecal material and disease into the surface water. Wildlife—and other campers—then use the contaminated source for drinking water. This can result in sickening consequences.

There are no outhouses in the backcountry of the Bighorn Mountains, so you will need to practice minimum-impact disposal techniques. Increasingly, land managers are asking (and in some places *requiring*) people to pack out human waste. Boaters on many western rivers have been doing this for years. Mountain climbers are now handed plastic bags for this purpose in several national parks. Thanks to the staff at Yosemite National Park, all backcountry visitors now have a clean, easy, and secure way to join the ranks and pack out waste. It is called the "poop tube."

You can make your own poop tube from a piece of 4-inch diameter PVC plastic pipe, the kind used for plumbing. Cut the pipe to length as needed for the number of days you'll be in the backcountry. A 2-foot section is enough for five to seven days for most folks. Then glue a cap on one end and a threaded adapter for a screw-on plug on the opposite end. Some travelers duct tape a piece of nylon webbing onto the side of the tube so it can be strapped onto the outside of a pack.

To use the tube, defecate into a paper lunch bag. Then sprinkle in a handful of kitty litter to absorb moisture and reduce odors. Shake the bag to distribute the kitty litter, roll it up, and slide it into the tube. Used toilet paper can go in the tube as well. Screw in the plug and you're done. At the end of the trip, empty the contents into a non-flush vault or "pit" toilet (ask land managers beforehand to recommend a specific outhouse). The paper bags will quickly decay (use only unwaxed bags to ensure they do) and won't clog the pump used to clean out the vault. Never put human waste into trash cans or dumpsters—it creates a health hazard and is illegal.

If you decide instead to use the cat hole method and bury your waste in the backcountry, follow a few simple guidelines:

- Look for an out-of-the-way site in stable soil at least 200 feet (about seventy paces) from surface water. Avoid places that show signs of flooding, carrying runoff, or groundwater.

- Make sure the site is at least 200 feet from campsites, trails, and other centers of human activity.

- Look for a site with a healthy layer of topsoil at least 6 inches deep. The ground should be moist (but not saturated) and easy to dig in.

- With a small hand trowel, dig a cat hole 6 to 8 inches deep. Keep the sod lid intact. Set it aside and pile all of the dirt next to the hole.

- Squat and aim for the hole. Deposit used toilet paper in the hole (or, preferably, bag it and pack it out).

- When covering the waste, use a stick to stir in the first handful or two of soil. This hastens the decomposition process. Add the remaining soil and replace the sod lid. Scrape leaves and duff around the site to camouflage your efforts. Remember to clean your hands thoroughly before handling food or cooking utensils.

- Unless local regulations state otherwise, it's usually best to dig individual cat holes rather than a group latrine. And always use the outhouse if one is provided.

WASHING

The key to cleaning up in the backcountry is to keep soap, oils, and all other pollutants out of the water. Mountain lakes and streams have a delicate balance of nutrient inputs and outputs. Soaps and dishwater dumped into alpine waterways encourage the growth of microbes that can deplete dissolved oxygen in the water, making it inhospitable to many species of fish. In addition, aquatic plants and fish are extremely sensitive to soap (even the biodegradable kind) and can die from contact with it.

To wash cooking and eating utensils, carry water in a clean bowl or pot at least 200 feet from water sources. Use little or no soap—water warmed on the stove will clean off most food and grease. Use a plastic scrubber and a little muscle for stubborn residues. Scatter wash water over the ground in an out-of-the-way spot at least 200 feet from surface water and 100 yards from any likely campsite. In bear country, pick out all food scraps before scattering the water and pack them out with other garbage.

For personal bathing, a good dousing and scrubbing with a washcloth will suffice for all but extended trips. Again, carry the water at least 200 feet from surface water. Remember, even biodegradable shampoos and soaps can be harmful to aquatic ecosystems and must be kept far away from surface water. There are also rinse-free soaps and shampoos on the market that are designed specifically for backpackers.

MINIMUM-IMPACT TECHNIQUES FOR HORSEMEN

Stock users must be particularly careful to minimize their impacts in the backcountry because poorly managed stock can be particularly damaging to the environment. Pack light in order to minimize the load on each animal. On the trail, it is imperative to keep all pack and saddle stock in a single-file line so the original trail does not expand into a multi-lane thoroughfare. When approaching a mudhole, stick to the center of the trail bed unless there is a great risk of injury to the animals. If possible, use llamas rather than horses or mules for carrying supplies. These animals weigh less and have more surface area on their hooves, thus they do less damage to the trail.

In camp, be sure pack and saddle stock are tied up in a responsible manner. Pack animals should never be tied directly to trees or shrubs, because they will dig or paw around the base of the trunk, killing the roots and thus the entire tree. Instead, set up a "high-line," in which a length of rope is tied between two trees to form a portable hitch-rail. The stock can then be secured at intervals to the high-line. Remember to locate the high-line on well-drained ground and change its location every day if you plan to camp at the same spot for more than one night.

Animals turned out to graze in natural openings should be hobbled or picketed. The locations of the picket pins should be rotated every several hours, so the animal does not have a chance to damage any one spot. Portable electric fences have become a favored method for maintaining stock in one place. The total weight of the fence and the installing equipment is typically less than 20 pounds for a fence that will surround a one-acre plot. Remember, these fences must be moved periodically to prevent a concentration of damage in one area. When using an electric fence, train the stock at home before coming into the backcountry. It is also a good idea to picket or hobble lead animals within the fence in case a passing deer knocks it down.

Feeding stock animals in the wilderness is one of the greatest challenges faced by stock users. Finding adequate forage in the backcountry can be a problem in some areas, and stock parties should bring along sufficient feed for their livestock in case grazing cannot be found. Hay is one of the best feeds, but it is heavy and bulky and thus impractical for short-term expeditions. In addition, all hay brought onto the Bighorn National Forest must be certified weed-seed free. Responsible stockmen feed their mounts weed-seed free hay for several days before traveling to the wilderness. This allows weed seeds from the home pasture to pass out of the digestive tract before the backcountry is reached. Pelletized rations are popular and contain all the nutrition needed by livestock. However, pelletized feeds do not fill animals up enough to satisfy their hunger and should be supplemented by grazing the animals. A hungry animal will paw restlessly and damage the environment, while a content animal will do much less damage.

Finally, stock users should be aware that livestock are just as susceptible to altitude sickness as humans. Allow several days of acclimation before riding your animals at high altitudes.

BACKCOUNTRY REGULATIONS AND PERMITS

REGULATIONS AND GUIDELINES SPECIFIC TO THE CLOUD PEAK WILDERNESS

- Backcountry campers and day hikers must obtain a self-registration permit when hiking on any route that enters the Cloud Peak Wilderness. Permits are available free of charge at ranger stations and some major trailheads. We have marked self-registration stations where permits can be obtained with an xx symbol on the maps in this book.

- Camping is not permitted within 100 feet of any lake or stream. Some of the high lakes do not have any level ground around them that qualifies them as a legal campsite. It is absolutely forbidden to camp at sites posted "closed to camping."

- Campfires are not permitted within 300 feet of streams, trails, or lakeshores, or above 9,200 feet elevation in the Cloud Peak Wilderness. All campfires must be completely extinguished before departure.

- All man-made structures, such as hitch racks, tent frames, and fire rings, must be completely dismantled after use.

- It is prohibited to short-cut switchbacks.

- All trails in the wilderness are closed to mountain bikes and motorized vehicles. Helicopters, airplanes, and hang gliders may not land (or take off) within the wilderness.

- The group size limit for all parties is 10 people and 15 head of stock (12 people if Leave No Trace training has been completed). In addition, a party may not possess more than 15 head of stock. Larger groups must split into parties of 25 (people plus horses) or less and remain at least 0.5 mile apart at all times.

- Horses and other pack animals must not be hitched, hobbled, picketed, or tethered within 100 feet of lakes or streams. Hitching, tethering, hobbling, or picketing of pack or saddle stock must be done in such a way that it prevents injury to any living tree.

- Human waste must be packed out in the West and Middle Tensleep drainages.

GENERAL REGULATIONS AND GUIDELINES FOR THE BIGHORN NATIONAL FOREST

- Permits are not required for backcountry trips.

Subalpine firs in the growth form known as krummholz.

- Dispersed camping is allowed in all areas free of charge except where posted otherwise.

- All hay, straw, or mulch taken into the Bighorn National Forest must be certified weed free.

- Many roads and trails are closed to motorized vehicles year-round or during certain seasons. Consult the forest map for details.

- Mechanized and motorized equipment (including mountain bikes) is prohibited within the wilderness.

- Firearms are allowed throughout the national forest. Hunting is permitted pursuant to State of Wyoming regulations. According to state law, a licensed guide must accompany out-of-state hunters in wilderness areas.

- A Wyoming fishing license is required for all fishing within the public lands, including minors and catch-and-release.

REGULATIONS SPECIFIC TO BUREAU OF LAND MANAGEMENT AREAS

- Dispersed camping is permitted on all Bureau of Land Management (BLM) lands, unless posted otherwise.

- Mechanized vehicles and motorized equipment are prohibited off officially designated trails and roadways.

- Some trails or roadways may be closed seasonally or permanently to motorized vehicles. Consult the nearest BLM district office for current road and trail closures.

THE CLEAR CREEK WATERSHED

On the eastern side of the Cloud Peak massif, a series of timbered terraces leads up to the foot of the high granite domes. Dotted with lakes and ponds, this part of the Cloud Peak Wilderness is within easy reach of hikers and horsemen alike. From snowfields and alpine meadows, glittering brooks trickle down from the high country to feed the three forks of Clear Creek. This area is as popular with fishermen as it is with hikers, and solitude is in short supply at the more popular destinations. Most of the trails can be hiked in a single day, and only the Florence Pass Trail breaches the crest of the Bighorn Mountain divide.

Access to the eastern side of the Cloud Peak Wilderness is via US Highway 16, a scenic byway that starts in Buffalo and climbs over the divide to reach Tensleep and Worland. The soils of this region are quite rocky. Both trails and primitive roads tend to be choked with boulders. If you aren't driving a high-clearance four-wheel-drive vehicle, we recommend staying on the improved gravel roads marked on maps with solid lines as opposed to dashed lines. FR 33 makes a nice scenic drive down Crazy Woman Creek. The fire lookout on Sheep Mountain is accessed via an easy drive on FR 28.

Trail Park, along the way to Florence Pass.

1

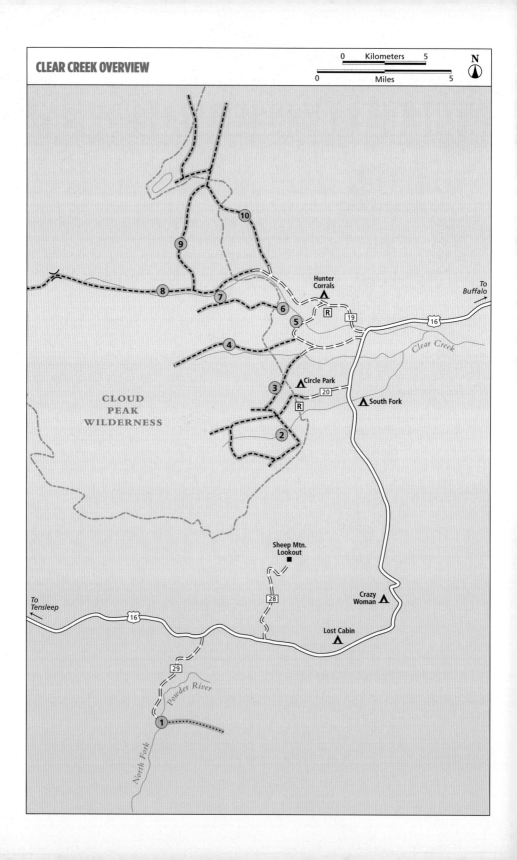

0   Kilometers   5

0   Miles   5

N

To
Buffalo

Hunter
Corrals

R   19

16

Clear Creek

CLOUD
PEAK
WILDERNESS

Circle Park

R   20   South Fork

Sheep Mtn.
Lookout
▪

Crazy
Woman

28

Lost Cabin

To
Tensleep   16

29

Powder River

North Fork

Hazelton Peak.

Developed campgrounds can be found where the highway crosses the Middle and South Forks of Clear Creek, as well as at the headwaters of Crazy Woman Creek. Also, there are campgrounds at or near the Circle Park and Hunter Trailheads. Permits are required for all visitors entering the Cloud Peak Wilderness for day trips or backpacks. These are available free of charge at the Circle Park Trailhead, Hunter Trailhead, and the Forest Service ranger station in Buffalo. Feel free to stop in at the ranger station to find out the latest trail conditions. There are several small lodges along the grade to Powder River Pass, but you will need to drive down to Buffalo to find most supplies.

1 HAZELTON PEAK

General description: A wilderness route to the summit of Hazelton Peak, 3.2 miles one way.
Difficulty: Moderately strenuous.
Route finding: Map and compass.
Best season: Mid-June to late September.

Visitation: Very light.
Elevation gain: 1,674 feet.
Maximum elevation: 10,534 feet (summit).
Topo map: Hazelton Peak.
Jurisdiction: Bighorn National Forest (Buffalo Ranger District).

FINDING THE TRAILHEAD

Leave US Highway 16 just east of Powder River Pass and exit onto FR 29. Follow FR 29, which starts out as a trunk road and deteriorates into a primitive, fair-weather road, for 4.8 miles to the roundabout at its end. The hike begins on the closed logging road that runs northeast from the far bank of the North Fork of the Powder River. GPS: 44.106103°N 107.089166° W

THE HIKE

This cross-country route penetrates a roadless area to the south of US 16 where sharp pyramids of granite rise high above the forests and meadows of the surrounding country. Elk congregate around the bases of these mountains during the calving season of early summer. The higher elevations are a mixture of tundra and frost-shattered granite, home to an abundance of pikas and alpine rodents. Raptors are commonly sighted here, soaring on the thermals as they search for their prey. Take along a full bottle of water, since the high-mountain springs may dry up during the height of summer.

The hike begins by following a closed logging road northeast across the headwaters of the Powder River's North Fork. At this point, the stream is no more than a winding meadow brook that you can leap across in places. On the far bank, follow the roadbed northeast as it climbs gently up a grassy hillock. Bear left at the first unmarked split in the road. Our road now runs atop a low finger ridge. There is a second junction atop the ridge. Stay right on timber sale road #4011, which runs out into a clearcut above a grassy park. Although the clearcut was replanted with seedlings in the late 1960s, grasses have taken over the opening and most of the seedlings have lost out in the competition for water.

At the far edge of the clearcut, follow an overgrown jeep trail southeast as it charts a level course across a long meadow. The route now leaves the established pathways and goes cross country as it heads up the meadow to reach the ridgeline. On the ridgetop is an uglier and more recent clearcut. Hike to its upper edge and follow the ridgeline southeast. It climbs gently at first, passing through uncut stands of timber and ridgetop meadows. Elk frequent the area during early summer and their trails make for rapid traveling up the ridge.

The pitch ultimately steepens, and soon the first outcrops of gneiss break through the spine of the ridge. The forest then gives way to a timberline meadow lit by the blooms of shooting star and alpine forget-me-not. Scattered about are patches of krummholz, which look like evergreen shrubs but are really trees pruned back by winter winds. Continue up the ridgeline to surmount the ridgetop, marked 10,201 feet on your topo map.

A rugged and nameless peak can now be seen to the north, with the granite domes of the Cloud Peak Wilderness rising beyond it. Near at hand, watch for pikas among the talus at the edges of the meadows. The pika spends all summer gathering an immense reserve of dried grass, which it stores beneath the boulders. The pika does not hibernate and this "hay" serves as a winter food supply for this tiny relative of the rabbit. Watch for raptors, which are commonly sighted in this area and depend upon the pika as a favored food source.

Knife-edge outcrops of bedrock rise from the ridge near its summit. At first you can find a grassy passage through the midst of the slabs, but ultimately it becomes necessary to traverse onto north-facing talus slopes and contour across the mountainside. Stringers of spruce rise at the far edge of the talus. Hike upward through the trees to regain the ridgetop.

The route now passes just to the south of point 10,201. It crests the spur ridge to reveal the first views of Hazelton Peak's summit of shattered stone, with a grassy bowl spread out below it. Chart an eastward course down past a spring at the upper edge of a stand of timber. From here, follow the upper edge of the meadow toward Hazelton Peak. The alpine tundra found here is quite fragile; walk on exposed rocks wherever possible.

At the far side of the bowl, climb straight up to reach the ridgetop just above a sharp outcrop of stone. From here, easy ridgeline traveling leads to a spot just below the summit. To attain the top, it becomes necessary to traverse across the rocks to the east of the summit, then scramble up the loose boulders to reach an old Geodetic Survey marker. The summit commands views in all directions, southward across the meadowy highlands at the tail of the Bighorns, westward across the Bighorn Basin toward the Absaroka and Wind River ranges, and far eastward across the high plains of the Powder River Basin. Prominent neighboring summits include Hesse Mountain to the north and Hazelton

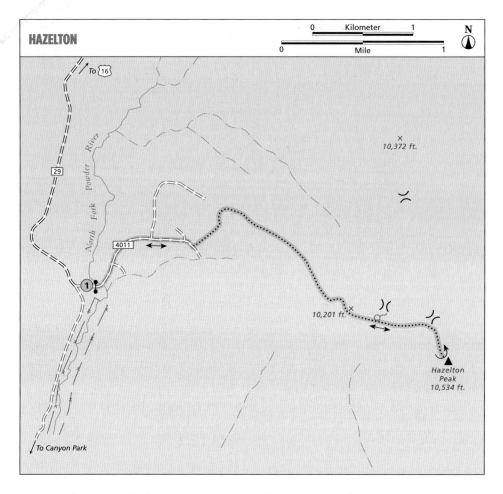

To 16

29

North Fork Powder River

4011

1

×
10,372 ft.

×
10,201 ft.

▲
Hazelton
Peak
10,534 ft.

To Canyon Park

Pyramid to the south, along with a panorama of high peaks stretching across the northern horizon.

MILES AND DIRECTIONS

0.0 Route leaves FR 29. Ford North Fork and follow closed road northeast.

0.2 Fork in old roads. Bear left (northeast).

0.5 Road junction. Bear right (east).

0.8 Route leaves old road and climbs northward.

1.2 Route reaches ridgetop.

2.0 Outcrops block the ridgeline. Route descends onto north slope.

2.3 Route reaches summit of spur ridge. Descend into basin to south.

2.9 Route reaches the ridgeline below Hazelton Peak.

3.2 Summit of Hazelton Peak.

2 THE SHERD LAKE LOOP

General description: A one-day loop trip visiting a number of subalpine lakes, 9.4 miles overall.
Difficulty: Moderate.
Route finding: No problem.
Best season: Early July to early October.
Visitation: Very heavy.
Elevation gain: 1,680 feet.

Elevation loss: 1,680 feet.
Maximum elevation: 9,400 feet (near Rainy Lake).
Topo maps: Hunter Mesa, Lake Angeline (position approximate), *Trails Illustrated* (position approximate).
Jurisdiction: Cloud Peak Wilderness (Bighorn National Forest).

FINDING THE TRAILHEAD

Follow US Highway 16 to mile 76.9, then turn west on the Circle Park Road (FR 20). Follow this road for 2 miles, bearing left at the forks (FR 384) and driving an additional 0.5 mile to the Circle Park Trailhead, where the hike begins. These roads are passable for all cars. GPS: 44.276728° N, 106.984542° W.

THE HIKE

This loop trail visits many of the tiny ponds and sparkling lakes of the South Fork of Clear Creek. During the ice ages, the upper reaches of this valley were a deposition zone for the South Clear Creek Glacier. The glacier deposited enormous quantities of sediment and gravel here, intermixed with chunks of glacial ice. As the buried ice melted, the surrounding sediment collapsed to form small, circular *kettle ponds.* Some of the larger lakes formed when ridges of glacial debris dammed up minor drainages. The Circle Park Trailhead offers some of the easiest access to the high country of the Cloud Peak Wilderness and as a result the Sherd Lake area receives lots of visitors. The loop trail can also be used to access Long Lake (page 11, Long Lake).

The hike begins by climbing a gentle incline robed in a sparse forest of young pines. As the trail ascends, note the varying stand ages and structures, which are all the result of past fires. There are dense stands of saplings where an intense wildfire burned off the overstory trees; sparse stands of old trees able to survive a ground fire; and young, full-formed trees dating from an older burn but untouched by more recent fires. Lodgepole stands are typically born of fire, and if left to nature, they will most often return to ashes. Their seedlings thrive only on open, sunny sites free of competition from grasses. The mature trees have *serotinous* cones, sealed with resin until the heat of a blaze melts the seal and allows the seeds to be released.

The slope ultimately steepens and after a brisk climb the path enters the Cloud Peak Wilderness. It now wanders upward among sinuous ridges, deposited here as Ice Age glaciers melted away. Gaps in the forest allow glimpses of the high peaks to the west, and soon the trail passes the first kettle ponds. These woodland pools formed when buried chunks of glacial ice melted away to form circular depressions, which then filled with water. Watch for water lilies and beaver on these quiet meres.

The trail emerges at a junction on the shore of Sherd Lake, larger than its neighbors but also set among the pines. Turn left to begin the loop. As the path follows the eastern shore of Sherd Lake, watch for superb views of Darton Peak, as well as glimpses of Bighorn Peak and Loaf Mountain to the south of it. The trail then enters the timber, passing

a number of small ponds as it tracks southward. After a short time, the route turns east, descending along a series of wooded hogbacks. At the bottom of the grade, a makeshift bridge spans Clear Creek's South Fork at the foot of South Fork Pond Number One. From here you can enjoy superb views of Bighorn Peak. The views only improve as the trail climbs into hills of broken rock where subalpine firs grow at scattered intervals.

A long and gradual descent now leads to a ford of Duck Creek, which is knee-deep during early summer. After passing through the woods, the trail crosses a boggy tributary clogged with willows. This is excellent moose habitat; keep an eye out for these immense and ungainly herbivores. After the crossing, the path turns westward beside the stream, then crosses a wooded flat where a maze of old jeep trails makes route-finding a challenge. Follow the cairns as the path ultimately emerges into grassy streamside meadows and follows them upward. A trail sign marks the spot where an abandoned roadway leads to FR 382; stay to the right.

The loop route recrosses the swampy watercourse and makes its way across the open flats to reach a second crossing of Duck Creek. The path then climbs into a burned-over wasteland of slag heaps left behind by the retreating glaciers. After a short distance, a spur path leads to the shallow and rocky basin that bears Trigger Lake. The main trail continues up the barren hogbacks as superb views of the peaks open up to the west.

Just before reaching a knee-deep ford of South Clear Creek, an unmarked spur leads west to a pond known as Her Lake. Really no more than a wide and shallow spot on the creek, this pond is pocked with boulders and offers a superb look at Bighorn Peak. The loop trail now wanders across burned-over and rocky flats before returning to a stand of mature conifers. Here, a short but rocky trail runs westward to the shore of Old Crow Lake. Arguably the prettiest of the South Fork Lakes, a loose subalpine forest surrounds

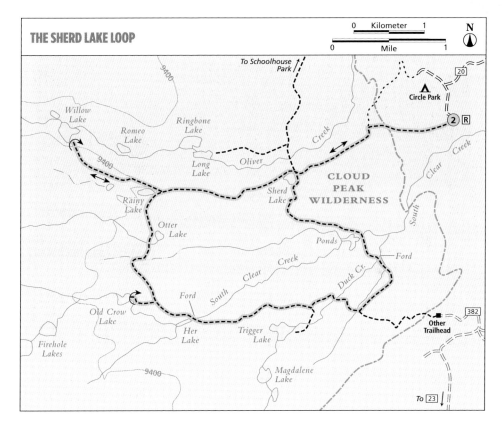

this circular tarn. It is guarded to the south by the rounded summit of Loaf Mountain and to the west by the imposing walls of Bighorn Peak.

The loop trail now runs northward through the trees, gliding downward at a steady clip. The descent steepens as the path enters the heart of the Duck Creek Burn, a fire which destroyed 10,000 acres of timber in 1943. Mountain views now stretch from Bighorn Peak in the south to Darton Peak in the north. The trail bottoms out at a small stream, then climbs again to enter a wooded draw. The path follows it eastward to reach a level shelf where Otter Lake is set amid lush meadows and sedge bogs in the burn.

The trail continues north, climbing steadily to gain the top of the South Fork-Oliver Creek divide. Here, Rainy Lake is set in a rockbound depression on the ridgetop and a spur trail runs westward to Willow Lake (see below). The loop trail now turns east, descending steadily down the wooded ridgeline for the final leg to Sherd Lake. Follow signs for Circle Park to return to the trailhead.

Willow Lake Option. From Rainy Lake, follow the footpath westward along the ridgetop, climbing steadily. The loose growth of pines ultimately opens up, revealing a broad vista of the high peaks to the west. To the south, the fallen snags of the Duck Creek Burn are scattered across the landscape like matchsticks, and to the north the more recent Lost Burn can be seen on the slopes beyond Oliver Creek. After a long ridgetop journey, the path finally drops onto north-facing slopes. Here, the pines and firs were spared from the two fires. The trail runs level for a time, then drops steadily through the

The Sherd Lake Loop offers abundant mountain views and innumerable subalpine lakes.

timber. It emerges beside an immense pile of boulders dredged up by the glacier that once carved out the valley of Oliver Creek.

Follow the cairns as the route fades out among the boulders. It finally makes a steep drop to reach the south shore of Willow Lake. This deep tarn is the largest of the Oliver Creek lakes and is surrounded by slopes of shattered rock swept bare by fire. Watch for moose in the brush above the lake's head.

MILES AND DIRECTIONS

- **0.0** Circle Park Trailhead.
- **0.6** Trail enters the Cloud Peak Wilderness.
- **0.8** Junction with old trail from Circle Park campground. Bear left.
- **1.7** Junction at foot of Sherd Lake. Turn left to begin loop.
- **2.7** Trail fords South Clear Creek at foot of pond.
- **2.9** Trail fords Duck Creek.
- **3.6** Junction with trail to FR 382. Bear right as trail runs northwest across boggy meadows.
- **3.9** Trail fords Duck Creek.
- **4.1** Junction with spur to Trigger Lake (0.2 mile, moderate). Stay right for loop.
- **5.1** Trail fords South Clear Creek at the foot of Her Lake.
- **5.4** Junction with spur to Old Crow Lake (0.2 mile, easy). Stay right for loop.
- **6.1** Otter Lake.
- **6.4** Rainy Lake. Junction with Willow Lake spur (1.0 mile, moderately strenuous). Turn right for loop.
- **7.7** Junction at foot of Sherd Lake. Turn right then left to finish hike.
- **9.4** Circle Park Trailhead.

3 LONG LAKE

General description: A day hike through the Lost Fire to a subalpine lake, 3 miles one way.
Difficulty: Moderate.
Route finding: No problem.
Best season: Early July to early October.
Visitation: Very heavy at the lake; otherwise light.

Elevation gain: 1,005 feet.
Maximum elevation: 8,925 feet.
Topo maps: Hunter Mesa, Lake Angeline (location approximate), *Trails Illustrated* (location approximate).
Jurisdiction: Cloud Peak Wilderness (Bighorn National Forest).

FINDING THE TRAILHEAD

Follow US Highway 16 to mile 79.3, then turn west on the Schoolhouse Park Road (FR 391). This road is rough but should be passable for all vehicles with high clearance. After 2.6 miles, turn left onto FR 387. Follow it 1.1 miles and turn left again onto FR 386. It is preferable to park in the grassy uplands. Adventurous drivers can attempt the steep grade to the road's end and save 0.5 mile of walking. GPS: 44.302571° N, 106.992885° W.

Long Lake.

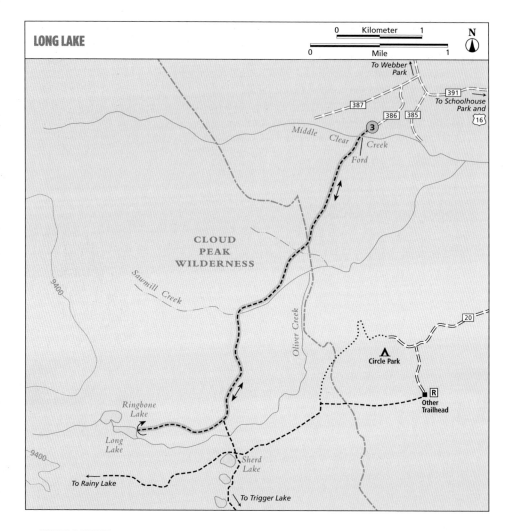

THE HIKE

This trail falls almost entirely within the Lost Fire, which burned through much of the forest on the east slope of the Cloud Peak massif in 1988. Visitors should expect boggy traveling and some route-finding challenges, as well as blown-down snags. This trail is not recommended for horses until the groundwater flows return to normal, which may take 10 years. The Long Lake Trail receives lighter usage than neighboring trails due to the roughness of the access road. The lake can also be approached via a quicker (but more heavily traveled) route from Sherd Lake (page 7, The Sherd Lake Loop).

The hike begins with a calf-deep ford of Middle Clear Creek. With some luck and agility, one might get across with dry feet. Next comes a gradual but marshy ascent up the bench to the south. Lupines and wild peas, both of which have symbiotic bacteria in their roots that pump nitrogen into the soil, underlie the charred snags. In this way, the early colonizers of burn sites speed up the return of the forest.

After cresting the divide, the path enters a grassy park facing southward toward Loaf Mountain. Lupines, wild pea, mountain aster, and larkspur light the way as the route follows the cairns southwest. A gentle climb leads into the valley of Sawmill Creek, a marshy basin that derives its name from an old tie-hack sawmill. The sawmill's remains burned during the 1988 fire. The trail now follows the valley upward for a time. It grows faint as it crosses the heart of the bogs and then rock-hops across the stream.

A well-defined and dry trail awaits on the far bank, carrying travelers upward through the snags at a brisk pace. Atop the initial grade you will find expansive views north-ward along the Bighorn Mountain front, with Ant Hill standing apart from the rounded domes. The path now meanders upward at a gentler pace, passing among stony hillocks as it makes its way toward Oliver Creek. There is a trail junction atop the Oliver Creek divide; to the left is Sherd Lake, while the right-hand trail leads to Long Lake.

The Long Lake Trail now winds along the edge of unburned timber, always within earshot of the stream, as the landscape becomes increasingly rocky. The lofty summits that rise to the west are Bighorn Peak and Darton Peak. The trail ends atop a promon-tory above Long Lake, which is guarded by the stony heights of Darton Peak. The lake offers fair fishing for cutthroat trout. Ringbone Lake lies just to the northwest and can be reached via a short but rocky scramble.

MILES AND DIRECTIONS

0.0   Trailhead. Ford Middle Clear Creek.

1.0   Trail enters Cloud Peak Wilderness.

1.6   Trail crosses Sawmill Creek.

2.5   Junction with cutoff trail to Sherd Lake (0.2 mile, moderate). Turn right for Long Lake.

3.0   Long Lake.

4 LAKE ANGELINE

General description: A day hike or short backpack to an alpine lake near the crest of the range, 5.8 miles one way.
Difficulty: Moderately strenuous.
Route finding: Some challenges.
Best season: Mid-July to early September.
Visitation: Moderate.
Elevation gain: 2,503 feet.

Elevation loss: 60 feet.
Maximum elevation: 10,550 feet (Lake Angeline).
Topo maps: Hunter Mesa, Lake Angeline (location approximate), *Trails Illustrated* (location approximate).
Jurisdiction: Cloud Peak Wilderness (Bighorn National Forest).

FINDING THE TRAILHEAD

Follow US Highway 16 to mile 79.3, then turn west on the Schoolhouse Park Road (FR 391). This road is rough but should be passable to all vehicles with high clearance. Bear right at all intersections and after 3 miles you will arrive in the south lobe of Webber Park. The hike begins by following this road westward. GPS: 44.312127° N, 106.995095° W.

THE HIKE

This trail climbs along Middle Clear Creek, eventually reaching a cirque lake set high in the alpine tundra near the Bighorn Mountain divide. The lower reaches of the trail fall

Lake Angeline.

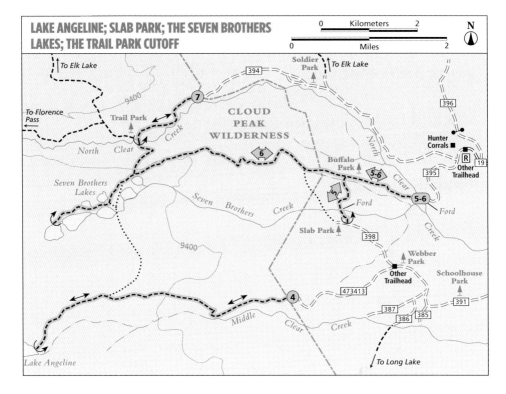

within the Lost Fire Burn of 1988. Expect to step over plenty of small blowdowns. The path is made up of round cobbles and boulders, so it is unpopular with horsemen.

From Webber Park, follow the jeep trail marked FR 391 westward into burned-over timber. Bear left at the fork as the track ascends a gentle slope to the north of Middle Clear Creek. As the road crests the ridgetop, initial views encompass the cliffs and domes at the head of the drainage. The old roadway then descends into the valley below to reach the boundary of the Cloud Peak Wilderness.

From here, a well-defined path follows the valley upward through a skeletal forest of snags. This area was at the heart of the Lost Fire in 1988 and only a few isolated groves of trees survived the blaze. After approaching the creek, the path ascends gradually into the subalpine zone, where the fire burned less fiercely due to a lack of dead wood. After climbing a steep pitch, an abandoned and all-but-invisible cutoff trail leads to the Seven Brothers Lakes.

The main trail now climbs into gently sloping uplands. Here, wet meadows are threaded with small rivulets where dwarfed willows grow. The firs shrink in stature as the trail climbs into alpine country, until only a few patches of shrub-like krummholz can be found in the protected swales. This is a land of bald domes covered in hardy alpine tundra of mountain avens and cushion-forming plants. Pikas are abundant here. Great cliffs and domes of granite rise along the crest of the range, silent and immutable.

Follow the cairns as the faint path threads its way among the hillocks and then crosses the outlet stream to reach the foot of Lake Angeline. This alpine gem is backed into a glacial cirque, which was carved out of the mountainside by a small glacier that has long since melted away. Anglers will find that the cold waters of the lake support a population of cutthroat trout.

MILES AND DIRECTIONS

0.0 Road junction in Webber Park. Hike west on FR 473413.

1.7 Road ends at Cloud Peak Wilderness boundary.

2.7 Trail approaches Middle Clear Creek.

4.0 Junction with abandoned trail to Seven Brothers Lakes. Stay left.

5.8 Lake Angeline.

5 SLAB PARK

See map on page 15.
General description: A side trip from Buffalo Park to Slab Park, 0.8 mile one way.
Difficulty: Moderate.
Route finding: Some challenges.
Best season: Mid-June to early October.

Visitation: Light.
Elevation gain: 130 feet.
Elevation loss: 70 feet.
Maximum elevation: 8,180 feet.
Topo maps: Lake Angeline, *Trails Illustrated* (location approximate).
Jurisdiction: Bighorn National Forest (Buffalo Ranger District).

FINDING THE TRAILHEAD

The trail departs from the Seven Brothers Lake Trail at a marked junction in Buffalo Park, 1.2 miles beyond the ford of North Clear Creek. GPS (Seven Brothers trailhead): 44.325576° N, 106.985628° W.

THE HIKE

This trail links FR 398 with Buffalo Park and the Seven Brothers Lakes Trail, passing among striking outcrops of stone and affording access to a high-mountain wetland. Since FR 398 is virtually impassable, most visitors approach from the Buffalo Park side (page 19, The Seven Brothers Lakes).

The hike begins with a crossing of North Clear Creek, which is knee-deep and turbulent during the early summer. Follow the old roadbed into Buffalo Park and hike two-thirds of its length to reach a signpost indicating the spot where the Slab Park Trail splits off. From this point, walk down across the untrodden grass to reach a cairn beside an intermittent stream. Here, a flagstone crossing has been made to get across the water and, on the far side, a distinct footpath rises into the burned-over timber.

The trail wanders upward, passing among knolls topped with twisted outcrops of gneiss. After a brief ascent, the path descends to ford Seven Brothers Creek. Low walls of gneiss that protrude from the hillsides flank this picturesque stream. On the south bank, the trail makes a short climb through the charred snags to reach Slab Park. This large opening is occupied by a sedge bog entirely saturated with water. The jeep track known as FR 398 enters the park at its eastern end and

Boggy meadows at Slab Park.

the abandoned cutoff route to the Seven Brothers Lakes departs from the northwestern side of the marsh.

MILES AND DIRECTIONS

0.0 Junction with Seven Brothers Trail in Buffalo Park.

0.05 Trail crosses small stream and starts to climb.

0.6 Trail fords Seven Brothers Creek.

0.7 Trail enters Slab Park. Follow east edge of trees.

0.8 Trail joins FR 398.

6 THE SEVEN BROTHERS LAKES

See map on page 15.
General description: A day hike or short backpack to a group of high lakes at the base of the peaks, 5.6 mile one way.
Difficulty: Moderately strenuous.
Route finding: No problem.
Best season: Late June to mid-September.
Visitation: Very heavy.

Elevation gain: 1,760 feet.
Elevation loss: 80 feet.
Maximum elevation: 9,600 feet (5th lake).
Topo maps: Hunter Mesa, Lake Angeline (location approximate), *Trails Illustrated* (location approximate).
Jurisdiction: Cloud Peak Wilderness (Bighorn National Forest).

FINDING THE TRAILHEAD

Follow US Highway 16 to mile 79.6, then drive west on the Hunter Creek Road (FR 19). After 2.3 miles, bear right to reach the Hunter Trailhead near the campground GPS: 44.338379° N, 106.977084° W. Most hikers park here. If you have four-wheel drive, you may continue up FR 394 for 0.2 mile, turn left onto FR 395, and follow it the remaining 1.2 miles over the hilltop and down to the beginning of the trail beside North Clear Creek. GPS: 44.325576° N, 106.985628° W.

THE HIKE

This trail leads from the Hunter Trailhead to a string of spectacular subalpine lakes in the headwaters of Seven Brothers Creek. These lakes are a popular destination for anglers and campers alike. Most visitors who attempt this trail start at Hunter Corrals and hike up the roads for 1.4 miles to reach the ford of North Clear Creek, taking in the ridgetop meadows and fine views of the high peaks along the way. Most stock users avoid the trail bed because it is rocky and rough. The lakes can also be reached via the Trail Park Cutoff (page 22), which ascends from the Florence Pass Trail.

If hikers drive all the way to the end of FR 395, the trek begins with a knee-deep ford of North Clear Creek. This willow-lined stream rushes down a slippery channel choked with boulders. On the far bank, an old roadbed winds around the hillside to enter Buffalo Park. This long and verdant meadow is dotted with the blossoms of lupine, blanketflower, and bistort. Groves of aspen line the intermittent stream that runs along the bottom of the park, but the slopes beyond bear only the silvery snags left behind by the Lost Fire.

The trail passes along the length of the meadow and is deeply rutted in places. Two-thirds of the way across, a signpost marks the junction with the Slab Park Trail, which is invisible in the meadow but well defined along most of its length. Near the head of Buffalo Park, the main trail begins to climb and it enters the Cloud Peak Wilderness as it passes into the burned-over timber.

The climb intensifies, becoming a steady slog up a bouldery channel. After the trail passes a drift fence, an old post marks the spot where the abandoned cutoff trail to Slab Park once joined the Seven Brothers Trail. The pitch of the slope soon steepens and the trail compensates by adopting a less aggressive angle of attack. Atop this initial grade is a level shelf where many of the conifers survived the fire. The respite is short-lived and soon the trail is again climbing up steep burned-over hillsides.

After the path gains the toe of a finger ridge, the climbing abates. The trail now follows the ridgetop westward, and periodic stands of surviving trees provide patches of shade. The path now dips onto the northern slope of a steep escarpment and glimpses through the trees reveal a broad sweep of high and rocky country guarding North Clear Creek.

After a long journey along the escarpment's edge, the path climbs back to the ridgetop and soon reaches the first of the Seven Brothers Lakes. This broad, deep-blue pool is surrounded by verdant forests and lined with a jumble of boulders. At its midpoint, a cutoff trail descends northward toward Trail Park on North Clear Creek.

The main trail wanders into the timber above the lake's head, a mixture of spruce, subalpine fir, whitebark pine, and lodgepole. Here, a trail junction marks a spur trail to the second and third lakes as well as access to the abandoned cutoff to Lake Angeline. The Seven Brothers Trail undertakes a steady climb, finally surmounting a knoll crowned by emerald subalpine meadows. It then drops to reach the fourth lake and follows its south shore. Soon the third lake can be seen in the basin below, stretching away toward forested ridges. Upon reaching the fifth lake, the path crests a grassy knob with superb views of the sixth (and largest) of the lakes. The stark domes and cliffs that guard the head of Seven Brothers Creek are ranged beyond it.

The path now descends to the densely wooded shoreline of this lake. Camping and horses are not allowed beyond this point so this fragile area can be restored to a pristine condition. Upon reaching the head of the lake, a path leads upward to the final lake in the chain. Here, wooded ridges close in around the valley, limiting views of the high peaks.

Rugged domes guard the sixth of the Seven Brothers Lakes.

MILES AND DIRECTIONS

0.0 Trail begins by fording North Clear Creek.

0.1 Trail enters Buffalo Park.

1.2 Junction with Slab Park Trail. Continue straight ahead.

1.5 Trail leaves Buffalo Park and enters Cloud Peak Wilderness.

1.7 Abandoned cutoff trail from Slab Park joins main route.

4.2 Lowermost of Seven Brothers Lakes. Junction with Trail Park cutoff. Stay left.

4.4 Trail descends to second and third lakes and continues toward Lake Angeline.

4.8 Fourth lake. Trail descends toward third lake.

5.1 Fifth lake.

5.4 Head of sixth lake.

5.6 Trail ends at uppermost of Seven Brothers Lakes.

7 THE TRAIL PARK CUTOFF

See map on page 15.
General description: A connecting trail between the Florence Pass Trail and the Seven Brothers Lakes, 0.9 mile one way.
Difficulty: Moderate.
Route finding: No problem.
Best season: Late June to mid-September.

Visitation: Very heavy.
Elevation gain: 310 feet.
Maximum elevation: 9,440 feet.
Topo maps: Lake Angeline (location approximate), *Trails Illustrated*.
Jurisdiction: Cloud Peak Wilderness (Bighorn National Forest).

FINDING THE TRAILHEAD

The trail begins at the east end of Trail Park GPS: 44.336237° N, 107.059423° W, 2.4 miles above Soldier Park on the Florence Pass Trail. It joins the Seven Brothers Trail at the lowermost of the Seven Brothers Lakes.

THE HIKE

For visitors with four-wheel drive, this trail offers a shorter and easier route to the Seven Brothers Lakes. On the other hand, the trail along North Clear Creek has many quagmires as a result of heavy horse use and solitude is in short supply. Hikers who value their vehicles will park at the Hunter Trailhead and walk up the jeep roads. Follow the Florence Pass routing to Trail Park and the beginning of the cutoff trail to Seven Brothers Lakes. A day hike or short backpack via this routing would cover 6.4 miles one way.

From Soldier Park, ford North Clear Creek and follow the boulder-choked road westward, climbing gradually through the bottoms of North Clear Creek. After 0.6 mile, an opening reveals views of the rugged but nameless peaks that guard the south side of the valley. The route then returns to the loose-knit forest, emerging again at Trail Park. This grassy expanse affords views all the way up the valley to Florence Pass, with massive domes and stark cliffs guarding the approach.

A trail sign points the way to Seven Bothers Lakes, but the path has been overtaken by the meadow and hikers will need to follow the edge of the trees down to ford North Clear Creek. The Trail Park cutoff now climbs into the lodgepoles on the far bank and soon turns eastward. Along the way, a talus slope breaks the forest canopy to allow spectacular aerial views of Trail Park with a ridge of high peaks beyond it stretching from Bomber Mountain in the west to Ant Hill in the east.

The trail now doglegs back to the west for a gentle stroll through the pines, which now are intermixed with subalpine fir. After 0.6 mile of easy traveling, a series of switchbacks leads up the short but breath-stealing final pitch to reach the lowermost of the Seven Brothers Lakes. Here, it joins the Seven Brothers Trail (see page 19 for details on the lakes and their connecting trails).

Looking across Trail Park to Bomber Mountain.

MILES AND DIRECTIONS

0.0   Junction, west end of Trail Park. I like south along edge of trees.

0.1   Ford of North Clear Creek.

0.9   Junction with Seven Brothers Trail. Lowermost of Seven Brothers Lakes.

8 FLORENCE PASS

General description: A day hike from the Hunter Trailhead to Trail Park, 5.5 miles one way, or a backpack over a high pass to Mistymoon Lake, 14.5 miles from Hunter Corrals or 11.4 miles from Soldier Park.
Difficulty: Moderate to Powell Creek; moderately strenuous beyond.
Route finding: No problem.
Best season: Mid-July to early September.

Visitation: Moderate.
Elevation gain: 3,070 feet (from Hunter Corrals).
Elevation loss: 640 feet.
Maximum elevation: 10,900 feet (Florence Pass).
Topo maps: Hunter Mesa, Lake Angeline, Lake Helen, *Trails Illustrated*.
Jurisdiction: Cloud Peak Wilderness (Bighorn National Forest).

FINDING THE TRAILHEAD

Follow US Highway 16 to mile 79.6, then drive west on the Hunter Creek Road (FR 19). After 2.3 miles, bear right to reach the Hunter Trailhead near the campground GPS: 44.338379° N, 106.977084° W. Most hikers park here.

THE HIKE

This trail is certainly one of the most scenic and popular routes in the Cloud Peak Wilderness. Florence Pass represents one of only three passes that bear trails across the Bighorn divide. It is an integral leg in many possible loop treks, and horse parties often use it for day trips into the high country. Horsemen should note that the trail is built on broken boulders above Medicine Park and may be impassable to inexperienced horses and riders. The gem-like meadows of North Clear Creek lead up to the stony heights near the pass, where even the tundra is sparse and ragged. Florence Lake occupies a barren cirque at the top of the divide. As the trail descends to Mistymoon Lake, it visits the Fortress Lakes in their tundra basin. At its terminus, the trail links up with routes leading to West Tensleep Lake, the Battle Park Trailhead, and Lake Solitude.

Hikers who want to spare their vehicles a severe thrashing will start the hike at the Hunter Trailhead. Cross the bridge and follow the jeep track up through an open meadow. Bear right at the first fork as the road climbs through the trees to emerge in hilltop meads. It soon winds through a stand of timber that burned during 1988. Beyond it is a pair of graves from which Soldier Park derives its name. One belongs to a Frenchman named Pierre Garde who died here while serving with an Army survey party in 1877. The other belongs to a Swedish lumberjack who expired in 1922. The gravediggers could hardly have chosen a prettier site to bury the pair. The bluff looks out over the wetlands of North Clear Creek, with the granite domes of Darton Peak, the Mather Peaks, and Bomber Mountain stretched beyond. After passing through a stretch of unburned timber, the road emerges in the grassy expanse of Soldier Park. Follow the road that runs west across the length of the meadow to enter the timber beyond.

Visitors who drive to Soldier Park will start hiking on the stony road leading westward into the forest along North Clear Creek. The jeep track becomes a pack trail as it enters the Cloud Peak Wilderness. Here, a small and grassy meadow allows early views of the Mather Peaks far up the valley. The path then enters the pines, and after a short distance the lodgepoles thin out and give way to the grassy expanse of Trail Park. This long

Medicine Park.

Cloud Peak from the vicinity of Florence Pass.

meadow stretches for 1.5 miles along North Clear Creek. Willows guard the watercourse, while the grassy swales are studded with the blossoms of prairie smoke and penstemon. There are superb views of the peaks that crowd the head of the valley.

A trail sign at the east edge of Trail Park marks the Trail Park cutoff to the Seven Brothers Lakes. There is a ford of the creek at the lower edge of the meadow. The main trail runs westward through the heart of the park, then winds upward into the lodgepoles to meet the trail to Ant Hill. The Florence Pass Trail then continues up the valley, staying mainly within the trees but making one more visit to Trail Park along the way.

The path ultimately descends to ford North Clear Creek beside a grassy opening that leads northwest to the swampy shores of Deer Lake. As the main trail follows the south bank of the stream, the lodgepoles give way to a subalpine forest of spruce, whitebark pine, and subalpine fir. Great walls of pale granite now rise skyward on either side of the valley, planed smooth by an immense glacier during the Pleistocene epoch.

After 5.7 miles, a knee-deep ford leads back to the north bank of the stream. The young firs growing in this area are subject to periodic avalanches that roar down from the steep walls above. The sparse trees yield excellent views of a stark southern crag of Bomber Mountain to the north of the creek, while the cliffs to the south are gouged with great rifts that bear tumbling waterfalls during the snowmelt season. The path now fords Powell Creek in the midst of a grove of stout spruce trees, the Bighorns' version of old growth.

The path then begins a steady climb, zigzagging up a meadowy slope. Here, the blue larkspurs and the graceful spires of subalpine fir provide a picturesque perch for viewing the immense waterfall that emerges from a basin between the Mather Peaks. After a vigorous climb, the trail drops down to the rim of Florence Canyon, a small gorge carved by North Clear Creek after the glaciers receded.

The trail continues up the valley to reach Medicine Park, a gemlike pocket of alpine tundra—smooth and flat like a billiard table. The fragile greenery contrasts sharply with the lifeless aprons of frost-shattered granite below the cliffs to the south. After crossing the park, the trail follows the streamcourse up through a narrow ravine where the blossoms of anemones and buttercups crowd the south-facing slope. At the head of the ravine, passage is blocked by a *terminal moraine*, a great heap of broken rubble pushed into place by a long-extinct glacier.

After threading a rocky course up the face of the moraine, the trail emerges into a harsh landscape of stone, mazes of moraines guarded by stark domes where the only color is provided by small clumps of krummholz fir and cushion-forming perennials. Soon the trees disappear altogether and the path enters a barren country of dark and brooding cliffs flecked with lingering snowdrifts and cornices. Three easy rock-hops afford crossings of North Clear Creek just below Florence Lake, a high alpine tarn of surreal beauty. The path follows the south shore of the lake, yielding excellent views of the summit of Bomber Mountain. Watch for marmots and much smaller pikas among the boulders beside the lake.

The trail then climbs the short and rather anticlimactic pitch to reach the rounded gap of Florence Pass, where a fragile veneer of tundra covers the rocks. It then descends at a steady clip, weaving among the granite outcrops as it drops into the alpine valley that bears the Fortress Lakes. Gunboat Lake is the largest of these, its turquoise waters crowded up against the sheer cliff that guards the south side of the valley. The trail levels off as it crosses the outlet stream that issues from Gunboat Lake, then wanders beside the shallow tarn to the north of the lake. The path then passes between the remaining Fortress Lakes and follows the stream that drains them.

The steady descent along this streamcourse will delight wildflower enthusiasts, as the brook is bordered by almost every timberline wildflower native to the Bighorn Mountains. The trail bottoms out at Mistymoon Lake, which is right at the timberline, and offers outstanding views of the surrounding summits, including Bomber Mountain and Cloud Peak. The Florence Pass Trail now crosses West Tensleep Creek to reach its terminus at a trail junction at the foot of the lake. From here, trails run south to West Tensleep Lake, west to the Battle Park Trailhead, and northwest to Lake Solitude.

MILES AND DIRECTIONS

0.0   Hunter Trailhead. Hike over bridge and up FR 394.

0.2   Road splits. Bear right.

2.2   Road reaches site of old graves.

2.5   Road enters Soldier Park. Follow road west.

3.1   Road leaves Soldier Park.

4.4   Road ends as trail enters Cloud Peak Wilderness.

5.5   Trail enters Trail Park. Junction with Trail Park cutoff to Seven Brothers Lakes. Continue straight ahead.

5.8   Trail exits Trail Park.

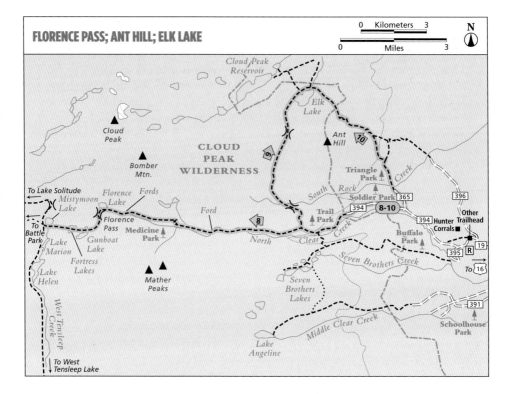

6.0 Junction with Ant Hill section of Solitude Trail. Bear left.

7.7 Ford leads to south bank of North Clear Creek.

8.8 Trail fords North Clear Creek to reach north bank.

9.7 Trail crosses Powell Creek.

10.3 Medicine Park.

11.8 First of three fords of North Clear Creek.

12.2 Trail makes final ford at the foot of Florence Lake.

12.5 Florence Pass. Trail starts descending.

13.2 Trail crosses outlet of Gunboat Lake.

13.5 Fortress Lakes.

14.3 Trail reaches shore of Mistymoon Lake.

14.5 Trail crosses outlet stream to reach junction with Mistymoon and Lake Solitude Trails.

9 ANT HILL

See map on page 28.
General description: A connecting trail between the Florence Pass Trail and Elk Lake, 5.3 miles overall.
Difficulty: Moderately strenuous.
Route finding: Some challenges.
Best season: Mid-July to early September.
Visitation: Light.
Elevation gain: 1,385 feet.

Elevation loss: 750 feet.
Maximum elevation: 10,620 feet (at pass behind Ant Hill).
Topo maps: Lake Angeline, Willow Park Reservoir (location approximate), *Trails Illustrated* (location approximate).
Jurisdiction: Cloud Peak Wilderness (Bighorn National Forest).

FINDING THE TRAILHEAD

Follow US Highway 16 to mile 79.6, then drive west on the Hunter Creek Road (FR 19). After 2.3 miles, bear right to reach the Hunter Trailhead near the campground GPS: 44.338379° N, 106.977084° W. The trail begins 2.9 miles above Soldier Park on the Florence Pass Trail just beyond Trail Park. It ends at Elk Lake, which is reached via a 5.2-mile hike from Soldier Park.

THE HIKE

This linking trail joins the Florence Pass Trail with Elk Lake via a high pass behind a mountain of shattered granite called Ant Hill. Considering its relative ease of access, the trail receives few visitors. Along the way it crosses the high meadows at the headwaters of South Rock Creek and affords superb views of the mountains along most of the route. The high tundra of the pass behind Ant Hill is one of the best spots in the Bighorn Mountains to observe marmots. From Hunter Corrals, a backpack to Elk Lake via this route would cover 11.3 miles one way. When combined with the Florence Pass and Elk Lake trails, it makes a two-day loop of 19.2 miles from Hunter Corrals.

From Trail Park, the path climbs vigorously through the trees to surmount a low *lateral moraine*. This landform is an old pile of rubble deposited along the side of a glacier as it moved down the valley. The glacier melted away thousands of years ago and the forest has colonized the old moraine. Atop the moraine is an open boulder field with south-west views of the Mather Peaks.

The trail then continues northward to reach the wooded slopes of an older and taller moraine. It climbs gently at first, then more urgently. The top of this moraine is a high watershed divide. Here, an old burn interrupts the forest and the basin of South Rock Creek stretches out ahead. Ant Hill is due north, while the outriders of Bomber Mountain rise above the head of the basin.

The path follows the base of the moraine westward for a while, then turns north to cross the basin. After an ankle-deep ford of South Rock Creek, the path crosses a grassy glade. It soon enters a series of meadows interspersed with groves of spruce and fir. The route now runs straight up the slopes ahead, toward the rounded pass behind Ant Hill. The trail may be faint in places—watch for cairns marking the way.

The trees become progressively shorter as the path ascends and soon they are reduced to scattered patches of dwarfed krummholz. Views expand to encompass a broad south-ward panorama of the Bighorns. Near the top of the divide, dwarfed snow willow and other tundra plants grow in a broad swath between hillocks of frost-shattered granite. Marmots are abundant in this area and are generally tolerant of humans who sit quietly and show patience. As the trail crests the pass, Ant Hill is hidden behind its closer twin and a rounded summit blocks northward views.

The blue expanse of Elk Lake becomes visible as the route follows cairns down the far side of the divide. The traveling is easy as the route rolls down the open tundra. As Penrose Peak becomes visible through a gap in the hills, the trail swings westward, contouring across the slopes and crossing a number of seasonal streams. It soon reaches the talus slopes that guard Elk Lake, then drops through a stand of spruce to reach the grassy meadows bordering its western shore. A signpost soon marks the spur trail to Cloud Peak Reservoir, while the main path continues around the lakeshore to reach a junction with the Elk Lake and Reservoirs routes at the outlet.

MILES AND DIRECTIONS

- 0.0 Trail departs from Florence Pass Trail.
- 0.5 Top of initial grade.
- 1.3 Trail fords South Rock Creek.
- 2.9 Pass below Ant Hill.
- 4.4 Trail reaches head of Elk Lake.
- 4.7 Trail departs for Cloud Peak Reservoir. Bear right.
- 5.3 Foot of Elk Lake. Junction with Elk Lake and Reservoirs trails.

10 ELK LAKE

See map on page 28.

General description: A day hike or short backpack to a subalpine lake set amid beautiful meadows, 5.2 miles one way from Soldier Park or 7.9 miles one way from Hunter Corrals.
Difficulty: Moderately strenuous.
Route finding: No problem.
Best season: Mid-July to early September.

Visitation: Moderate.
Elevation gain: 1,540 feet.
Elevation loss: 287 feet.
Maximum elevation: 10,080 feet (near the wilderness boundary).
Topo maps: Lake Angeline, Willow Park Reservoir, *Trails Illustrated.*
Jurisdiction: Cloud Peak Wilderness (Bighorn National Forest).

FINDING THE TRAILHEAD

 Follow US Highway 16 to mile 79.6, then drive west on the Hunter Creek Road (FR 19). After 2.3 miles, bear right to reach the Hunter Trailhead near the campground GPS: 44.338379° N, 106.977084° W. Most hikers park here. Hike up FR 394, bearing right at the forks. Expect washouts and lots of boulders as the road runs for 2.6 miles to reach the edge of Soldier Park. Turn right at the junction with FR 365 and drive to the north edge of the meadow, parking just inside the trees on the far side. The hike now follows the jeep track that runs north into the trees.

THE HIKE

This trail offers the most direct route to Elk Lake, a large and marshy pool that occupies a high shelf north of Ant Hill. The meadows surrounding this lake offer one of the finest mountain panoramas in the area. From Elk Lake, trails radiate southward toward the Florence Pass Trail, west to Cloud Peak Reservoir and Flatiron Lake, and north to Willow Park Reservoir.

If you don't have an ATV, the hike starts by following a narrow and rocky jeep track through formless hillocks robed in lodgepole pine. After many ups and downs, a steep descent leads to Triangle Park, where South Rock Creek flows through a lush and swampy opening filled with sedges. A thigh-deep ford of its slow-moving water leads to the trail that follows the northern edge of the park. Along the way are superb views of the cliffs and domes that stretch between Darton Peak and the Mather Peaks.

Leaving the park, the trail climbs steadily through the pines to reach the low saddle behind a rocky outcrop. A cutoff trail leads northeast toward the French Creek Swamps, while the main trail continues upward. It ultimately swings north across sparsely timbered slopes. On a clear day, you can see far out onto the High Plains from this area.

As it approaches the next spur ridge, the trail meets an incoming trail signed "Paradise Ranch." (This is the South Rock Creek Trail.) Watch for "glory holes" in this area. Prospectors dug these open pits along veins of exposed quartz hoping to find gold in paying quantities. The trail now zigzags upward through the pines to gain the top of the spur ridge. After following the ridgeline briefly, the path sags onto north-facing slopes robed in a shady woodland of spruce.

Open meadows augur the final pitch and the trail switchbacks upward beneath the silent gaze of Ant Hill. After crossing a rounded divide, the trail undertakes a shallow descent and soon enters the Cloud Peak Wilderness. As the faint track follows the cairns

down through the timberline meadows, a stunning panorama unfolds ahead. Elk Lake lies in a shallow depression ringed with meadows and beyond it rise the jagged peaks and dizzying walls of Bomber Mountain and Cloud Peak, as well as the rounded cone of Penrose Peak farther north.

The going is rocky as the trail approaches the lakeshore, and a knee-deep ford of Elk Creek awaits you at the foot of Elk Lake. This broad, shallow pool is a haven for breeding waterfowl. On the far bank of its outlet, the trail joins the Ant Hill and Reservoir routes at a signpost.

MILES AND DIRECTIONS

0.0 Old road runs north from Soldier Park.

0.8 Road ends at the edge of Triangle Park. Follow trail northwest.

0.9 Trail fords South Rock Creek.

1.1 Trail leaves Triangle Park.

1.7 Junction with cutoff to South Rock Creek Trail in saddle. Bear left.

2.6 Junction with South Rock Creek Trail. Bear left.

4.0 Top of grade.

4.2 Trail enters Cloud Peak Wilderness.

5.2 Trail fords outlet at foot of Elk Lake to join Ant Hill and Reservoirs trails.

ADDITIONAL TRAILS

A seldom-used road climbs 2 miles from US Highway 16 to reach **Cull Watt Park**, a hilltop meadow to the east of the Bighorns. The best views of the mountains are from the first hundred yards; trees obscure westward views from Cull Watt Park.

A motorbike route (trail #134) starts in the **French Creek Swamps** and runs west to reach Soldier Park.

A stock drive trail runs from the French Creek cow camp to **Johnson Park**.

An old connecting trail once ran from Seven Brothers Lakes to **Lake Angeline**. The Forest Service has since closed the route for management purposes and use of it is discouraged.

An old roadbed (trail #082) connects the Reservoirs section of the Solitude Trail with **Cloud Peak Reservoir**. The roadbed, now used as an all-terrain vehicle trail, is in excellent shape and offers easy hiking.

TENSLEEP AND PAINT ROCK CREEKS

To the west of the Cloud Peak massif, rolling uplands dotted with broad meadows lead to the high peaks. Large alpine lakes are nestled within the deep, glacier-carved valleys of West Tensleep and Paint Rock creeks. Elsewhere, sparkling streams course down through wet meadows and verdant grasslands en route to the deep rifts of Tensleep Canyon and Paint Rock Canyon. The massive half-domes and sheer granite cliffs that stretch from Bighorn Peak and Cloud Peak dominate the landscape and are visible even from the distant foothills. A network of interconnected trails offers excellent possibilities for both day hikes and extended loop trips in this area.

Good gravel roads lead along the edge of the mountains, providing easy access to the western and southern reaches of the Cloud Peak Wilderness. From US Highway 16, FR 27 follows West Tensleep Creek to the West Tensleep Trailhead, which serves as the gateway for almost half of all visitors to the entire Cloud Peak Wilderness. FR 24 wanders 17 miles through the foothills en route to the Battle Park Trailhead. This latter trailhead is a popular base camp for horse parties. From the north, FR 17 winds for 26

Mistymoon Lake is a popular and often crowded destination.

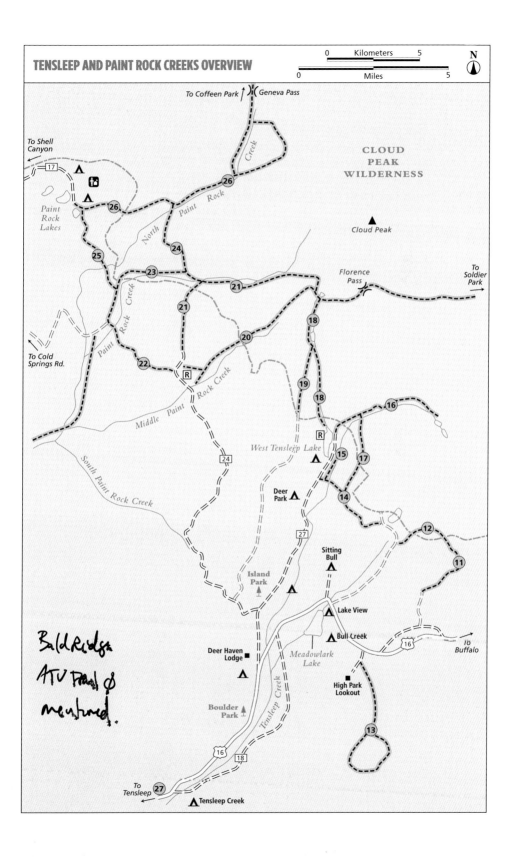

TENSLEEP AND PAINT ROCK CREEKS OVERVIEW

Kilometers

Miles

N

To Coffeen Park — Geneva Pass

CLOUD
PEAK
WILDERNESS

To Shell
Canyon

17

Paint
Rock
Lakes

26

26

North Paint Rock Creek

24

25

23

21

Paint Rock Creek

21

22

To Cold
Springs Rd.

R

Middle Paint Rock Creek

24

South Paint Rock Creek

Cloud Peak

Florence
Pass

To
Soldier
Park

18

20

19

18

16

R

West Tensleep Lake

15

17

14

Deer
Park

12

11

27

Island
Park

Sitting
Bull

Lake View

Bull Creek

16

To
Buffalo

Deer Haven
Lodge

Meadowlark
Lake

High Park
Lookout

13

Boulder
Park

Tensleep Creek

16

18

To
Tensleep

27

Tensleep Creek

Bald Ridge
ATV Trail ∅
mentioned.

miles to reach the Lower Paint Rock Trailhead. Primitive roads throughout the Tensleep and Paint Rock watersheds have a tendency to liquefy even after a light rain—watch the forecast carefully before setting out on one of these roads. Roadside attractions along US 16 include Tensleep Canyon, man-made Meadowlark Lake, and the James T. Saban fire lookout.

Developed campgrounds can be found in the lower reaches of Tensleep Canyon, along the shores of Meadowlark Lake, and at Sitting Bull Park just to the north of this lake. Other campgrounds can be found along the road to West Tensleep Lake and dispersed camping is allowed at the Battle Park Trailhead. Self-registration permits are required for all excursions into the Cloud Peak Wilderness. Pick one up at the West Tensleep or Battle Park Trailheads. Hikers bound for the Paint Rock Lakes can obtain a permit at the self-registration station near the Shell Creek Ranger Station, or at the Edelman or Paint Rock Lake trailheads. Tensleep has limited accommodations and supplies. You will need to travel to Worland or Buffalo to find a full-scale grocery store and most backpacking equipment.

11 BABY WAGON CREEK

General description: A wilderness route for a day hike or short backpack to Maybelle Lake, 4.3 miles one way.
Difficulty: Moderate.
Route finding: Map and compass.
Best season: Early July to early September.

Visitation: Light.
Elevation gain: 695 feet.
Elevation loss: 520 feet.
Maximum elevation: 9,970 feet.
Topo maps: Meadowlark Lake, Powder River Pass, *Trails Illustrated*.
Jurisdiction: Cloud Peak Wilderness (Bighorn National Forest).

FINDING THE TRAILHEAD

Follow US Highway 16 to mile 51.8, then drive northwest on FR 422. Follow this trunk road 0.5 mile to reach FR 419, just west of a gravel pit. This fair-weather four-wheel-drive track runs north for 1.8 miles to end at the edge of the meadows, where the trail begins. GPS: 44.186073° N, 107.144989° W.

THE HIKE

Ten thousand years ago, the East Tensleep Glacier extended down from the heights of Bighorn Peak, blocking the valley of Baby Wagon Creek. As the ice receded, a *lateral moraine,* or ridge of glacial debris, was left behind to mark where the sides of the glacier had been. The moraine dammed the valley, forming a shallow lake. Over the centuries, this lake filled in with silt, and grasses and sedges thrived on the mudflats. These flats have become the wet meadows of Baby Wagon Creek, some of the most extensive meadows in the Bighorn Mountains. The challenging route described here visits the lush and beautiful meadows of Baby Wagon Creek. The path is poorly marked and overgrown by meadow in many places. You will need skill with a topographic map and compass in order to make the trek. At the end of the trail is Maybelle Lake, where anglers can fish for cutthroat trout. Self-register if you intend to follow this trail into the Cloud Peak Wilderness.

The trail begins in the vast meadows of Baby Wagon Creek, pocked with sedge swamps and guarded by the rocky grandeur of Bighorn Peak to the north and Loaf Mountain to the east. From the road's end, follow the beaten tracks along the southern edge of the meadow. Posts mark the track with "TRAIL" signs. The track passes two boggy ponds on its way to a gap in a series of grassy knolls.

After passing through the gap, hike to the top of the next knoll, marked by a "TRAIL" post. This is a tricky junction: Misleading posts with orange diamonds lead north to the Virginia Creek Trail. Take a bearing on the summit of Loaf Mountain, then bring your gaze down to pinpoint a yellow-tipped post at the end of a distant, sinuous knoll. The trail runs toward this spot, crossing Baby Wagon Creek at a trail post where a rock-hop is possible without getting wet feet. The route then approaches the yellow-post knoll and runs along its southern base. Watch for signs of beaver activity along Baby Wagon Creek and for the marmots that live colonially within warrens dug into the knoll.

At the end of the knoll, the route crosses a swampy clearing and enters the forest, where it becomes visible as a trail. (It may take some time to locate it—cairns or blazes do not mark the path.) This path ascends steadily through the forest, climbing the lower slopes of Loaf Mountain. It eventually disappears as the trees give way to grassy glades.

Wet meadows along
Baby Wagon Creek.

Continue straight uphill, following the bottom of a shallow vale, until you reach an open meadow overlooked by a small but rocky peak (marked 10705 on the topographic map). Ascend into the grassy saddle behind a rocky knob, where a cairn marks the abandoned (and faint) road that is the next incarnation of the Baby Wagon Trail.

Follow the old road north as it descends steadily through the trees. It ultimately strikes Virginia Creek and follows it downstream. After crossing Virginia Creek, the trail grows faint as it ascends gradually across the meadows and then returns to the forest. After climbing over a timbered hilltop, the path descends to emerge on a grassy swell with a sweeping view of Bighorn Peak and the wet meadows at the head of East Tensleep Creek.

The trail runs northwest to ford the creek (hikers might find a log crossing just downstream). Here it enters the Cloud Peak Wilderness. Follow the fence posts north along the edge of the sedge bogs, bearing for the swampy shoreline of Maybelle Lake. Just before reaching the lake, the trail turns west at a large cairn to cross a rocky finger ridge. The path is faint here, but is (belatedly) marked by small cairns and blazes. After rounding the ridge, the path descends into the wooded cirque that bears Lake McLain. The Maybelle Lake Trail departs from its foot.

MILES AND DIRECTIONS

0.0 Baby Wagon Creek Trailhead. Follow old jeep trail east.

0.5 Junction with Virginia Creek snowmobile trail. Bear northeast.

0.9 Route fords Baby Wagon Creek.

1.5 Route leaves meadows and starts climbing through forest.

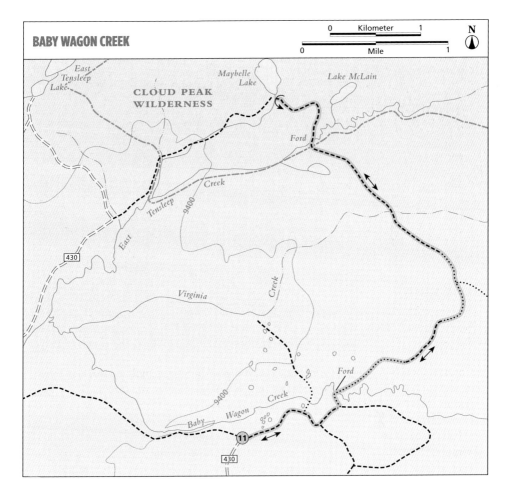

BABY WAGON CREEK

0 Kilometer 1
0 Mile 1

N

East Tensleep Lake

CLOUD PEAK WILDERNESS

Maybelle Lake

Lake McLain

Ford

Tensleep Creek

9400

East

430

Virginia

Creek

9400

Baby Wagon Creek

Ford

11

430

2.2 Route reaches high saddle.

2.9 Route crosses Virginia Creek.

3.7 Route fords East Tensleep Creek and enters Cloud Peak Wilderness.

3.9 Trail leaves marshes and runs west.

4.3 Maybelle Lake.

12 MAYBELLE LAKE

General description: A day hike to Maybelle Lake, 1.6 miles one way.
Difficulty: Moderate.
Route finding: Some challenges.
Best season: Early July to early September.
Visitation: Light.

Elevation gain: 420 feet.
Maximum elevation: 9,610 feet.
Topo maps: Meadowlark Lake (trail not shown), *Trails Illustrated*.
Jurisdiction: Cloud Peak Wilderness (Bighorn National Forest).

FINDING THE TRAILHEAD

Take US Highway 16 to Meadowlark Lake, and from the lake's northeastern shore, turn east onto FR 430. This rough and often muddy jeep trail runs about 4 miles along East Tensleep Creek to reach a signpost marked "Trail 079" at the base of a rocky grade. The trail runs east from this point. GPS: 44.207374° N, 107.162605° W.

THE HIKE

This footpath makes a short and shallow ascent to a cirque lake at the foot of Bighorn Peak. Although the trail tread is visible in most places and is marked with cairns and blazes, it can be challenging to follow in places. Rock piles along the route make it unsuitable for horses.

From the trail sign marked "McLain Trail," follow the trail marker posts (*not* the tire tracks) eastward along the edge of a grassy meadow. The trail becomes apparent as it dips

Maybelle Lake.

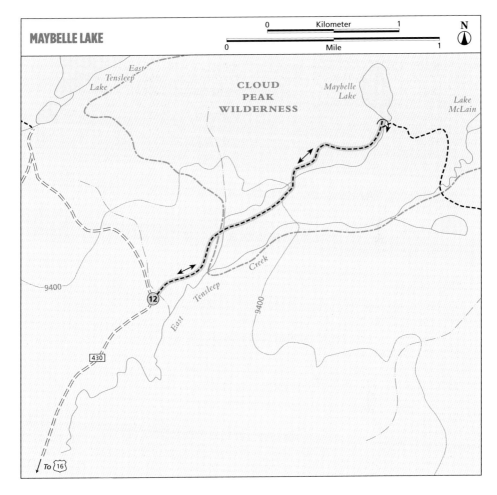

CLOUD PEAK WILDERNESS

East Tensleep Lake

Maybelle Lake

Lake McLain

9400

Tensleep Creek

East

9400

12

430

To 16

just inside the trees at the meadow's edge. As the path climbs steadily, grasses give way to willows in the clearing and a barren shoulder of Bighorn Peak rises ahead.

The path soon rock-hops across a stream that drains an open marsh, entering the Cloud Peak Wilderness as it does so. The path now visits rocky glades among the spruce trees, following the stream to a boggy crossing where the watercourse is scarcely noticeable. A level trek then leads to a round, lush sedge meadow. After skirting it, the path climbs the final pitch through a wooded draw to reach Maybelle Lake. This deep tarn is surrounded by subalpine forest and guarded by a stony buttress of Bighorn Peak.

MILES AND DIRECTIONS

0.0   McLain Trailhead.

0.6   Trail crosses substantial stream.

1.0   Second stream crossing.

1.6   Maybelle Lake.

13 PASTURE PARK

General description: A day hike or short backpack along old roadways, 10 miles overall. **Difficulty:** Moderately strenuous. **Route finding:** Some challenges. **Best season:** Early July to early September. **Visitation:** Light.	**Elevation gain:** 1,535 feet. **Elevation loss:** 1,535 feet. **Maximum elevation:** 8,960 feet (trailhead). **Topo maps:** Meadowlark Lake, Onion Gulch. **Jurisdiction:** Bighorn National Forest (Tensleep Ranger District).

FINDING THE TRAILHEAD

 Take US Highway 16 to mile 48.7, between Meadowlark Lake and Powder River Pass. From this point, drive south on FR 429, following signs for High Park Lookout. After 0.5 mile, the trail is the closed jeep track that veers left from the main road just beyond its junction with FR 433. GPS: 44.150784° N, 107.192101° W.

THE HIKE

This hike follows old jeep roads into the wild meadows surrounding the headwaters of Leigh Creek. Leigh Creek was named for Gilbert Leigh, a titled Englishman and friend of a Powder River cattle baron. He met his demise on a hunting trip in Tensleep Canyon in 1884. According to historians, Leigh apparently woke up in the night, walked over to some bushes to relieve himself, and promptly walked right off the edge of a cliff. His "bushes" turned out to be the tops of tall trees growing at the base of the rock. Elk use this area as a calving ground and summer range. Keep an eye out for these impressive animals during the twilight hours.

The trek begins on an old jeep trail that runs southward across the lush meadows of High Park. Lupines, shooting stars, and buttercups light the way. A backward glance reveals Bighorn Peak and the rocky summits surrounding it and to the west is High Park Lookout atop a wooded point. The cattle industry has left its distinctive footprint here: Fences, watering ponds, and corrals are scattered across the landscape.

The trail soon crests a rolling divide and descends into the Leigh Creek watershed. The high peaks disappear, but to the west are tors and palisades of Tensleep sandstone. Watch for elk and white-tailed deer as the trail approaches the edge of the timber. It then drops into a shallow gulch, where stands of whitebark pine are interspersed with grassy glades.

Soon a small brook appears in the gulch. As it merges with the headwaters of Leigh Creek, the trees open up into a grassy vale bordered by lodgepole pine. The route leads down this vale, splashing across the shallow stream several times and crossing boggy spots where springs contribute to the flow of the creek. Soon after passing a drift fence, the trail reaches a large park where aspens join the lodgepoles guarding the meadows. Scan one last time for elk before the old road contours southwest, fording another small brook and wandering across slopeside meadows.

The trees soon recede, to be replaced by a vast sagebrush meadow splashed with the blossoms of larkspur, forget-me-not, and lupine. This meadow owes its existence to the dry southern exposure of the slope; the north-facing slopes on the opposite side of Leigh Creek are clad densely in pines. The route tracks high across the open slope,

Pasture Park (middle distance) and the high peaks of the Bighorns.

ultimately reaching a series of small ponds where waterfowl and red-winged blackbirds make their nests. The path now deteriorates and becomes little more than a pale-green swath through the sage as it stays high on the benches.

As the sandstone palisades close in to form the head of Leigh Canyon, the track descends for a calf-deep ford of Leigh Creek. It then winds around a hillock and drops onto a grassy flat guarded by spruce trees. A faint track continues down Leigh Creek, but our route follows the old roadbed that heads uphill from this spot. It climbs into a lush meadow and promptly disappears. Watch for the path as it climbs eastward along the edge of the timber.

The track tops out on a meadowy divide and meets FR 436, two ruts running through the sagebrush. Turn left (north) on this road and follow it around a low summit as broad vistas reveal the surrounding country. Far to the west is the Absaroka Range, while to the east are the Hazelton Pyramid and the rugged peaks that surround it. The Mather Peaks massif rises along the northern skyline, flanked to the right by Bighorn Peak. Looking southward across the valley of Canyon Creek, there are good views of the Gold Mine Fire of 1988.

The road soon descends into a saddle with a circular cattle trough and reaches an intersection. The main road drops southeast toward Canyon Creek, while our route follows the closed road that runs northward. It surmounts a small hill and then follows a wooded ridgeline to emerge at Pasture Park. This broad grassland is almost free of sagebrush and the blossoms of lupine, shooting star, and forget-me-not carpet the opening.

As the route tracks across the lower portion of the meadow, reefs of Tensleep sandstone rise on the far side of Leigh Creek. After passing a cattle trough, the path descends to pass through a drift fence opposite a stand of aspen. Entering the forest, the rocky track

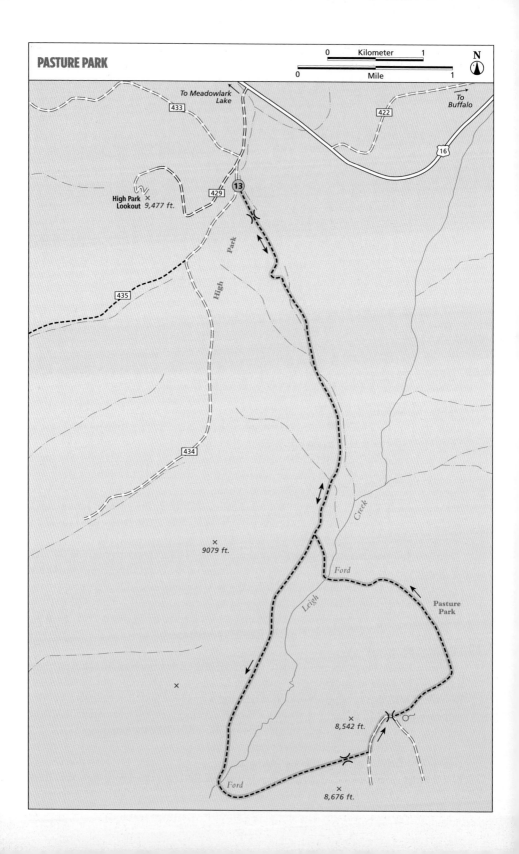

PASTURE PARK

0 Kilometer 1

0 Mile 1

N

To Meadowlark
Lake

To
Buffalo

433

422

16

429

13

High Park
Lookout 9,477 ft.

435

434

High Park

Creek

9079 ft.

Ford

Leigh

Pasture
Park

8,542 ft.

8,676 ft.

Ford

drops briskly through the lodgepoles, strikes a meadowy brook, and follows it to Leigh Creek. A calf-deep crossing ensues, after which the path climbs up the north edge of the open slope to rejoin the original trail. Turn right to retrace your steps to the trailhead.

MILES AND DIRECTIONS

0.0   Trailhead in High Park. Follow closed jeep trail southeast.

0.8   Trail leaves High Park and starts descent.

2.5   Trail enters large park above Leigh Creek. Return leg joins from east. Stay right.

4.2   Trail fords Leigh Creek.

5.3   Trail tops out at junction with FR 436. Turn left on road.

5.5   Road junction at watering trough. Continue straight ahead.

6.0   Trail enters Pasture Park.

6.6   Trail leaves Pasture Park and descends toward Leigh Creek.

7.2   Ford of Leigh Creek.

7.5   Trail meets original leg. Turn right to return.

10.0   Trail returns to trailhead in High Park.

combo w/ lost twin lakes...?

14 **THE HIGH LINE TRAIL**

General description: A day hike or short backpack to East Tensleep Lake, 4.5 miles one way.
Difficulty: Moderate.
Route finding: Some challenges.
Best season: Early July to early September.
Visitation: Very light.

Elevation gain: 1,410 feet.
Elevation loss: 600 feet.
Maximum elevation: 9,710 feet (East Tensleep Lake).
Topo maps: Meadowlark Lake, *Trails Illustrated.*
Jurisdiction: Bighorn National Forest (Buffalo Ranger District).

FINDING THE TRAILHEAD

Take US Highway 16 west from Meadowlark Lake to reach the old Deer Haven Lodge. Turn north on FR 27. Follow this good road north for 1.2 miles to a fork; bear right to stay on FR 27. Follow it for 5 miles to reach Deer Park. Park just beyond the bridge. GPS: 44.244924° N, 107.221828° W.

THE HIKE

Do not be fooled by the name of this trail; it doesn't follow high ridgetops with sweeping views in all directions. Instead, it climbs across the rolling and timbered hills to the south of the Cloud Peak massif, visiting the wet meadows of Bear Park along the way. The trek ends at East Tensleep Lake, a large natural lake that extends northward into the high peaks.

East Tensleep Lake.

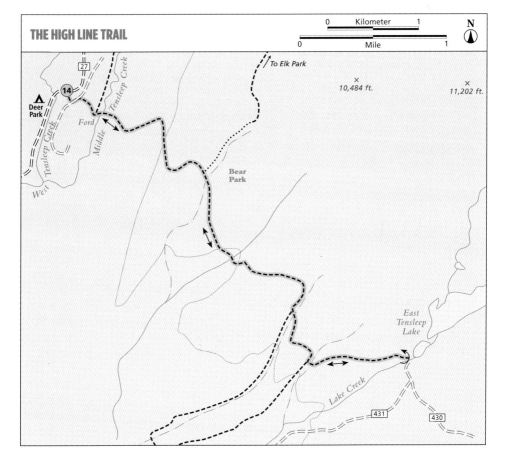

0   Kilometer   1

0   Mile   1

N

To Elk Park

× 10,484 ft.

× 11,202 ft.

27

14

Deer Park

Ford

West Tensleep Creek

Middle Tensleep Creek

Bear Park

East Tensleep Lake

Lake Creek

431

430

The footpath begins by running east, but soon turns north onto an abandoned road-bed. Watch for blazed trees as the trail turns east once more, surmounting a low ridge and then descending to the meadowy bottoms of Middle Tensleep Creek. A signpost marks the spot where the High Line splits away to the right. Go right and you will find a second sign at the footbridge over Middle Tensleep Creek.

The trail then climbs vigorously up the timbered slopes beyond. It ultimately levels off and runs through the forest to reach the boggy clearing of Bear Park. This meadow offers limited views of the neighboring peaks and at the time of this writing it was used as a summer pasture for domestic sheep. The Elk Park route enters the far northern end of the park, unmarked by cairns. Follow the signposts to pick up the High Line as it follows an old road that departs from the park's south end.

The old road now runs southward through the trees, passing a jumble of boulders where pikas make their homes. It then drops steadily through the timber, finally reaching bottom in a grassy valley. The trail disappears here. Hike east across the head of the meadow to pick up the old road on the far side. It climbs vigorously up the next ridge as several fainter jeep tracks veer away to the south. Atop the ridge are pleasant glades, and the High Line now turns south, descending through lush pocket meadows.

In the second meadow is a signpost. Here, the High Line leaves the road and follows a pack trail east and then south again (follow the cairns, posts, and blazes). After crossing another finger ridge, the path strikes a grassy brook and follows it down to a poorly marked junction with trail #068. Turn east at the double posts as the High Line climbs vigorously into wooded uplands.

The gradient eases and soon the rushing of Lake Creek can be heard through the timber. The path emerges at a signpost beside a swampy clearing. One must wade across the swamp to reach FR 430. The steep hill above the meadow is an old terminal moraine that dams the basin of East Tensleep Lake. To reach the lake, scramble up the moraine, then follow the east shore of a small mere that is connected to the large lake. East Tensleep is a large, sinuous body of water that lies at the base of many-lobed Bighorn Peak. Beyond it are impressive domes of granite, replete with sheer cliffs chiseled by glacial action.

MILES AND DIRECTIONS

0.0   Deer Park Trailhead.

0.5   Junction with Tensleep Falls Trail. Bear right.

0.6   Trail crosses a bridge over Middle Tensleep Creek.

1.7   Bear Park.

3.3   Junction with old jeep trail. Turn left.

3.7   Junction with trail #068. Turn left.

4.5   Foot of East Tensleep Lake.

15 TENSLEEP FALLS

General description: A short day hike along Middle Tensleep Creek, 2 miles overall.
Difficulty: Easy.
Route finding: No problem.
Best season: Late June to mid-September.
Visitation: Very light.
Elevation gain: 80 feet.

Elevation loss: 265 feet.
Maximum elevation: 9,100 feet (West Tensleep Trailhead).
Topo maps: Lake Helen (trail not shown), *Trails Illustrated* (trails shown incompletely).
Jurisdiction: Bighorn National Forest (Tensleep Ranger District).

FINDING THE TRAILHEAD

Take US Highway 16 west from Meadowlark Lake to reach the old Deer Haven Lodge. Turn north on FR 27. Follow this good road north for 1.2 miles to a fork; bear right to stay on FR 27. Follow it for 6.9 miles to a fork; bear right here to reach the West Tensleep Trailhead at the road's end GPS: 44.261709° N, 107.212447° W. For through hikers, the trail winds up at Deer Park GPS: 44.244924° N, 107.221828° W, page 46, The High Line Trail.

Tensleep Falls.

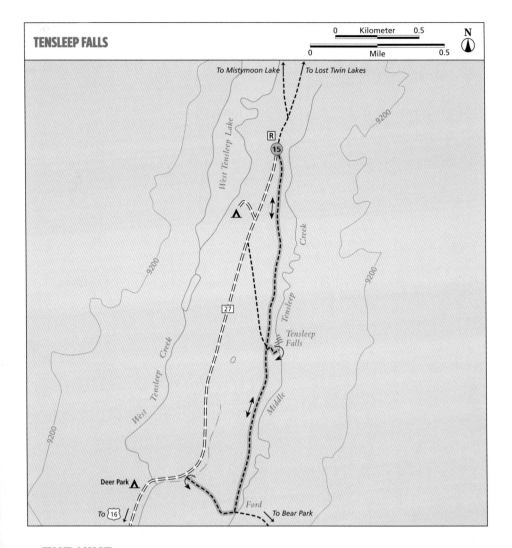

THE HIKE

This trail follows Middle Tensleep Creek, visiting an impressive waterfall and scenic meadows along the way. It is a short and easy trip, but it has not received much use in the past since the destination is relatively obscure. The round trip to the falls is 1.6 miles. Hikers with only one vehicle tend to turn around at the falls and retrace their steps on the return leg.

From the West Tensleep Trailhead, this wide path glides southward toward the shady riffles of Middle Tensleep Creek. As the stream drops into broad meadows, the trail maintains its altitude, following the top of a pine-clad ridge. Upon reaching the lower end of the meadow, the stream carves a narrow cleft in an outcrop of granite, then plunges 20 feet over a sheer drop and into an emerald pool. A spur path descends for a better view of the falls.

The main trail continues southward, dropping gradually across a wooded slope. From time to time, the trees open up for a view of the meadows below. At the junction with the High Line Trail, take a stroll out to the banks of the creek for a picturesque view of the Mather Peaks. To complete the trek, follow the High Line westward as it climbs a wooded ridge, follows an old road south for a brief time, then turns west again to meet FR 27 just north of Deer Park.

MILES AND DIRECTIONS

0.0   West Tensleep Trailhead.

0.7   Spur trail to base of falls (0.1 mile, moderate).

0.8   Junction with trail from West Tensleep campground. Continue straight ahead.

1.5   Junction with High Line Trail. Turn right.

2.0   Deer Park Trailhead.

16 THE LOST TWIN LAKES

General description: A day hike or backpack to the Lost Twin Lakes, 6.1 miles one way.
Difficulty: Moderately strenuous.
Route finding: Some challenges.
Best season: Early July to mid-September.
Visitation: Heavy.

Elevation gain: 1,490 feet.
Elevation loss: 410 feet.
Maximum elevation: 10,410 feet.
Topo maps: Lake Helen, *Trails Illustrated.*
Jurisdiction: Cloud Peak Wilderness (Bighorn National Forest).

FINDING THE TRAILHEAD

Take US Highway 16 west from Meadowlark Lake to reach the old Deer Haven Lodge. Turn north on FR 27. Follow this good road north for 1.2 miles to a fork; bear right to stay on FR 27. Follow it for 6.9 miles to a fork; bear right here to reach the West Tensleep Trailhead at the road's end. GPS: 44.261709° N, 107.212447° W.

THE HIKE

The Lost Twin Lakes are among the most scenic of the hundreds of lakes in the Cloud Peak Wilderness. These alpine gems are set in a glacial cirque, guarded by the towering walls and domes of Bighorn Peak. The trek can be approached as a day trip or a backpack. Campers should plan to stay in the grassy basin below the lakes because there are no legal campsites in the lake basin.   From the trailhead, hike north and take the right-hand path, marked "Middle Tensleep Trail #65." An old road soon drops toward the grassy bottoms of Middle Tensleep Creek, while our trail continues to follow the crest of a low ridge where lodgepole pines attain diameters approaching 3 feet. It is rare for lodgepoles to attain such old-growth size, since when they reach maturity, they are prone to fire and bark beetles.

The ridge that the trail is following is an old *medial moraine*, a mound of gravel deposited at the point where two glaciers merged together. To the west is Bald Ridge, a much taller lateral moraine that the West Tensleep Glacier pushed up along its far edge.

The path soon dips eastward, dropping to the head of a broad meadow beside Middle Tensleep Creek. Above the head of the clearing is a striking double waterfall, which the trail passes just before it enters the Cloud Peak Wilderness. A steep climb through the trees leads to the top of a granite knoll. Here, panoramic views of rounded summits stretch from the Mather Peaks in the north to Bighorn Peak in the south.

The trail dips to cross an elevated meadow, and it is here that the unmarked Elk Park route heads southward. The main trail follows a northern tributary up another sharp incline and at the top is the shelf that bears Mirror Lake. Hike east from a signpost to reach the foot of the lake or follow the main trail across the outlet stream to gain access to the southern shore. Darton Peak can be seen from the west end of the lake, while the south side offers views of the Mather Peaks.

The Lost Twin Lakes Trail now follows the edge of yet another meadow, then climbs along the rim of a small gorge carved by the stream after the glaciers receded. Above this gulch is an upper basin of sedge meadows. It offers views of the cliff-girt peaks that line a hanging cirque bearing the Lost Twin Lakes. The trail ahead is unsuitable for horses. Horse users should picket their mounts here and proceed on foot.

The path now crosses the swampy streamcourse and climbs vigorously to surmount a granite headwall. A meadowy basin lies beyond, and the trail grows a bit faint as it follows the eastern edge of the valley. The path then climbs a steep pitch across the bedrock, finally topping a rise above the lowermost of the Lost Twin Lakes. Awe-inspiring cliffs tower 1,600 feet above the water, carved from the massive dome of Bighorn Peak by relentless glacial erosion. A narrow veneer of vegetation borders the lower lake, while the upper lake is completely rockbound. To preserve the pristine quality of these alpine lakes, camp out of sight well below the lake basin.

MILES AND DIRECTIONS

0.0   West Tensleep Trailhead.

0.1   Junction with Mistymoon Trail. Bear right.

1.5   Falls on Middle Tensleep Creek.

1.6   Trail enters Cloud Peak Wilderness.

2.5   Elk Park route departs to the south.

2.9   Trail crosses outlet of Mirror Lake.

The lower of the Lost Twin Lakes.

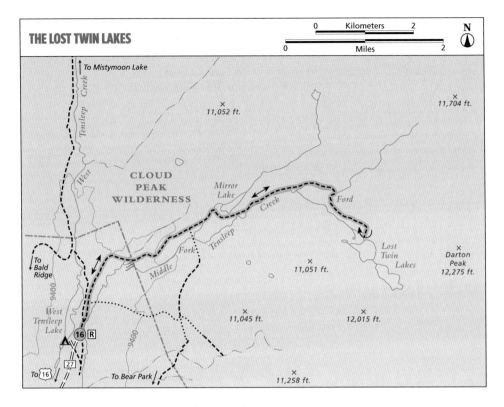

3.3 Trail passes south shore of Mirror Lake.

5.0 Trail fords Middle Tensleep Creek.

6.1 Lost Twin Lakes.

17 ELK PARK

General description: A wilderness route from Middle Tensleep Creek to Bear Park via Elk Park, 3.5 miles.
Difficulty: Strenuous.
Route finding: Map and compass.
Best season: Early July to mid-September.
Visitation: Very light.
Elevation gain: 1,050 feet.

Elevation loss: 920 feet.
Maximum elevation: 10,120 feet (Elk Park).
Topo maps: Lake Helen, Meadowlark Lake (trail not shown), *Trails Illustrated*.
Jurisdiction: Cloud Peak Wilderness (Bighorn National Forest).

FINDING THE TRAILHEAD

Take US Highway 16 west from Meadowlark Lake to reach the old Deer Haven Lodge. Turn north on FR 27. Follow north for 1.2 miles to a fork; bear right to stay on FR 27. Follow it for 6.9 miles to a fork; bear right to reach the West Tensleep Trailhead at the road's end. GPS: 44.261709° N, 107.212447° W. Hike up the Lost Twin Lakes Trail 2.5 miles to an open meadow just after the first major grade. Hike south across the meadow, fording Middle Tensleep Creek and a tributary stream to reach a level shelf at the southeast corner of the clearing. The route starts here. It ends at the north end of Bear Park, which is reached via a 1.7-mile hike on the High Line Trail.

THE HIKE

This primitive trail links the trail to Lost Twin Lakes with the High Line Trail via a grassy shelf high on the mountainsides. The resulting loop of 7.7 miles can be made in a long day trip or as an overnighter. Backpackers should be aware that water is not available in Elk Park. The non-system trail is no longer maintained and is difficult to follow in places.

From the upper shelf on the south bank of Middle Tensleep Creek, the faint track climbs southward through a spruce woodland. It soon emerges into an old burn. At the top of the grade, the path passes through the pocket meadows that occupy a gap in the granite hills. On the far side is a vale drained by an intermittent stream. Follow the streamcourse downward for a short distance, then seek out the path as it angles upward across granite slopes. As the slopes level off, the trail enters a lush glade at the foot of a talus slope.

At the far edge of the glade, the path turns upward into the rocks, climbing at a murderous pace. There are some old, eroded switchbacks in places, but even these are steep. Eventually, the grade eases and the trees thin out. The path levels off as it reaches Elk Park, emerging from the timber at a cairn in a grassy arm of meadow. This high and windswept steppe is perched on the shoulder of a rocky summit and has superb views northward of the Mather Peaks. Sheep have grazed Elk Park heavily. It is also a summer range for elk, which are sometimes spotted in the drainage to the south. There is little cover in the heart of the park and thus it is a poor place to be caught in a thunderstorm.

Cross the lower edge of Elk Park on a southward bearing, staying just below a rocky knoll in the midst of the meadows. Cairns and posts mark the route as it crosses the western slope of the knoll and then drops through fields of fractured boulders to descend into the drainage beyond. The trail now drops briskly across rocky slopes, passing copses of fir and aspen. In the valley below, a small brook pours over a slanted waterfall and meanders

Looking north toward
Mather Peaks.

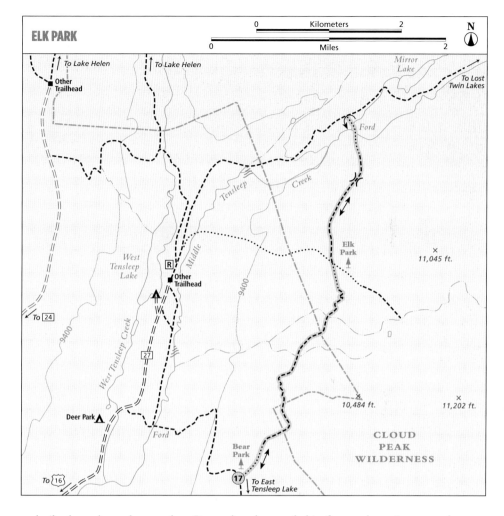

Kilometers

Miles

N

To Lake Helen
Other Trailhead
To Lake Helen
Mirror Lake
To Lost Twin Lakes
Ford
Tensleep
Creek
Elk Park
11,045 ft.
West Tensleep Lake
R
Middle
Other Trailhead
9400
To 24
9400
West Tensleep Creek
27
10,484 ft.
11,202 ft.
Deer Park
Ford
CLOUD PEAK WILDERNESS
Bear Park
To 16
17
To East Tensleep Lake

lazily through a sedge meadow. Rugged peaks mantled in fractured granite tower above the valley's head.

The path crosses the stream at the foot of a bog, then ascends to the hill marked "9818" on the topo map. After cresting this hill, the trail descends on a southwesterly course, staying above groves of aspen that grow on the south-facing slope. The trail bottoms out at the foot of a second wet meadow. Cross its lower edges to pick up the trail again.

It follows a rocky draw at first, then climbs steeply up the far wall of the valley. The path tops out on a tableland of broken rock, weaving a devious course through and sometimes over the boulders (watch carefully for cairns). Soon the trees close in and the traveling gets easier.

After leaving the Cloud Peak Wilderness, the path drops down a sharp slope to reach the long strip of wet meadow that leads to Bear Park. Water can generally be found at this park and domestic sheep are often present as well. The High Line Trail enters Bear Park from the west and departs from its southern tip, bound for East Tensleep Lake.

MILES AND DIRECTIONS

0.0 Route leaves Lost Twin Lakes Trail.

0.1 Trail fords outlet stream from Mirror Lake and Middle Tensleep Creek.

0.5 Trail crosses low saddle.

0.9 Trail begins climb to Elk Park.

1.1 Trail emerges at Elk Park. Hike south across the clearing.

1.4 Trail leaves Elk Park and starts descending.

1.7 Trail crosses small stream.

2.1 Trail crosses second stream and starts climbing.

2.5 Trail reaches top of grade.

2.9 Trail leaves Cloud Peak Wilderness.

3.1 Trail enters Bear Park

3.5 Route joins High Line Trail.

18 MISTYMOON LAKE

General description: A day hike or backpack to Lake Helen (4.9 miles), Lake Marion (6.2 miles), or the head of Mistymoon Lake (7.2 miles).
Difficulty: Moderate.
Route finding: No problem.
Best season: Mid-July to early September.
Visitation: Extremely heavy.

Elevation gain: 970 feet.
Elevation loss: 200 feet.
Maximum elevation: 10,250 feet (Mistymoon Lake).
Topo maps: Lake Helen, *Trails Illustrated*.
Jurisdiction: Cloud Peak Wilderness (Bighorn National Forest).

FINDING THE TRAILHEAD

Take US Highway 16 west from Meadowlark Lake to reach the old Deer Haven Lodge. Turn north on FR 27. Follow this good road north for 1.2 miles to a fork; bear right to stay on FR 27. Follow it for 6.9 miles to a fork; bear right here to reach the West Tensleep Trailhead at the road's end. GPS: 44.261709° N, 107.212447° W.

THE HIKE

Mistymoon Lake is one of the premier destinations in the Cloud Peak Wilderness. This high alpine lake offers rather tepid fishing, but the surrounding grandeur makes up for it. Do not plan on a fire since wood is scarce, and this area is above the 9,200-foot fire limit. The trailhead is easy to access, and as a result the trail tends to be crowded. Wise hikers will avoid it on the weekends. Lakes Helen and Marion are equally scenic and make fine day-hiking destinations, but camping opportunities are limited. Visitors who stay over-night should be conscientious and select a campsite hidden from the trail.

From the trailhead, hike north through the pines and take an immediate left as the Mistymoon Lake Trail glides down to the shore of West Tensleep Lake. The grassy crest of Bald Ridge rises beyond the lake, culminating in a rocky peak far to the north. At the head of the lake is a pastoral landscape of grassy bottoms, and the trail follows the east bank of West Tensleep Creek through these meadows. A brief climb through the pines leads to a bridge over the creek, and on the far side is a grassy clearing that affords the first views of the peaks at the head of the valley. It is here the faint West Tensleep cutoff trail climbs to the west to reach the top of Bald Ridge.

The main trail resumes its northward course, climbing modestly through the pines as it moves away from the creek. The trail levels off in an isolated meadow that reveals the summits flanking Bighorn Peak. The path makes a brief return to West Tensleep Creek at a spot where deep sloughs wander through a series of emerald meadows. The landscape grows rocky as the mountains crowd in around the stream and a sparse growth of spruce and pine rises between the granite balds. Expect periodic views of the rugged foothills as the gradient increases to a modest climb.

At the top of the rise is a junction with the Bald Ridge Trail and just beyond it lies Lake Helen. Its lower end is narrow and choked with boulders, while at the upper end the waters spread broad and cobalt beside alpine meadows. There are superb views of Cloud Peak straight up the valley and massive, granite-ribbed peaks rise on both sides of the lake. The subalpine forest soon dissipates into a few scattered groves of fir. These

Lake Helen.

trees become progressively smaller as the trail continues up the valley. The path wanders among granite outcrops to reach the glistening waters of Lake Marion, a smaller clone of Lake Helen.

The path then rises through the alpine meadows to reach Mistymoon Lake. This broad, circular tarn sits at the base of rocky peaks. It is surrounded by alpine tundra dotted with krummholz clumps of fir, huddled low to the ground to escape the icy winter blasts. Watch for marmots and pikas on the slopes surrounding the lake. The Florence Pass Trail runs eastward from the outlet stream, while the Mistymoon Trail continues around the western shore. Along the way, a signpost marks the departure of the Middle Paint Rock Trail. The Lake Solitude Trail descends from a saddle to the north shore of Mistymoon Lake, merging with the terminus of the Mistymoon Trail.

MILES AND DIRECTIONS

- **0.0** West Tensleep Trailhead.
- **0.1** Junction with Lost Twin Lakes Trail. Bear left.
- **1.0** Head of West Tensleep Lake.
- **1.3** Trail fords West Tensleep Creek.
- **1.4** Junction with Bald Ridge cutoff. Bear right.
- **2.8** Junction with abandoned Yost Trail.
- **4.6** Junction with Bald Ridge Trail. Continue straight ahead.
- **4.9** Trail reaches foot of Lake Helen.
- **5.3** Head of Lake Helen.

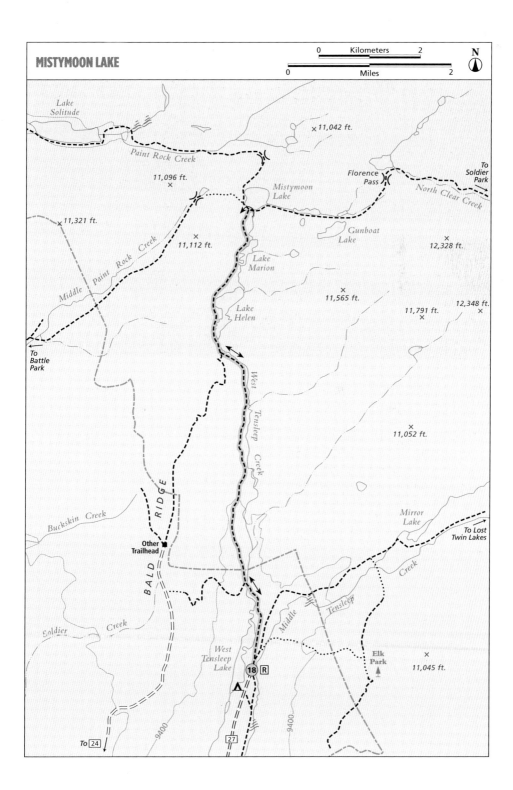

MISTYMOON LAKE

Kilometers
0   2

Miles
0   2

N

Lake
Solitude

Paint Rock Creek

× 11,042 ft.

Florence
Pass

To
Soldier
Park

North Clear Creek

11,096 ft.
×

Mistymoon
Lake

× 11,321 ft.

Middle Paint Rock Creek

× 11,112 ft.

Lake
Marion

Gunboat
Lake

12,328 ft.
×

Lake
Helen

11,565 ft.
×

11,791 ft.
×

12,348 ft.
×

To
Battle
Park

West Tensleep Creek

11,052 ft.
×

Buckskin Creek

B A L D   R I D G E

Mirror
Lake

To Lost
Twin Lakes

Other
Trailhead

Soldier   Creek

West
Tensleep
Lake

Middle   Tensleep   Creek

Elk
Park

11,045 ft.
×

18 R

9400

To 24

27

9400

Mistymoon Lake.

6.2   Lake Marion.

7.0   Foot of Mistymoon Lake. Junction with trail to Florence Pass.

7.1   Junction with Middle Paint Rock Creek.

7.2   Head of Mistymoon Lake. Lake Solitude Trail climbs away northward.

19 BALD RIDGE

General description: A connecting trail from Bald Ridge to Lake Helen, 3.1 miles.
Difficulty: Moderate.
Route finding: Some challenges.
Best season: Mid-July to early September.
Visitation: Light.

Elevation gain: 179 feet.
Elevation loss: 215 feet.
Maximum elevation: 10,165 feet.
Topo maps: Lake Helen, *Trails Illustrated*.
Jurisdiction: Cloud Peak Wilderness (Bighorn National Forest).

FINDING THE TRAILHEAD

Take US Highway 16 west from Meadowlark Lake to reach the old Deer Haven Lodge. Turn north on FR 27. Follow this good road north for 1.2 miles to a fork, then veer left onto FR 24. Follow this gravel trunk road for 1.7 miles, then turn right onto FR 411. This rough road requires a four-wheel-drive vehicle in dry weather. If rain is in the forecast, don't even try it with a tank. Follow this road (go straight at all junctions) for 8.2 miles to reach the end of the trail. GPS: 44.282348° N, 107.234914° W.

Cloud Peak as seen from the crest of Bald Ridge.

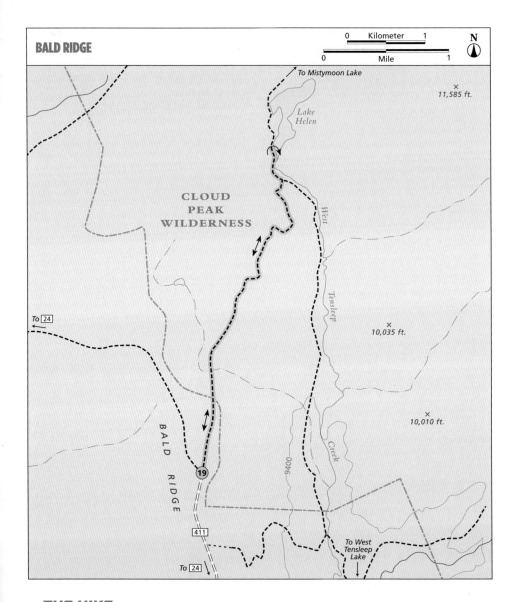

CLOUD
PEAK
WILDERNESS

BALD RIDGE

To Mistymoon Lake

Lake
Helen

West

Tensleep

Creek

9400

To 24

19

411

To 24

To West
Tensleep
Lake

×
11,585 ft.

×
10,035 ft.

×
10,010 ft.

0   Kilometer   1
0   Mile   1

N

THE HIKE

This trail offers the fastest and most scenic route to Mistymoon Lake and the other tarns along West Tensleep Creek. On the down side, a four-wheel drive is required to reach the trailhead and when the weather is wet, only a helicopter can get you there. As a result, the trail receives few visitors and makes a fine option for enterprising souls who seek to avoid the crowds.

The trail begins by running northward atop a treeless, windswept escarpment that represents an enormous lateral moraine left behind by the West Tensleep Glacier. The path crosses rolling tundra, rising and falling as it makes its way toward the base of a nameless summit. All along the way are astounding views of the Cloud Peak massif with its bald domes broken up by sheer cliffs.

The path ultimately angles downward through great outcrops of granite, and the first subalpine firs form small, scattered copses among the rocks and meadows. The trees rise in stature as the trail makes its way downward, passing a stagnant pond. The trail jogs eastward briefly, providing views of the rounded summits that surround Bighorn Peak. It then surmounts a small hill and descends steadily through a thickening forest. The trail joins the Mistymoon Trail at a marked junction just 0.3 mile below Lake Helen.

MILES AND DIRECTIONS

0.0 Bald Ridge Trailhead.

0.5 Trail enters Cloud Peak Wilderness.

2.8 Junction with Mistymoon Trail just south of Lake Helen.

3.1 Lake Helen

20 MIDDLE PAINT ROCK CREEK

General description: A short backpack from the Battle Park Trailhead to Mistymoon Lake, 5.9 miles.
Difficulty: Moderately strenuous.
Route finding: Some challenges.
Best season: Mid-July to early September.
Visitation: Light.

Elevation gain: 1,490 feet.
Elevation loss: 370 feet.
Maximum elevation: 10,560 feet.
Topo maps: Lake Helen, Lake Solitude (trail not shown), *Trails Illustrated*.
Jurisdiction: Cloud Peak Wilderness (Bighorn National Forest).

FINDING THE TRAILHEAD

Take US Highway 16 west from Meadowlark Lake to reach the old Deer Haven Lodge. Turn north on FR 27. Follow this good road north for 1.2 miles to a fork and veer left onto FR 24. Follow this gravel trunk road for 15.4 miles to reach a small meadow, where ATV Trail 066 departs to the right. The hike begins on this ATV trail. GPS: 44.300313° N, 107.303363° W.

THE HIKE

Of the routes that run into the Cloud Peak Wilderness from the Battle Park Trailhead, this one receives the fewest visitors. The trail is faint in some places, but the scenic rewards along the way make up for any route-finding difficulties. This trail makes an excellent two-day loop when combined with the Lake Solitude route (page 69). The trail leads into the grassy upper vale of Middle Tensleep Creek, climbs over a pass, and drops into the basin that bears Mistymoon Lake. The Lily Lake Trail provides an alternate for the first leg of this hike, but this latter trail is open to ATVs.

The trail begins by following a draw northeast along the rolling meadows stretching to the base of the mountains. Elk Mountain rises prominently to the northeast, while the domed massif of Bomber Mountain is visible through the gap of the Middle Paint Rock Valley.

Follow the ATV trail eastward past Lily Lake. This broad mere is ringed on three sides by timber. On the eastern shore, the meadows lead right up to the base of Elk Mountain. After passing the lake, the ATV trail makes a sharp swing to the south, while the Middle Paint Rock Trail follows trail markers and posts eastward.

This path descends to cross a boggy slough, then climbs a bit to strike the north bank of Middle Paint Rock Creek. After following the stream for a short distance, watch for a cairn and a trail marker that indicate the faint crossing. The creek can be jumped easily here. Hikers who miss this crossing can strike the trail by hiking due south from a second ford where the valley constricts.

At first, the trail runs northeast along the edge of the timber. It soon wanders inland along the spine of a grassy rise. At the top of a modest grade, the path enters the Cloud Peak Wilderness. There are breathtaking views of the peaks ahead. Elk Mountain presents a façade of fractured granite to the north of the valley, while ahead a pair of nameless and barren summits guards the southern approach to a high pass.

The trail soon makes an insanely steep climb up a side gully, passing into the alpine landscape of krummholz and tundra. Wildflowers light the way and pikas scurry among the boulders near the trail. The grade ultimately levels off for a pleasant tundra stroll along the headwaters of the creek. There is a mirror-like tarn at the head of the valley and a second pool awaits at the top of the divide. Cloud Peak rises regally to the northeast, while the rugged backside of Bomber Mountain lies just to the south of it. This latter peak was named after a World War Two B-17 bomber that crashed into the peak during a storm on its way to England. The wreckage was not found until a herder noticed the sun reflecting off the fuselage several years later.

The trail now descends steadily across the alpine tundra, obvious at first but then growing faint as it follows widely spaced cairns. It runs roughly southeast to join the Mistymoon Trail at a signpost on the southwestern shore of Mistymoon Lake. This circular alpine lake is right at the timberline, surrounded by tundra interspersed with clumps of krummholz rising from the tundra. Impressive peaks surround the lake, and the awe-inspiring scenery explains the large number of people that visit the area. From here, trails run northwest to Lake Solitude, east to Florence Pass, and south to West Tensleep Lake.

MILES AND DIRECTIONS

0.0   Trail leaves FR 24.

1.3   Lily Lake.

1.7   Trail leaves ATV trail. Turn left.

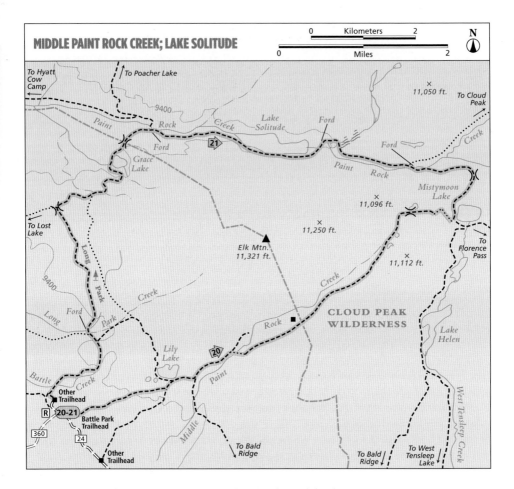

MIDDLE PAINT ROCK CREEK; LAKE SOLITUDE

2.0 Trail fords Middle Paint Rock Creek to reach south bank.

3.2 Trail enters Cloud Peak Wilderness.

5.2 Trail crosses pass into Tensleep watershed.

5.9 Trail junction beside Mistymoon Lake.

21 LAKE SOLITUDE

See map on page 68.
General description: A backpack to Lake Solitude (6.2 miles) and Mistymoon Lake (10.1 miles).
Difficulty: Moderate.
Route finding: No problem.
Best season: Mid-July to early September.

Visitation: Moderate.
Elevation gain: 2,100 feet.
Elevation loss: 1,065 feet.
Maximum elevation: 10,450 feet.
Topo maps: Lake Solitude, Lake Helen, *Trails Illustrated.*
Jurisdiction: Cloud Peak Wilderness (Bighorn National Forest).

FINDING THE TRAILHEAD

Take US Highway 16 west from Meadowlark Lake to reach the old Deer Haven Lodge. Turn north on FR 27. Follow this good road north for 1.2 miles to a fork; veer left onto FR 24. Follow this gravel trunk road for 16.3 miles to reach the Battle Park Trailhead at its end. GPS: 44.308785° N, 107.312244° W.

THE HIKE

This is the primary route into the Cloud Peak Wilderness from the Battle Park Trailhead. It runs north through broad meadows, climbs over a ridge, and descends to Grace Lake. The trail runs north to the main fork of Paint Rock Creek and follows it to Lake Solitude, the largest of the natural lakes in the Bighorn Mountains. Above the lake, the trail runs up the valley into alpine country, finally crossing a pass to bring the traveler to Mistymoon Lake. This trail receives heavy use from horses as far as the head of Lake Solitude. As a consequence, it becomes quite muddy after a rainstorm.

The trail begins with a descent through the lodgepoles to cross Battle Creek, then climbs modestly through open glades on a northeasterly tangent. At the top of the grade is the broad, grassy saddle that marks the south end of Long Park. Here, a trail splits away to the right, bound for Middle Paint Rock Creek. The main trail descends to a rock-hop over Long Park Creek, then crosses a small tributary stream. The path glides up into the heart of Long Park, a vast grassland bordered with pines and guarded by the imposing summit of Elk Mountain. As the trail climbs northward, the more distant summits of Mount Woolsey and then Cloud Peak appear above the intervening ridgetop.

The trail levels off atop a grassy divide and follows it to the toe of a ridge that falls away to the west. Here, an open meadow reveals the barren ranges to the north and an unmarked track drops westward toward Lost Lake. The main trail turns northeast, dropping through pocket meadows, and then following the base of a steep boulder field.

The path levels off as it reaches a marshy basin, where it meets a confusing array of trails at the edge of a meadow. Bear right as the Lake Solitude Trail descends eastward through spruce and fir to reach the south shore of Grace Lake. This large woodland mere is ringed with lily pads and affords some limited mountain views. The trail rounds its western shore, then climbs a low ridge to enter the Cloud Peak Wilderness. From here, a steep descent across several grassy benches leads to a junction with the Paint Rock Trail on a shelf above Paint Rock Creek.

The trail now runs eastward, parallel to the creek. The forest found here is transitional between the montane woodland of lodgepole pine and the subalpine forest of spruce and

Waterfalls above
the head of
Lake Solitude.

fir. The forest opens up near Lake Solitude and the trail winds among a series of grassy hillocks. Great mounds of granite rise to the north of the stream, the outliers of the high peaks at the core of the range.

There is a grassy rise at the foot of Lake Solitude and it offers a glimpse of Cloud Peak's rounded summit. Massive walls of granite march right down to the water's edge on the north shore. The trail will follow the nominally gentler terrain to the south of the lake. It passes below slender cascades before venturing out across a jumble of massive boulders that tumbled down from the heights. After negotiating this obstacle, the path runs through the forest to reach the broad meadows at the head of the lake. There are well-worn camp spots along the edge of the trees.

The path crosses the meadows to make a knee-deep ford of Paint Rock Creek, turns east, and starts to climb. It soon reaches a bridge over a tributary stream, which tumbles through a series of stunning waterfalls on its way down from the granite heights. The trail now climbs briskly to avoid a narrow gorge where blade-shaped slabs of granite rise above Paint Rock Creek. Dazzling arrays of wildflowers bloom from chinks in the rock and on the lush slopes beyond. Look back to take in an aerial view of Lake Solitude.

After a rock-hop leads to the south bank of Paint Rock Creek, the trail winds upward across meadowy knolls interspersed with groves of subalpine fir. The path rounds a final, rocky knob to emerge above the timberline, and now Cloud Peak and Bomber Mountain can be seen in all their glory. A substantial stream with a small waterfall courses down from a rocky defile to the north and joins the main valley here. This stream is actually the head of Paint Rock Creek, and the scramble route to the summit of Cloud Peak follows it upward to the tops of the domes.

The trail continues to climb through the alpine tundra, then swings south into a broad gap filled with meltwater pools. After crossing the divide into the West Tensleep drainage, Lake Marion appears in the distance and soon Mistymoon Lake appears in the basin below. The trail descends to the north shore of Mistymoon and runs around its west side, joining the Middle Paint Rock Trail en route to the foot of the lake. From here, the Mistymoon Trail runs south, while the trail to Florence Pass climbs eastward.

MILES AND DIRECTIONS

0.0 Battle Park Trailhead.

0.2 Trail crosses head of Battle Creek.

0.8 Trail enters Long Park.

1.2 Trail crosses Long Park Creek.

2.4 Trail leaves Long Park.

2.7 Top of grade. Trail starts downward.

4.3 Grace Lake.

4.7 Trail enters Cloud Peak Wilderness.

5.0 Junction with Paint Rock Trail. Turn right.

6.2 Trail reaches foot of Lake Solitude.

7.1 Trail reaches head of Lake Solitude and fords inlet.

7.5 Waterfalls.

8.5 Trail fords Paint Rock Creek.

9.5 Trail crosses pass into West Tensleep drainage.

10.1 Head of Mistymoon Lake. Mistymoon Lake Trail follows western shore of lake.

22 BATTLE PARK

General description: A linking trail from the Battle Park Trailhead to Hyatt Cow Camp, 4.5 miles one way.
Difficulty: Moderately strenuous (west to east); moderate (east to west).
Route finding: No problem between Battle Park and Hyatt Cow Camp; map and compass beyond.
Best season: Mid-July to mid-September.

Visitation: Very light.
Elevation gain: 225 feet.
Elevation loss: 1,475 feet.
Maximum elevation: 9,140 feet.
Topo maps: Lake Solitude (trail not shown), *Trails Illustrated* (location incorrect).
Jurisdiction: Bighorn National Forest (Tensleep Ranger District).

FINDING THE TRAILHEAD

Take US Highway 16 west from Meadowlark Lake to reach the old Deer Haven Lodge. Turn north on FR 27. Follow this good road north for 1.2 miles to a fork; veer left onto FR 24. Follow this gravel trunk road for 15.7 miles to reach a large meadow with a wilderness-permit registration station. The trail departs from the Battle Park trailhead at the end of the road. GPS: 44.308785° N, 107.312244° W.

Battle Park.

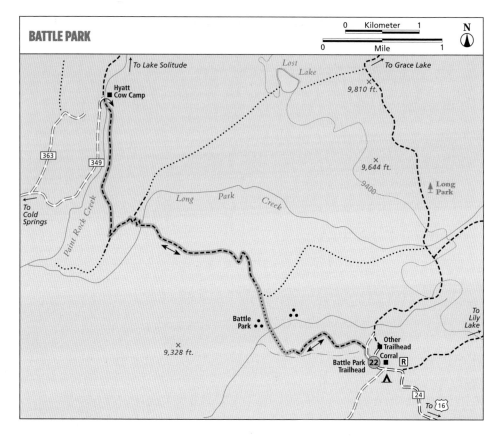

0   Kilometer   1

0   Mile   1

N

To Lake Solitude

Lost Lake

To Grace Lake

Hyatt
■ Cow Camp

×
9,810 ft.

363

349

×
9,644 ft.

9400

▲ Long
  Park

To
Cold
Springs

Long   Park   Creek

Paint Rock Creek

Battle
Park ● ●

To
Lily
Lake

×
9,328 ft.

Other
■ Trailhead

Corral

Battle Park (22) ■   R
Trailhead

24

To 16

THE HIKE

The hike starts by running west through the timber from the Battle Park Trailhead. The route follows blazes as it descends westward through the pines. After passing some granite outcrops, the path drops into a grassy draw that leads downward into Battle Park.

The trail is invisible as it crosses the grasslands of Battle Park. Cattle graze here in the summer and a small herd of resident elk may be spotted during the twilight hours. Hike north-northwest across the meadows, which are guarded to the west and south by picturesque buttes. There are two cabin ruins here, one on the west side of the basin and the other just inside the trees at the spot where Battle Creek enters the meadows. The trail enters the timber on the west side of a grassy cove that marks the northern edge of the park.

From here, a well-defined pathway leads through the level forest and descends into a basin. It passes aspen groves and outcrops of granite on the way to the basin's floor, then turns northwest. The forest opens up into broad meadows as the trail approaches Long Park Creek. Make the rock-hop across the creek and climb the finger ridge beyond. The trail now enters the trees, descending briefly before it emerges into the sagebrush meadows that border Paint Rock Creek. The final leg of the trail leads across a diverse landscape of sagebrush meadows, old-growth spruce bottoms, and stands of aspen. The trail fords the creek and meets FR 349 below the Hyatt Cow Camp. Skirt the camp and make the calf-deep ford of Paint Rock Creek to reach the end of FR 349. From here, the

Paint Rock Trail runs north toward Lake Solitude. Soon it joins the Kinky White Trail, which leads to the Paint Rock Lakes.

MILES AND DIRECTIONS

0.0   Trail runs west from Battle Park trailhead.

0.2   New trail leaves roadbed. Turn left.

1.0   Route enters Battle Park.

1.3   Route crosses Battle Creek.

1.7   Trail leaves Battle Park.

2.9   Trail crosses Long Park Creek.

4.5   Hyatt Cow Camp.

23 PAINT ROCK CREEK

General description: A linking trail from Hyatt Cow Camp to a junction with the Poacher Lake and Lake Solitude Trails, 4.9 miles.
Difficulty: Moderate.
Route finding: No problem.
Best season: Early July to mid-September.

Visitation: Very light.
Elevation gain: 1,220 feet.
Maximum elevation: 9,130 feet.
Topo maps: Lake Solitude, *Trails Illustrated*.
Jurisdiction: Cloud Peak Wilderness (Bighorn National Forest).

FINDING THE TRAILHEAD

The trail can be reached by four-wheel-drive vehicle via a long and arduous journey to the end of FR 349 (page 257, Paint Rock Canyon). The beginning of the trail can also be reached via the Battle Park Trail (4.5 miles) or from the Paint Rock Lakes via the Kinky White Trail (6.2 miles). The end of the Paint Rock Trail can be reached from the south via the Lake Solitude routing (5 miles) or by combining the Cliff Lake and Poacher Lake Trails (8.7 miles overall).

Along the Paint Rock Trail.

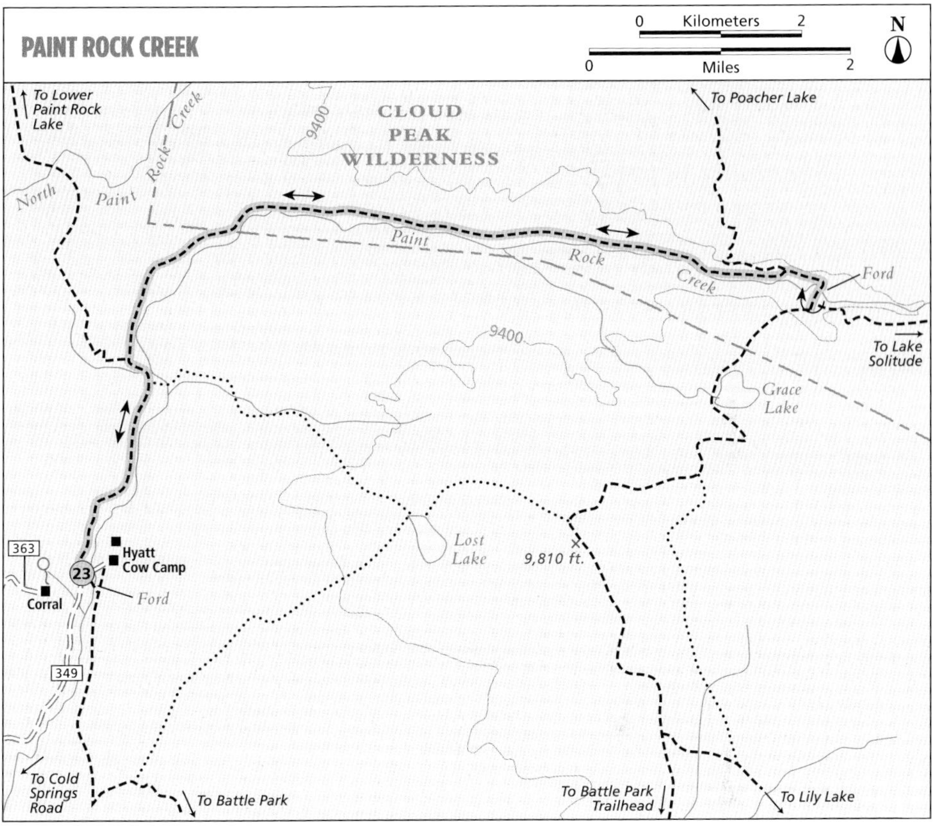

PAINT ROCK CREEK

To Lower Paint Rock Lake
To Poacher Lake
CLOUD PEAK WILDERNESS
9400
North Paint Rock Creek
Paint Rock Creek
Ford
To Lake Solitude
9400
Grace Lake
363
23
Hyatt Cow Camp
Corral
Ford
Lost Lake
9,810 ft.
349
To Cold Springs Road
To Battle Park
To Battle Park Trailhead
To Lily Lake

THE HIKE

This section of trail connects the Hyatt Cow Camp with the trail to Lake Solitude. The route along Paint Rock Creek is pleasant and scenic, but not spectacular. This trail offers connections with the Kinky White Trail to the Paint Rock Lakes as well as the Poacher Lake Trail. A short stretch of road hiking leads from the trailhead to link up with the upper end of the Paint Rock Canyon Trail.

Great groves of old-growth spruce line Paint Rock Creek where it passes the Hyatt Cow Camp. The Paint Rock Trail, however, sticks to the sagebrush meadows at the base of the hills as it runs northward. Impressive bluffs of granite flank the creek, and groves of aspen add a splash of color with their emerald summer foliage and golden autumn hues.

The trail climbs modestly at first, then with great vigor as it ascends to a narrow gap between mounds of granite. After gaining the gap, the trail enters an elevated basin where pine and spruce grow on a fertile floodplain. The trail crosses a broad meadow as the valley bends to the east and on the far side it enters the Cloud Peak Wilderness.

For the next few miles, the trail is choked with boulders that become stepping stones when rain turns the soil into a sticky muck. A dense forest of spruce shades the creek, while low cliffs of granite rise above its north bank. The valley widens as it approaches a major northern tributary and grassy meadows offer glimpses of the summit of Elk Mountain.

After crossing a second tributary, the valley walls close in around the foaming rapids of Paint Rock Creek. The path soon climbs onto a steep and open slope, ultimately rising to the wooded hilltops where it meets the Poacher Lake segment of the Solitude Trail. The main trail continues eastward, passing beneath massive formations of granite on its way to a knee-deep ford of Paint Rock Creek. Here, on a shelf above an open park, the path joins the trail to Lake Solitude, which lies 2.1 miles to the east.

MILES AND DIRECTIONS

0.0 End of FR 349.

1.1 Junction with Kinky White Trail. Continue straight ahead.

1.8 Trail enters Cloud Peak Wilderness.

4.7 Junction with Poacher Lake Trail. Bear right.

4.9 Junction with Lake Solitude Trail.

24 POACHER LAKE

General description: An extended trip from Paint Rock Creek to Teepee Pole Flats, via Poacher Lake, 3.8 miles.
Difficulty: Moderate.
Route finding: No problem.
Best season: Early July to late August.

Visitation: Light.
Elevation gain: 810 feet.
Elevation loss: 825 feet.
Maximum elevation: 9,770 feet.
Topo maps: Lake Solitude, Shell Lake, *Trails Illustrated.*
Jurisdiction: Cloud Peak Wilderness (Bighorn National Forest).

FINDING THE TRAILHEAD

Hike the Lake Solitude Trail 5.1 miles from Battle Park to Paint Rock Creek, ford the creek, and hike west for 0.2 mile to reach the Poacher Lake Trail. The far end is reached via a 4.9-mile hike on the Cliff Lake Trail from Lower Paint Rock Lake.

THE HIKE

This surprisingly scenic trail links the main fork of Paint Rock Creek with Teepee Pole Flats on North Paint Rock Creek. Here, the trail is joined by trails to the Paint Rock Lakes to the west and Geneva Pass to the east. The fastest access to the trail is via the Cliff Lake route from Lower Paint Rock Lake or via the Lake Solitude Trail from the Battle Park Trailhead.

Wet meadows on the way to Poacher Lake.

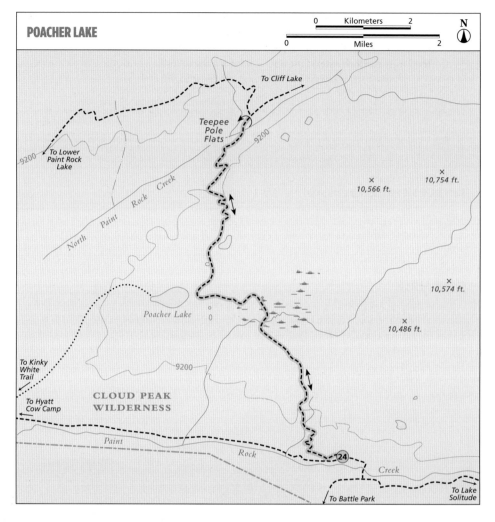

The trail begins by wandering westward and climbing gently the bluffs to the north of Paint Rock Creek. As it zigzags upward along the bases of granite outcrops, the path offers unobstructed views of Elk Mountain to the southeast. The path then enters a closed-canopy forest of lodgepole pine and climbs at a steady rate. It passes several grassy pockets that offer glimpses of the low summits to the east. At the top of the grade is a rounded ridgetop where the forest was thinned by lightning strikes and wind throw.

There is an abrupt transition from pine to spruce and fir as the path descends onto the north side of the ridge. This is explained by the cooler and moister climate found on north-facing slopes. A shallow descent leads into a broad, marshy basin that stretches eastward to the base of the mountains. Here, the trail crosses a substantial stream and turns west along an open finger ridge at the edge of the marsh. This ridge is a small *lateral moraine*, made of gravel deposited along the edge of a long-extinct glacier. Look back for a fine view of the terminal moraine the path followed across the marsh. It marks the endpoint of a glacial surge.

The trail now makes a level journey through a shady forest of spruce en route to Poacher Lake. This broad but shallow pool is bordered by marshes and meadows that make it a magnet for wildlife. The path now turns northeast, passing through the trees to reach a long meadow extending northeast from the lakeshore. An imposing range of summits now rises to the north, beyond North Paint Rock Creek.

The path threads its way between granite formations, passing a rockbound pond before it begins to descend toward Teepee Pole Flats. A sparse woodland is interspersed with granite slabs that offer additional views to the north. The path now descends briskly through the forest, bearing northeast for Teepee Pole Flats. Here, the braided channels of North Paint Rock Creek course through verdant meadows lit by wildflowers. An ankle-deep ford leads across the stream to reach the end of the trek, marked by a signpost on the trail that runs from Paint Rock Lakes to Cliff Lake and Geneva Pass.

MILES AND DIRECTIONS

0.0   Trail leaves Paint Rock Trail.

0.5   Trail crosses small stream.

1.5   Trail crosses marshy brook.

2.3   Poacher Lake.

3.8   Trail fords North Paint Rock Creek to reach junction with Cliff Lake Trail.

25 THE KINKY WHITE TRAIL

General description: A connecting trail from Lower Paint Rock Lake to the main fork of Paint Rock Creek, 6.2 miles total.
Difficulty: Moderate (north to south); moderately strenuous (south to north).
Route finding: Some challenges.
Best season: Mid-July to mid-September.
Visitation: Light.

Elevation gain: 310 feet.
Elevation loss: 1,320 feet.
Maximum elevation: 9,250 feet (scarp above North Paint Rock Creek).
Topo maps: Spanish Point, Lake Solitude (trail not shown), *Trails Illustrated* (trail shown incorrectly).
Jurisdiction: Bighorn National Forest (Medicine Wheel Ranger District).

FINDING THE TRAILHEAD

Drive east from Shell on US Highway 14 to mile 31.3. Turn right on FR 17 and follow this trunk road east and then south for 25.5 miles. The portion of the road that crosses private land gets sloppy after it rains. The trailhead is the parking area just before the campground at the head of Lower Paint Rock Lake. GPS: 44.395415° N, 107.381130° W.

THE HIKE

This connecting trail provides a surprisingly scenic hike between the Paint Rock Lakes and Hyatt Cow Camp. At its terminus, the trail links up with trails leading to Battle Park, up the main fork of Paint Rock Creek toward Lake Solitude, and with a short section of road that leads to the upper end of the Paint Rock Canyon Trail. The Kinky White Trail traverses a diverse mixture of meadows, climax coniferous forest, and aspen stands. There are broad vistas from a ridgetop at the trail's midpoint.

The trail begins by rounding the head of Lower Paint Rock Lake to reach a junction with the trail to Cliff Lake (page 86). Bear right at the junction, following the Kinky White Trail along the eastern shore of the lake. As it departs from the foot of the lake, the trail enters a shady forest of lodgepole pine. It soon passes a beaver pond on Trout Creek, then bends southeast past a kettle lake formed eons ago by a melting chunk of glacial ice.

After a short jaunt along a finger ridge, the path descends across a small vale where an intermittent stream courses through a pocket meadow. The trail now descends gradually through the timber, emerging as it crosses a small brook to enter Anthony Park. This rolling expanse of grassland is flanked by low hills. The trail disappears in the open meadow; follow the guideposts along the northeast edge of the clearing to pinpoint the spot where the trail enters the trees once again.

The trail soon crosses Sheep Creek and glides up a wooded rise. At the top of the slope, the path emerges atop a steep escarpment high above the valley of North Paint Rock Creek. Here, open slopes are populated by isolated groves of aspen and you can take in sweeping views of the surrounding country. To the south is Paint Rock Canyon and the sedimentary bluffs that guard it while to the east are the cloud-scraping peaks of granite that rise within the Cloud Peak Wilderness. Elk Mountain is the prominent summit to the south while the tops of both Cloud Peak and Black Tooth Mountain rise to the east above the intervening summits.

Looking southward toward the head of Paint Rock Canyon.

The trail traverses eastward across the slope as it descends, rendering fine views of the meadows along North Paint Rock Creek. It bottoms out in a heavily timbered depression. The small ridge that defines this vale was once a lateral moraine of the Paint Rock Glacier, which carved out the valley below. The path now runs southwest along the depression, descending gradually. It finally drops onto the rolling sage meadows of the valley floor. Once again, it becomes necessary to follow the guideposts as the path skirts the western edge of a broad sedge bog, then wanders among wooded hillocks. It seeks an open slope of sagebrush for its descent to the North Fork of Paint Rock Creek. This pretty stream flows through a shady woodland of spruce. A calf-deep ford leads across the slippery cobbles to the far bank.

The path now climbs gradually through the trees, then strikes a grassy meadow and follows it southward. (An informal route runs northeast from this meadow, bound for Poacher Lake.) A low but rugged summit of granite rises to the east, while the wooded point straight ahead represents the summit of Cement Mountain. The trail passes a weedy marsh, then swings east through an open saddle to enter the watershed of Paint Rock Creek's main fork.

The sagebrush meadows give way to aspen groves as the path drops into a vale occupied by a tributary stream. It levels off briefly, then makes a vigorous descent through the spruce to reach the valley floor. Here, it meets the Paint Rock Creek Trail at a signpost amid the sagebrush, 1.1 miles north of Hyatt Cow Camp.

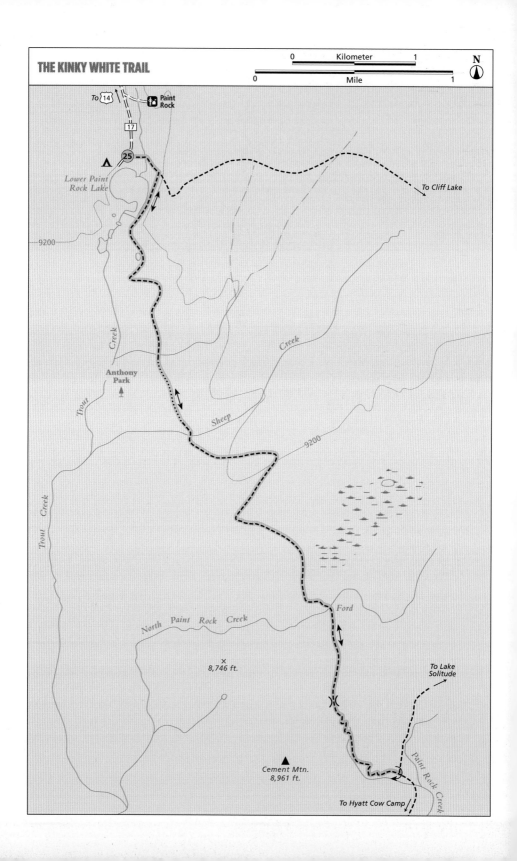

0   Kilometer   1

0   Mile   1

N

To 14

Paint
Rock

17

25

Lower Paint
Rock Lake

To Cliff Lake

9200

Creek

Creek

Trout

Anthony
Park

Sheep

9200

Trout   Creek

Ford

To Lake
Solitude

North Paint Rock Creek

X
8,746 ft.

Paint Rock Creek

Cement Mtn.
8,961 ft.

To Hyatt Cow Camp

MILES AND DIRECTIONS

0.0   Lower Paint Rock Lake Trailhead.

0.2   Junction with Cliff Lake Trail. Continue straight ahead.

0.5   Trail leaves foot of Lower Paint Rock Lake.

1.3   Trail crosses nameless stream to enter Anthony Park. Follow posts southeast.

1.6   Trail leaves Anthony Park.

1.7   Trail crosses Sheep Creek.

2.2   Top of scarp above North Paint Rock Valley. Trail starts to descend.

3.5   Trail fords North Paint Rock Creek.

4.0   Trail crosses saddle to enter drainage of Paint Rock Creek.

6.2   Junction with Paint Rock Creek Trail.

26 CLIFF LAKE

General description: A backpack to Cliff Lake (8.9 miles) and through the upper lake basin of North Paint Rock Creek to the Geneva Pass Trail (11.6 miles).
Difficulty: Moderately strenuous.
Route finding: No problem.
Best season: Mid-July to late August.

Visitation: Heavy.
Elevation gain: 2,275 feet.
Elevation loss: 1,465 feet.
Maximum elevation: 10,300 feet.
Topo maps: Spanish Point, Cloud Peak, Shell Lake, *Trails Illustrated*.
Jurisdiction: Cloud Peak Wilderness (Bighorn National Forest).

FINDING THE TRAILHEAD

Drive east from Shell on US Highway 14 to mile 31.3. Turn right on FR 17 and follow this trunk road east and then south for 25.5 miles. The portion of the road that crosses private land gets sloppy after it rains. The trailhead is the parking area just before the campground at the head of Lower Paint Rock Lake. GPS: 44.395415° N, 107.381130° W.

THE HIKE

This trail begins at the Paint Rock Lakes and follows North Paint Rock Creek deep into the heart of the Cloud Peak Wilderness. The upper lake basin at the head of the valley is not to be missed. The trail offers two different chances to join the Geneva Pass Trail, which runs north over the divide to reach Coffeen Park.

Hike to the far edge of the meadow above Lower Paint Rock Lake, where the trail begins with a steady climb up a heavily timbered hillside. The path turns east after cresting the ridge. It strikes grassy vales and follows them upward for a time before resuming its eastward course. The trail ultimately makes its way across high sage meadows to enter the vast pastures of Sheep Creek. Rocky summits now rise in plain view to the north.

After crossing Sheep Creek, the path climbs into a sparse woodland and soon reaches the wilderness boundary. The trees close in as the trail progresses eastward. Before long, the trail is traveling atop a level plateau robed in rich spruce-fir woodland. The forest ends abruptly as the path climbs into a notch between two bald hillocks. This opening allows a view of the mountains to the south and the arid slopes support an astonishing diversity of wildflowers.

The trail now wends its way through a maze of granite hills, clad in pine and occasionally interrupted by wet meadows. Sporadic views of the peaks to the east improve as the trail nears Teepee Pole Flats. Here, the path descends to North Paint Rock Creek, which runs through a narrow, grassy vale between the hills.

After passing a junction with the Poacher Lake Trail, the Cliff Lake route follows the meadows upstream, occasionally climbing onto pine-studded hillsides. There is a knee-deep ford at the upper end of the pastures. Beyond it the trail climbs more vigorously across grassy hillsides and through subalpine forests. The mountains reveal themselves at a junction with the Geneva Pass Trail. Stay right as the trail now climbs beside a rushing tributary stream.

After a stiff climb through a stand of subalpine fir, the trail emerges amid a series of grassy balds. It winds upward, following the pretty mountain brook that drains Cliff Lake. The first pool to be encountered at the foot of the cliffs is a shallow, narrow pond. Cliff

Still waters at Cliff Lake.

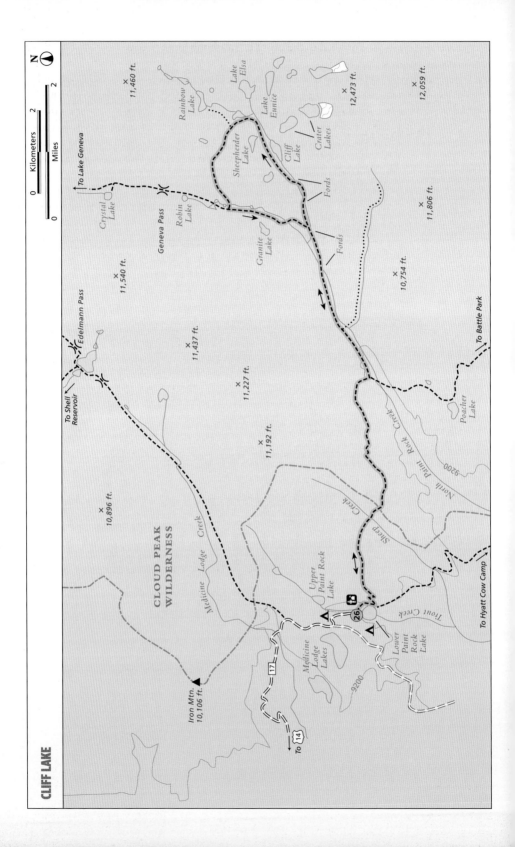

CLIFF LAKE

CLOUD PEAK WILDERNESS

N

Kilometers
0   2

Miles
0   2

To Lake Geneva

× 11,460 ft.

Rainbow Lake

Lake Elsa

Lake Eunice

Crater Lakes

× 12,473 ft.

Sheepherder Lake

Cliff Lake

Fords

× 12,059 ft.

Crystal Lake

Geneva Pass

Robin Lake

Granite Lake

Fords

Fords

× 11,806 ft.

Edelmann Pass

To Shell Reservoir

× 11,540 ft.

× 11,437 ft.

× 11,227 ft.

× 10,754 ft.

To Battle Park

× 11,192 ft.

Medicine Lodge Creek

× 10,896 ft.

Iron Mtn. 10,106 ft.

North Paint Rock Creek

Peacher Lake

9200

Sheep Creek

Upper Paint Rock Lake

26

17

Medicine Lodge Lakes

Lower Paint Rock Lake

Trout Creek

To Hyatt Cow Camp

9200

14

To

Lake lies beyond it, bordered to the north by subalpine forest and to the south by a sheer wall of granite rising 700 feet above the water. The best views are from the head of the lake, where the trail climbs onto meadowy hillocks above the wetlands at the east end.

The trail then continues upward along the stream, passing a slender waterfall that descends across the rounded face to the south. The route now leads onto open moors where trees are scarce and rocky knobs rise from the rolling tundra. Soon the broad mirror of Lake Elsa can be seen to the southeast, and before long the path reaches the shore of Lake Eunice. Soon thereafter, a cairn marks the old trail that climbs the tundra escarpment to the east to reach Rainbow Lake.

The main trail turns northwest at this cairn, climbing into the granite hills. It now reveals stunning views of Black Tooth Mountain, which rises beyond the glacier-carved crags of the divide. Sheepherder Lake can be seen to the southeast as the path winds upward across the meadows and past isolated stands of fir. The trail tops out at a high saddle, then turns west to cross a small rill. The path rises into a second pass for final views of Black Tooth Mountain.

The path ultimately strikes a westward-running vale and follows it to North Paint Rock Creek. After a shallow ford, the path rises to meet the Geneva Pass Trail 2 miles below Geneva Pass.

MILES AND DIRECTIONS

0.0   Lower Paint Rock Lake Trailhead.

0.2   Junction with Kinky White Trail. Turn left.

1.9   Trail crosses Sheep Creek.

2.3   Trail enters Cloud Peak Wilderness.

4.9   Teepee Pole Flats. Junction with Poacher Lake Trail. Turn left.

6.9   Trail fords North Paint Rock Creek.

7.5   Junction with end of Geneva Pass Trail. Bear right.

8.3   Trail fords outlet of Cliff Lake.

8.9   Trail reaches north shore of Cliff Lake.

9.7   Lake Eunice. Junction with route to Rainbow Lake. Bear left.

10.1   Trail reaches top of high saddle.

11.5   Trail fords headwaters of North Paint Rock Creek.

11.6   Junction with Geneva Pass Trail.

27 **THE SALT LICK TRAIL**

General description: A day hike on a loop trail to the rim of Tensleep Canyon (1.5 miles round-trip).
Difficulty: Moderately strenuous.
Route finding: No problem.
Best season: May and late August to mid-October.
Visitation: Moderate.

Elevation gain: 660 feet.
Elevation loss: 660 feet.
Maximum elevation: 5,700 feet.
Topo maps: Old Maid Gulch (trail not shown).
Jurisdiction: BLM Worland Field Office.

FINDING THE TRAILHEAD

 Drive east from Tensleep for about six miles on US Highway 16. The trailhead is on a short spur road on the north side of the highway, near a geological sign for the Madison Formation. GPS: 44.070515° N, 107.348650° W.

THE HIKE

This is a hike best saved for cooler weather. The highway and rural residences on the valley floor are constant companions as you climb; this is no wilderness trek. There is no water along the trail and lots of exposure to the sun on the vigorous climb to the canyon rim, so prepare accordingly and bring plenty of water of your own.

The hike begins with a steady, often steep grade up through the junipers and yuccas. The first ponderosa pines signal the approach to the loop junction. We describe the route in a counterclockwise direction, so turn right at the marked intersection. The trail steepens past prickly pear cactus and cheatgrass, which are markers of past overgrazing by livestock. The trail reaches the base of the caprock of Tensleep Sandstone, then dips and climbs as it continues northward. The trail soon reaches a junction with a faint path that runs north along the base of the cliffs; turn left here to follow the loop hike. Our route heads steeply upward, to gain the canyon rims amid widely spaced ponderosas. From this lofty vantage point, you can enjoy panoramic views of Tensleep Canyon below.

The path now rises gently as it runs westward through the pines, then descends into the lower reaches of the canyon of Salt Lick Creek. The descent soon steepens, and the loose woodland offers fine views of this picturesque canyon. Alternating descents and short climbs, the path leads southward until it reaches Tensleep Canyon once again. The trail now crosses drier, south-facing slopes high above the canyon floor, skirting the base of the caprock. Soon the path bends north to complete the loop, leading to a foot-pounding descent back to the starting point.

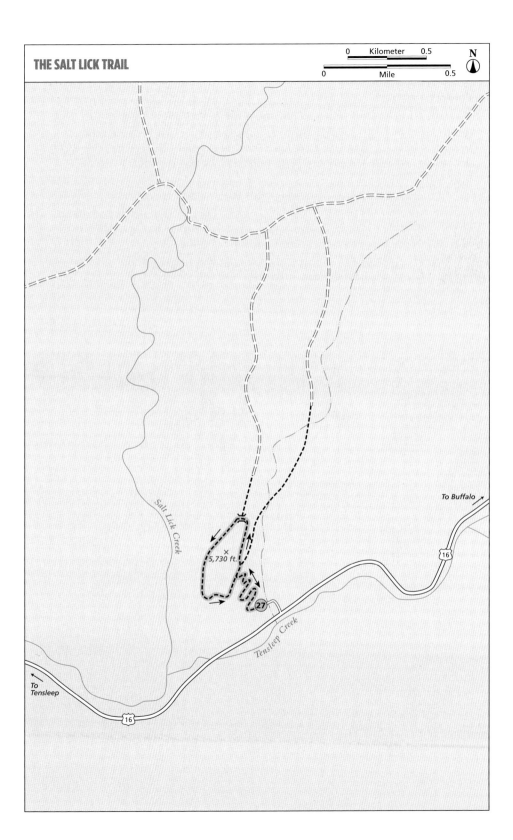

THE SALT LICK TRAIL

0   Kilometer   0.5

0   Mile   0.5

N

To Buffalo

16

Salt Lick Creek

× 5,730 ft.

27

Tensleep Creek

16

To Tensleep

16

ADDITIONAL TRAILS

An ATV road runs from FR 24 to **Lily Lake**, where it meets the Middle Paint Rock Trail. The ATV road then swings south through the high country and eventually ends at the Bald Ridge Trailhead.

The **Bald Ridge cutoff** climbs steadily from the head of West Tensleep Lake to a poorly marked spot at the top of Bald Ridge, just south of the Bald Ridge Trailhead.

An unofficial trail leads down to **Lost Lake** from the ridgetop just north of Long Park. A long-abandoned trailbed leads west from this lake to join the Paint Rock Trail near its junction with the Kinky White Trail.

The unmaintained trails that ring **Sitting Bull Park** follow a series of old jeep routes through riparian areas and past privately leased cabins. They are hard to follow in places.

A connecting trail runs along **Willow Creek** from the Tyrell Work Center to join the High Line Trail just west of East Tensleep Lake. It receives little use.

The **Virginia Creek Trail** is a snowmobile route that runs across the meadows of Baby Wagon Creek, descends through a marshy woodland, and peters out in the meadows beside Virginia Creek.

Rimrock high above Tensleep Canyon.

THE NORTHERN HINTERLANDS OF THE CLOUD PEAK MASSIF

The northern half of the Cloud Peak Wilderness is wilder and more remote than the southern reaches. Fewer trails penetrate into the mountains. These trails receive less maintenance and thus tend to be more primitive. In contrast to the southern marches of the Bighorns, the northernmost end of the Cloud Peak massif features pyramid-shaped peaks of frost-shattered granite. If you are looking for a place in the Cloud Peak Wilderness to find solitude or undertake an off-trail expedition, the northern hinterlands offer a good place to start.

Road access is fair to poor along the northern edge of the wilderness. FR 17 on the west side and FR 26 to the north and east provide access to a handful of trails. The Red Grade Road (FR 26 from Big Horn to Big Goose Park) is steep, winding, and rough. It is not recommended for trailers or low-clearance vehicles. Most of the trailheads can only be reached via primitive four-wheel-drive roads that may be rocky or have deep potholes. These trailheads become impassable to all vehicles in wet weather. An extensive network of ATV trails extends up to the boundary of the Cloud Peak Wilderness around Bighorn and Park Reservoirs. To the east of the wilderness, Willow Park Reservoir and Penrose Park are also hotbeds of ATV use. Be prepared to share the trail with motorized vehicles in these areas. Road-based attractions include Shell Canyon and Falls as well as the ruins of a historic tie flume along the upper South Tongue River.

Developed campgrounds can be found at the Paint Rock Lakes, along the upper reaches of the South Tongue River, and in the vicinity of Big Goose Park. Primitive campgrounds can be found at Shell Reservoir, Coffeen Park, Park Reservoir, and Little Goose Creek. These primitive camping areas are reached via four-wheel-drive roads. If your trip will carry you into the Cloud Peak Wilderness, you will need to self-register for a permit. Do this at the Shell Creek Ranger Station, the Coney Lake and Coffeen Park Trailheads, or Poverty Flat on FR 26 near the east boundary of the National Forest. The ranger stations at Shell Creek, Paint Rock Lakes, and Big Goose are staffed intermittently. Stop in at Shell Falls or Sheridan for current trail conditions. Shell, Big Horn, Dayton, and Ranchester offer gas, restaurants, and a limited range of supplies. Full services are available in Sheridan and Greybull.

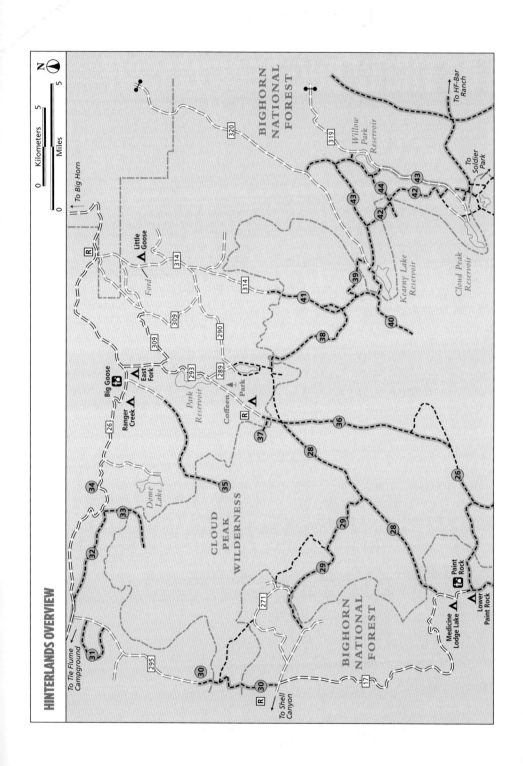

HINTERLANDS OVERVIEW

N

0 Kilometers 5
0 Miles 5

To Big Horn

BIGHORN NATIONAL FOREST

320

319

Willow Park Reservoir

To Soldier Park

To HF-Bar Ranch

43

44

42

43

42

39

40

41

38

Kearny Lake Reservoir

Cloud Peak Reservoir

R
Little Goose

Ford

314

314

309

309

290

Big Goose

East Fork

293

289

Park Reservoir

Ranger Creek

26

Coffeen

Park

R

37

36

28

34

35

33

32

Dome Lake

CLOUD PEAK WILDERNESS

29

28

26

29

31

271

Paint Rock

Medicine Lodge Lake

Lower Paint Rock

BIGHORN NATIONAL FOREST

To Tie Flume Campground

295

30

30

R

17

To Shell Canyon

28 **EDELMAN PASS**

General description: A backpack from FR 17 to Coffeen Park over two high passes, 11 miles overall.
Difficulty: Moderately strenuous.
Route finding: No problem.
Best season: Mid-July to early September.
Visitation: Light.
Elevation gain: 1,270 feet (west to east).

Elevation loss: 2,020 feet (west to east).
Maximum elevation: 10,465 feet (pass west of Emerald Lake).
Topo maps: Spanish Point, Shell Lake, Park Reservoir, Dome Lake (trail shown incompletely), *Trails Illustrated*.
Jurisdiction: Cloud Peak Wilderness (Bighorn National Forest).

FINDING THE TRAILHEAD

 Drive east from Shell on US Highway 14 to mile 31.3. Turn right on FR 17 and follow this trunk road east and then south for 24 miles. The portion of the road that crosses private land gets sloppy after it rains. Watch for the marked trailhead parking area on the right side of the road, 0.5 mile beyond Medicine Lodge Creek. GPS: 44.410684°N, 107.385686° W. The trail leaves FR 17 about 0.3 mile to the north. The hike ends at the Coffeen Park Trailhead GPS: 44.518912° N, 107.245332° W; page 119.

THE HIKE

This trail is one of the major routes across the high divide of the Cloud Peak Wilderness. It offers a fine sampling of the attractions of the wilderness, combining the broad grasslands along Medicine Lodge Creek with the alpine tundra surrounding Emerald Lake and the timbered valley of Edelman Creek. The trail can be linked with the Geneva Pass and Cliff Lake routes for an excellent loop trip.

The trek begins by wandering up a grassy dale that is drained by a small spring creek. After a short distance, the track crosses the stream and climbs to the top of a long and grassy rise beside Medicine Lodge Creek. The entire valley is blanketed in open prairie: high, wide, and handsome. It is a horseman's paradise. As the path proceeds up the valley, ranks of granite peaks rise to guard both sides of the drainage. There is an ankle-deep ford of Medicine Lodge Creek near the head of the valley.

The trail now begins an ascent to a nameless pass, climbing through subalpine meadows dotted with copses of fir. At the head of the drainage, the ascent steepens en route to a windswept gap where boulders and tundra create a desolate landscape. This pass leads into the head of the Shell Creek watershed, where the aquamarine waters of Emerald Lake are stretched beneath tundra-clad summits. A string of high tarns, known as the Lakes of the Rough, stretches to the northwest.

After a short but vigorous descent, the path makes its way across the narrow and rocky isthmus at the foot of Emerald Lake. It meets the Shell Creek Trail just before crossing the outlet stream. The low gap to the northeast is Edelman Pass and the trail grows faint as it passes through this saddle.

A steep and rocky descent leads down into a basin of subalpine marshes. Snow lingers late on this stretch of the trail. Scan the talus beside the trail for the reclusive pika and listen for its plaintive bleats. After passing the marshes, the trail drops again to reach a circular basin where the ruins of prospectors' cabins are guarded by rugged summits.

Emerald Lake and Edelman Pass.

The trees begin to close in as the trail drops through a series of sharp descents. It finally bottoms out as the valley widens. Here the valley floor is carpeted with flower-strewn glades. The path soon passes beside a broad swamp. Look back for fine views of the surrounding peaks. The trail fords Edelman Creek just below the wetland and soon a spur path runs east to reach Devils Lake. This small mere is backed up against a rugged cliff, and its waters support a population of pan-sized brook trout.

The main trail now wanders among hillocks and past stagnant ponds, and soon it returns to the west bank of Edelman Creek. Following another sojourn to the east bank, the path reaches an old mine site beside a substantial tributary on the west slope of the valley. The ruins of an old log cabin stand atop a tailings heap at the mouth of an open tunnel. Just beyond this point, the abandoned trail to Thayer Lake drops to the valley floor.

The Edelman Pass Trail soon makes a calf-deep ford of Edelman Creek. Just beyond it is a second ford, this time of the East Fork of Big Goose Creek. After a knee-deep crossing, the trail ends at a junction with the Geneva Pass Trail. The trailhead at Coffeen Park is only 1.1 miles north of this point, while Geneva Pass lies to the south.

MILES AND DIRECTIONS

0.0 Trail leaves FR 17.

0.3 Trail crosses small spring creek.

0.5 Trail enters Cloud Peak Wilderness.

2.6 Trail fords Medicine Lodge Creek.

5.0 Trail crosses pass to enter Shell Creek drainage.

EDELMAN PASS

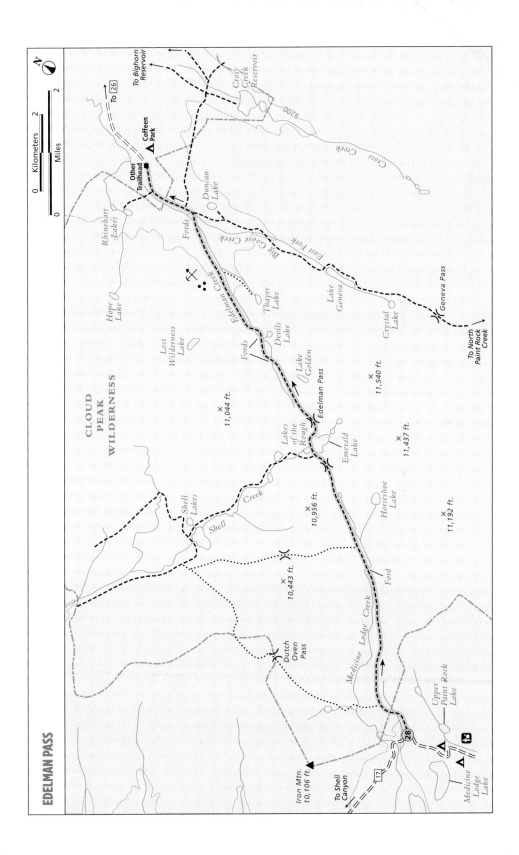

N

Kilometers
0   2

Miles
0   2

To Bighorn
Reservoir

Cross
Creek Reservoir

To 26

Coffeen
Park

Other
Trailhead

Rhinehart
Lakes

Duncan
Lake

Cross Creek

9200

Fords

Big Goose Creek

East Fork

Geneva Pass

To North
Paint Rock
Creek

Hope
Lake

Edelman Creek

Thayer
Lake

Lake Geneva

Crystal
Lake

Lost
Wilderness
Lake

Fords

Devils
Lake

CLOUD
PEAK
WILDERNESS

×
11,044 ft.

Lake
Golden

Edelman Pass

×
11,540 ft.

Lakes
of the
Rough

Shell
Lakes

Shell Creek

Emerald
Lake

×
10,956 ft.

×
11,437 ft.

Horseshoe
Lake

×
11,192 ft.

×
10,443 ft.

Dutch
Oven
Pass

Ford

Medicine Lodge Creek

Iron Mtn.
10,106 ft.

To Shell Canyon

17

28

Upper
Paint Rock
Lake

Medicine
Lodge Lake

5.4 Foot of Emerald Lake. Junction with Shell Creek Trail. Continue straight ahead.

5.5 Trail crosses headwaters of Shell Creek.

5.7 Edelman Pass. Trail starts descending.

6.7 Trail crosses Edelman Creek and follows west bank.

7.5 Trail crosses to east bank of Edelman Creek.

7.6 Junction with trail to Devils Lake (0.2 mile, easy). Bear left for Coffeen Park.

7.7 Trail returns to west bank of Edelman Creek.

8.7 Ruins of old mine.

8.8 Junction with abandoned trail to Thayer Lake. Continue straight ahead.

9.6 Trail makes final ford of Edelman Creek.

9.8 Trail fords East Fork of Big Goose Creek.

9.9 Junction with Geneva Pass Trail. Bear left for Coffeen Park.

11.0 Coffeen Park Trailhead.

29 SHELL CREEK

General description: A day hike or backpack to the Lakes of the Rough, connecting with the Edelman Pass Trail at Emerald Lake (6.6 miles one way).
Difficulty: Moderately strenuous.
Route finding: Some challenges.
Best season: Mid-July to early September.

Visitation: Light.
Elevation gain: 1,455 feet.
Elevation loss: 340 feet.
Maximum elevation: 10,270 feet (Emerald Lake).
Topo maps: Shell Reservoir, Spanish Point, Shell Lake, *Trails Illustrated.*
Jurisdiction: Cloud Peak Wilderness (Bighorn National Forest).

FINDING THE TRAILHEAD

Drive east from Shell on US Highway 14 to mile 31.3. Turn right on FR 17 and follow this trunk road east and then south for 10 miles. The portion of this road that crosses private land gets sloppy after it rains. At the bottom of Crooked Creek Hill is a junction; bear left onto FR 271. After 0.8 mile of climbing, bear left at the junction. High-clearance vehicles can make it another 2.5 miles to the foot of Shell Reservoir. Intrepid four-wheelers can then ford the foot of the lake (up to your door handles) and follow the steep and rocky road up to Lake Adelaide. Continue across meadows that turn to mud bogs in the rain, reaching a road junction 3.1 miles beyond Shell Reservoir. Park here GPS: 44.507362° N, 107.379659° W and walk south on the road to start the hike.

THE HIKE

This rather obscure trail offers a wilder alternative to the Edelman Pass Trail, visiting the Lakes of the Rough on its way to Emerald Lake and Edelman Pass. The difficulty of the access road guarantees that this rugged and scenic valley will have fewer visitors than other nearby drainages.

To begin the hike, follow the old roadway south as it climbs over a wooded knob and descends through a rocky course to reach Buckley Creek. Cross this small stream and make the knee-deep ford of Shell Creek, which is a sluggish stream at this point. Turn left on the far bank as the Shell Creek Trail departs from the roadway, running southeast through the grasslands that flank Shell Creek. This substantial stream meanders lazily through the meadows, often widening to form small lakes and ponds.

Before long, the trail ascends onto the grassy knolls to the west of the stream. From there, you will have superb views of the rugged peaks on the far side of the valley. The trail continues to follow the terraces all the way to its junction with the abandoned Dutch Oven Pass Trail. Here, the Shell Creek Trail climbs briskly through an open woodland of spruce and fir to surmount a minor hillock. It then descends to the shore of Shell Lake. From the lakeshore, you will have mountain vistas in all directions.

The trail runs northeast to cross the outlet stream, then follows the north shore to reach the stream that drains Little Shell Lake. This smaller sister to Shell Lake lies 100 yards upstream from this point. The trail then enters the defile that bears Shell Creek and follows its north bank through a subalpine forest. After a short climb, the trail emerges into a stark landscape of granite mounds. After cresting a rise, the valley widens suddenly and the bottoms are filled with brilliant green marshes. Shell Creek loops through the wetland and hulking peaks rise beyond.

The trail skirts the edge of the marsh, then continues upstream. Shell Creek is now a splashing mountain brook bordered by blossom-filled meadows. As a tributary stream enters from the east, the trail makes a pair of rock-hop crossings of Shell Creek. The path then passes a second bog and climbs eastward into the subalpine timber.

The trail levels off atop a wooded shelf, which bears the traveler to the first of the Lakes of the Rough. These pretty alpine tarns lie below rounded faces of granite, connected to each other by Shell Creek like pearls on a string. The streamside thickets of willow provide summer forage for moose, which are sighted in this area from time to time. A gentle stroll up Shell Creek leads to the second lake, where the trees become sparse.

Beyond the second lake is a vigorous climb that leads up past the treeline to the alpine zone. Here, lush swards of tundra cover the landscape and the only trees are the scattered clumps of wind-blasted fir. Look back down the valley to view the endless ranks of barren peaks stretching northward along the crest of the Bighorn Mountains. Leveling off, the trail passes a final, shallow tarn before reaching Emerald Lake. This large alpine lake is surrounded by hulking summits clad in tundra. The trek ends at a junction with the Edelman Pass Trail. To the east is the low gap of Edelman Pass, while to the southwest is a higher pass that leads to Medicine Lodge Creek.

MILES AND DIRECTIONS

0.0 Parking area at junction of FR 271 and FR 280. Follow FR 280 south.

0.3 Road fords Buckley Creek.

0.5 Road fords Shell Creek. Turn left onto trail on far bank.

0.8 Trail enters Cloud Peak Wilderness.

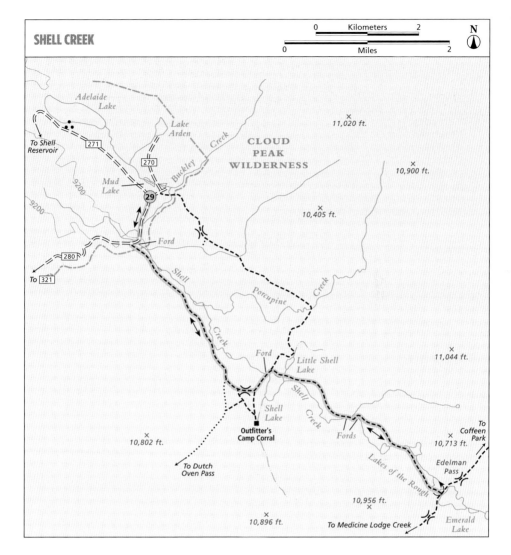

0   Kilometers   2

0   Miles   2

N

2.3   Junction with abandoned trail to Dutch Oven Pass. Bear left.

3.0   Junction with spur to outfitter's camp. Bear left.

3.4   Trail crosses outlet of Shell Lake. Junction with trail to Porcupine Creek. Follow trail along northeast shore of lake.

3.7   Trail crosses outlet of Little Shell Lake.

4.7   Trail makes two quick fords of Shell Creek.

5.3   Trail reaches lowermost of Lakes of the Rough.

5.4   Trail fords Shell Creek to follow west bank.

5.8   Second lake.

6.4   Third lake.

6.6   Trail reaches foot of Emerald Lake. Junction with Edelman Pass trail.

30 THE OLD MAIL TRAIL

General description: A long day hike following a historic stagecoach road from the Crooked Creek divide to Moraine Creek, 5.1 miles one way.
Difficulty: Moderate.
Route finding: Some challenges.
Best season: Early July to mid-September.
Visitation: Light.

Elevation gain: 625 feet.
Elevation loss: 179 feet.
Maximum elevation: 9,144 feet (Crooked Creek divide).
Topo maps: Shell Reservoir, *Trails Illustrated* (trail shown partially).
Jurisdiction: Cloud Peak Wilderness (Bighorn National Forest).

FINDING THE TRAILHEAD

Drive east from Shell on US Highway 14 to mile 31.3. Turn right on FR 17 and follow this trunk road east past the Shell Creek Ranger Station (mile 2.8) and then south for 10 miles. The portion of the road that crosses private land gets sloppy after it rains. Park at the junction with FR 271 GPS: 44.505728° N, 107.454436° W and hike down the lower of two road grades that descend to the north. To reach the north trailhead, drive north from the Shell Creek Ranger Station on FR 277 (a primitive road) for 2 miles. Turn right on FR 226 and follow it for 1.5 miles to the trailhead just beyond the ford of Willett Creek. GPS: 44.554825° N, 107.464137° W.

THE HIKE

This hike follows the old Big Horn Toll Road, which served as a mail and stagecoach route between Big Horn and Hyattville during the late 1800s. This road was abandoned in 1901 when the railroad built a spur line south from Lovell. The route leads down the pastoral valley of Crooked Creek, where cattle graze in summer, then enters the Cloud Peak Wilderness as it crosses the valley of Shell Creek. The route then climbs to uplands, passing glacial landforms on its way to the Woodchuck Pass road. The ford of Shell Creek is virtually impassable during spring runoff.

From the pass above Crooked Creek, follow the lower of two road grades northward into the valley of Crooked Creek. The broad, level bottomlands of this valley are robed in a pastoral grassland and the route takes the form of a broad, green track through the sagebrush. Cattle use this area for summer pasture and contaminate the creek. Don't use it as a source of drinking water.

At the north end of the valley, the stream drops rapidly into the forest. The trail follows its west bank to reach a gate with trail signs. The Cloud Peak Wilderness lies beyond this gate. Turn west as the old wagon road descends across steep slopes timbered in spruce and fir. Expect some steep ups and downs in places where erosion and slumping have damaged the roadbed.

As it nears the floor of the Shell Creek Valley, the old road doglegs back to the east. It becomes faint and tricky to follow as it crosses the meadows above a shallow mere. The route soon turns north, threading its way among swamps and low mounds of granite. Watch for cairns and blazes in this area. The trail ultimately approaches the eastern shore of the mere, then turns northeast and becomes quite obvious as it drops across timbered slopes to reach the Shell Creek bottoms. Shell Creek is a pretty stream that runs through a sun-dappled stand of tall spruce. The route follows it upstream to reach a thigh-deep but slow-moving ford.

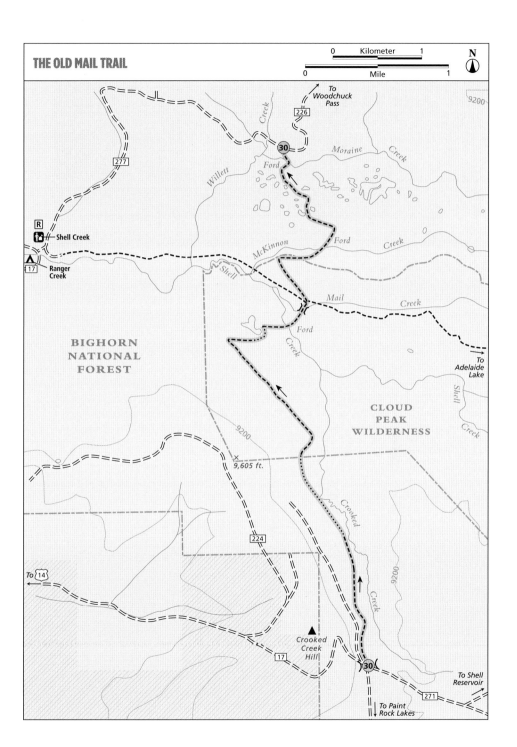

THE OLD MAIL TRAIL

0   Kilometer   1

0   Mile   1

N

To Woodchuck Pass

226

Moraine Creek

9200

30

277

Willett Creek

Ford

McKinnon

Ford Creek

R

Shell Creek

Shell

Mail   Creek

17

Ranger Creek

Ford

To Adelaide Lake

BIGHORN NATIONAL FOREST

Shell Creek

CLOUD PEAK WILDERNESS

9200

x
9,605 ft.

224

Crooked Creek

To 14

9200

Crooked Creek Hill

17

30

To Shell Reservoir

271

To Paint Rock Lakes

The valley of Crooked Creek.

On the far side, a well-beaten track runs north across sage flats and then pine-bordered glades to join the Adelaide Lake Trail. Cross the bridge over Mail Creek and then seek out the road grade that climbs northwest across sage-covered slopes. This well-traveled track ascends steadily into an aspen grove. The track leaves the Cloud Peak Wilderness upon reaching the far side of this grove.

The old wagon road now climbs through several sagebrush meadows before the lodge-pole pines close in. It soon crosses McKinnon Creek, a small stream where pleasant glades are populated by a few old aspens. The trail then continues upward through the timber to surmount the top of an old glacial moraine. After a steady climb, the trail tops out on a wooded shelf and wanders among woodland ponds. After a short journey, it reaches the grassy clearing that marks the confluence of Moraine and Willett creeks. An ankle-deep ford leads across Moraine Creek, after which the route continues along the edge of the meadow to reach FR 226.

MILES AND DIRECTIONS

- **0.0** Trailhead. Follow lower roadway toward Crooked Creek.
- **1.6** Trail leaves Crooked Creek Valley and enters Cloud Peak Wilderness. Beginning of descent toward Shell Creek.
- **2.9** Trail reaches shore of nameless lake.
- **3.1** Trail fords Shell Creek.
- **3.3** Trail crosses Mail Creek.
- **3.4** Two junctions with the Adelaide Lake Trail. Follow old road grade that climbs northwest.
- **3.9** Trail leaves Cloud Peak Wilderness.
- **4.2** Trail crosses McKinnon Creek.
- **5.0** Trail fords Moraine Creek.
- **5.1** Trail joins FR 226.

31 BRUCE MOUNTAIN

General description: An off-trail loop route to the summit of Bruce Mountain, 5 miles total.
Difficulty: Moderately strenuous.
Route finding: Map and compass.
Best season: Mid-July to early September.
Visitation: Very light.

Elevation gain: 820 feet.
Elevation loss: 820 feet.
Maximum elevation: 10,280 feet (summit of Bruce Mountain).
Topo map: Shell Reservoir.
Jurisdiction: Bighorn National Forest (Medicine Wheel Ranger District).

FINDING THE TRAILHEAD

From US Highway 14 south of Burgess Junction, take FR 26 southeast for 11 miles to reach the Woodchuck Pass Road (FR 226). Follow this fair-weather road across a stream ford and onward for 1.4 miles to park at a microwave station on the right side of the road. GPS: 44.611778° N, 107.413075° W. The hike turns around at the terminus of FR 268 near Calvin Lake. GPS: 44.622728° N, 107.413755° W.

THE HIKE

This off-trail route makes an excellent day trip, wandering across the trackless expanse of alpine tundra atop Bruce Mountain. Along the way are striking formations of granite in the high country and fine fishing opportunities at Calvin Lake. From the heights, visitors will enjoy sweeping vistas of the surrounding mountains.

From the starting point, follow the telephone poles across the open country that leads up to Woodchuck Pass. Before long, a grassy avenue leads up the ridge to the west; follow it to the ridgeline. After crossing the ridgetop, the route enters a meadowy basin guarded to the north and west by outcrops of granite. Contour across the floor of the basin, then climb the ridge that guards its south side.

At the top of the grade is an open promontory with superb views of Elk Mountain to the east. More high peaks are ranged to the south of this summit, beyond the valley of Shell Creek. The route now follows the rounded, grassy ridgetop toward the summit of Bruce Mountain. Views open up to the west along the way, featuring Antelope Butte and the distant cleft of Shell Canyon.

Steer to the left (west) of the first three tors of granite that rise from the ridgetop. The route then follows a grassy slope to the east of the final outcrop to gain the top of Bruce Mountain. There are two summits, represented by outcrops of stone that rise above the bald pate of the mountaintop. A cairn marks the southeastern summit, which is an easy walk-up when approached from the north. The northwestern summit is best approached from the northeast, but to gain the top requires some scrambling. From here, one can look northwest across the high, open country that stretches toward Bald Mountain. Lookout Mountain is the ragged summit to the north, and in the distance the High Plains stretch away to the eastern horizon.

The route then drops onto a grassy flat to the north of the summit, then runs northeast along a ridgetop to approach a rocky summit robed in trees. Initially, the route follows the southeast slope of the ridge, but later it drops onto the north slope to avoid a rocky knob. After returning to the ridgeline, a wrinkled face of granite rises ahead. Drop eastward here, following the lower edge of a talus apron below it. Next, contour across the

Atop Bruce Mountain.

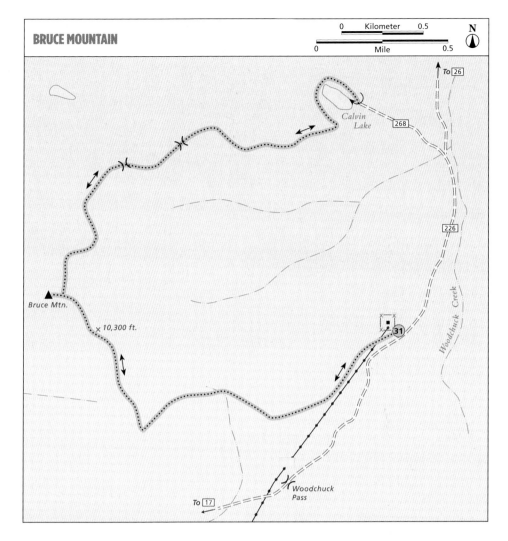

slope, picking your way through stands of subalpine fir and piles of granite boulders. The traveling gets easier as the woodland opens up, and soon the route passes below a jagged backbone of granite. Continue across the slopes, climbing to gain the ridgeline at a convenient location. The ridgetop is level at first, but later it drops off steeply as the blue waters of Calvin Lake appear below.

The route now doglegs sharply to the northwest, descending across steep slopes and bearing for the head of the lake. This is dangerous country. Descend only where it is absolutely safe. Traverse westward to find an easier way down. On the lakeshore you will strike a primitive angler's path. Follow it around the head of Calvin Lake and then eastward past the far shore. A brief descent leads from the foot of the lake to the end of FR 268. This steep road drops down 0.3 mile to reach the Woodchuck Pass road (FR 226), 0.8 mile north of the starting point.

Outcrops of gneiss atop Bruce Mountain.

MILES AND DIRECTIONS

0.0   Hike begins at relay station. Hike toward Woodchuck Pass.

0.3   Trail starts westward ascent.

0.8   Grassy bowl to the southeast of summit. Climb ridgetop to the southwest.

1.1   Route reaches the toe of the ridge.

1.8   Summit of Bruce Mountain. Route descends ridge northward.

2.7   Trail crosses saddle to north side of ridge.

2.9   Saddle leads back to south side of ridge.

3.3   Route leaves ridgetop for descent to Calvin Lake.

3.6   Route reaches head of Calvin Lake.

3.8   Trail reaches foot of Calvin Lake. Follow trail eastward.

3.9   Trail reaches end of FR 268. Follow roads back to starting point (1.1 miles).

32 ROCK CHUCK PASS

General description: A short day hike to Rock Chuck Pass (1.3 miles one way) or a wilderness route to the Coney Lake Trailhead (3.4 miles overall).
Difficulty: Moderate.
Route finding: Some challenges to Rock Chuck Pass; map and compass beyond.
Best season: Mid-July to mid-September.

Visitation: Very light.
Elevation gain: 525 feet (to Rock Chuck Pass).
Elevation loss: 960 feet (beyond Rock Chuck Pass).
Maximum elevation: 9,840 feet (Rock Chuck Pass).
Topo maps: Woodrock, Dome Lake, *Trails Illustrated* (partially shown).
Jurisdiction: Bighorn National Forest (Tongue Ranger District).

FINDING THE TRAILHEAD

Follow US Highway 14 south from Burgess Junction to mile 42.6. Drive east on FR 26, a good trunk road that wends its way through the mountains for 12.5 miles to reach Sawmill Pass. The hike begins on a jeep track that veers right (south) from the road beyond an interpretive sign and just before (west of) the summit of Sawmill Pass GPS: 44.627424° N, 107.377195° W. For through-hikers, the trek ends at the Coney Creek Trailhead, 3.8 miles east of Sawmill Pass. GPS: 44.614690° N, 107.323741° W.

THE HIKE

This route offers a short day hike through pristine meadows to reach an open pass with superb southward views of the high summits of the Cloud Peak Wilderness. Beyond Rock Chuck Pass, the trail tread has disappeared almost completely. A skillful navigator can follow the terrain down to a trail junction near the Coney Creek Trailhead.

The hike begins on a trail that runs south from the road, climbing up the spine of a low and forested ridge. It soon strikes the East Fork of the South Tongue River, which at this elevation is no more than a small mountain brook. The trail runs upstream, and soon the firs and spruces give way to open meadows dotted with the blossoms of phlox, lupine, and buttercup. A backward glance reveals the rocky summit of Bruce Mountain.

The trail now disappears in the meadows. Follow the broad, open avenue between the trees. It leads all the way to the gentle, grassy swell of Rock Chuck Pass. Here, between two rocky summits, there are superb views southward toward Black Tooth Mountain and the other high summits of the Cloud Peak massif. It is wise to turn around here if you are unsure of your route finding abilities.

If you elect to continue along the route of the long-vanished trail, take a sighting on the grassy clearing on Snail Creek, which occupies the valley directly below the pass. Hike straight down the drainage on an eastward heading, passing through loose woodland established after a wildfire. The route heads straight for the northern edge of the meadow on Snail Creek, then follows the edge of the timber until it comes to a well-beaten trail. Follow this trail through the trees to join the Coney Lake Trail, then turn left to cover the remaining distance to its large trailhead on FR 26.

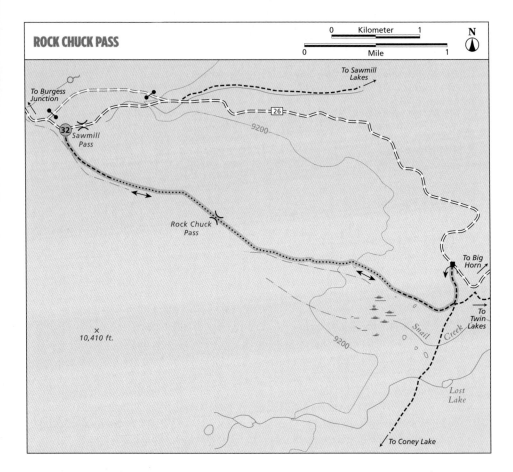

MILES AND DIRECTIONS

0.0 Trailhead at Sawmill Pass.

1.3 Rock Chuck Pass. Wilderness route descends eastward.

2.1 Route passes marshes of Snail Creek.

3.1 Junction with Coney Lake Trail. Turn left to finish hike.

3.4 Coney Lake Trailhead.

33 CONEY LAKE

General description: A day hike to Stull Lakes (1.6 miles) or Coney Lake (3.7 miles).
Difficulty: Easy to Stull Lakes; moderate beyond.
Route finding: No problem.
Best season: Mid-July to mid-September.

Visitation: Moderate.
Elevation gain: 640 feet.
Elevation loss: 240 feet.
Maximum elevation: 9,300 feet.
Topo maps: Dome Lake (trail not shown), *Trails Illustrated*.
Jurisdiction: Cloud Peak Wilderness (Bighorn National Forest).

FINDING THE TRAILHEAD

Follow US Highway 14 south from Burgess Junction to mile 42.6. Drive east on FR 26, a good trunk road that wends its way through the mountains for 16 miles to reach the well-marked Coney Creek Trailhead on the north side of the road, 3.8 miles beyond Sawmill Pass. GPS: 44.614690° N, 107.323741° W. The trail runs south on the opposite side of the road.

THE HIKE

This popular trail visits several woodland lakes in the northern quadrant of the Cloud Peak Wilderness. The mountains are less impressive here and the lakes become the main attraction. Bring mosquito repellent, as the insects tend to be abundant in this area.

Coney Lake.

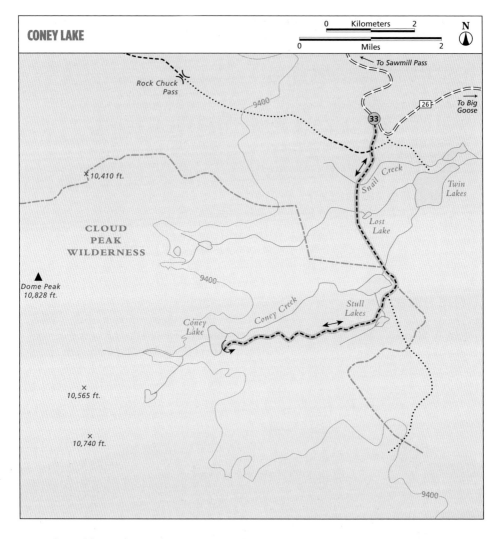

The trail begins by wandering southward among a maze of hillocks timbered in spruce. It soon meets the trail that links Rock Chuck Pass and Twin Lakes, then continues south to cross two small brooks. The first one is Snail Creek, while the second one (larger and nameless) feeds into Lost Lake, which appears in the meadowy depression just beyond the stream crossing. The path then crosses a level woodland of lodgepole pines to reach a rock-hop crossing of Coney Creek. Just beyond the crossing is the larger of the Stull Lakes, a broad, deep pool that reflects the rugged peaks flanking Rock Chuck Pass. There are several spurs that access the lakeshore just beyond the wilderness boundary. The path then climbs a bit to visit the smaller lake, which is a shallow mere surrounded by wet meadows.

Leaving the Stull Lakes, the trail climbs a short, steep pitch to reach the top of a finger ridge, then follows its level surface westward. A second steep ascent leads to the top of a high and rocky divide that yields southward views of Elk Peak. The path climbs and falls atop this rocky ridge, passing a lush meadow just before reaching Coney Lake. Large boulders are scattered across the surface of this broad and shallow tarn. A nameless peak of 11,100 feet rises beyond the water and brook trout dimple its quiet surface.

MILES AND DIRECTIONS

0.0   Coney Creek Trailhead.

0.2   Junction with Rock Chuck Pass Trail. Continue straight ahead.

0.5   Trail crosses Snail Creek.

1.5   Trail crosses Coney Creek.

1.6   Big Stull Lake.

2.0   Little Stull Lake.

3.7   Coney Lake.

34 SAWMILL LAKES

General description: A short day hike to Sawmill Reservoir, 1.1 miles one way.
Difficulty: Easy.
Route finding: No problem.
Best season: Mid-July to mid-September.
Visitation: Light.

Elevation gain: 70 feet.
Elevation loss: 280 feet.
Maximum elevation: 8,440 feet.
Topo maps: Walker Mountain, Dome Lake (trail not shown).
Jurisdiction: Bighorn National Forest (Tongue Ranger District).

FINDING THE TRAILHEAD

Follow US Highway 14 south from Burgess Junction to mile 42.6. Drive east on FR 26, a good trunk road that wends its way through the mountains for 18 miles to reach the West Fork of Big Goose Creek, 5.7 miles beyond Sawmill Pass. GPS: 44.612968° N, 107.298749° W. The trail runs down the west bank of the creek.

THE HIKE

This short trail accesses two lakes and a reservoir in a wooded fold in the foothills. The trail begins with a gentle descent along the banks of Big Goose Creek's West Fork. It soon seeks the spine of a narrow, pine-clad ridge that maintains its altitude as the valley floor drops away. This finger ridge is an old lateral moraine left behind by the Dome

Largest of the Sawmill Lakes.

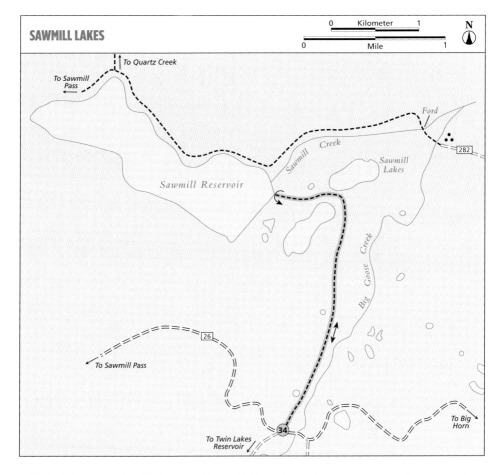

Lake Glacier. During Pleistocene times, this broad but thin ice sheet crept down the valley from the high peaks to the south, depositing mounds of rocky debris along its margins as it inched northward.

After a steady descent, an old burn opens up the trees to reveal the larger of the Sawmill Lakes, bordered by spruce swamps reminiscent of the muskeg bogs of the Alaskan taiga. The ridge soon winds around the foot of the lake, revealing aerial views of the smaller lake to the south. A spur path soon departs for this lake, while the main trail undertakes a brief, westward climb to gain the top of the earth-fill dam at the foot of Sawmill Reservoir.

MILES AND DIRECTIONS

0.0   Trailhead.

0.7   Big Sawmill Lake.

0.8   Little Sawmill Lake.

1.1   Trail reaches dam of Sawmill Reservoir.

35 GEDDES LAKE

General description: A day hike to Geddes Lake, 5.5 miles one way.
Difficulty: Moderate.
Route finding: No problem.
Best season: Mid-July to mid-September.
Visitation: Moderate.
Elevation gain: 1,390 feet.

Elevation loss: 150 feet.
Maximum elevation: 9,320 feet (Geddes Lake).
Topo maps: Park Reservoir, Dome Lake, *Trails Illustrated*.
Jurisdiction: Cloud Peak Wilderness (Bighorn National Forest).

FINDING THE TRAILHEAD

Follow US 14 south from Burgess Junction to mile 42.6. Drive east on FR 26, a good trunk road that wends its way through the mountains for 23.5 miles to reach Little Goose Park. Turn right (south) on FR 299. After 0.8 mile, bear left at the junction and follow the road (four-wheel drive recommended) another 1.2 miles to the meadow beside Babione Creek. Bear left at the final fork to descend to the ford of Babione Creek, where the walking begins. GPS: 44.576561° N, 107.230400° W.

THE HIKE

This hike follows jeep trails to Weston Reservoir, then enters the Cloud Peak Wilderness and travels through pristine country en route to Geddes Lake. There is excellent habitat for moose and mosquitoes along the way; watch out for both. The old trail that once

Geddes Lake.

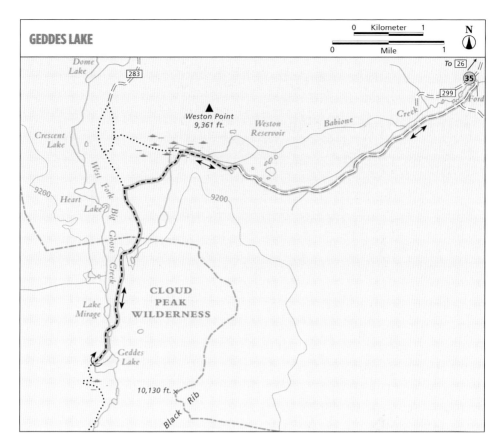

climbed from Geddes Lake to the high country near Elk Pass has been abandoned, and now it is challenging to follow.

The hike begins on a rocky road that makes a ford of Babione Creek and then runs upstream to a junction. The road to the left runs to Park Reservoir; stay right for Geddes Lake. The old road parallels Babione Creek through a shady forest of spruce and pine. After several rocky grades, the road arrives at the upper reaches of Babione Creek. Here, the forest is interrupted by sunny glades dotted with wildflowers. The road then climbs over a low divide and drops into a boggy forest where mosquitoes lurk in ambush. A brief rise leads to the shore of Weston Reservoir. The road ends here, and motor vehicles are not allowed beyond this point.

The trail follows the south shore toward the head of the reservoir, then passes the meadows above its head. Moose are commonly seen in this area. The low-slung summits of Elk Peak and its snow-dappled neighbors can now be seen to the west. After an unmarked junction with an abandoned trail beside Babione Creek, the Geddes Lake Trail heads southward, climbing into the pine-clad hills. It ultimately crosses an imperceptible divide and drops toward the West Fork of Big Goose Creek.

The pines thin out as the trail follows this valley toward its head. The path becomes a mere avenue through the boulders as it passes Lake Mirage, a shallow and boulder-strewn pond. The trail crosses the West Fork at the foot of the next mere, larger and deeper than the first. It then wanders southward through loose subalpine woodland. A small spring in a clearing offers a fine spot to camp. Just beyond it, the trail reaches the western shore of Geddes Lake. The forested slopes of the Black Rib rise to the east. It is necessary to do some cross-country scrambling in order to view the higher summits to the south and west. The old trail into the high country beyond the lake has been abandoned for many years.

MILES AND DIRECTIONS

0.0 Ford of Babione Creek.

2.6 Road ends at Weston Reservoir. Follow trail west.

2.9 Trail leaves head of Weston Reservoir.

3.7 Junction with abandoned trail. Bear left.

3.8 Junction with abandoned trail. Turn left.

4.9 Lake Mirage.

5.1 Trail fords West Fork of Big Goose Creek.

5.5 Geddes Lake.

36 GENEVA PASS

General description: A day hike from Coffeen Park to Lake Geneva (3.4 miles) or Crystal Lake (4.9 miles); or a backpack to the Cliff Lake Trail (8.4 miles).
Difficulty: Moderate to Lake Geneva; moderately strenuous beyond.
Route finding: No problem.
Best season: Mid-July to mid-September.

Visitation: Heavy.
Elevation gain: 1,775 feet.
Elevation loss: 615 feet.
Maximum elevation: 10,275 feet (Geneva Pass).
Topo maps: Park Reservoir, Cloud Peak, Shell Lake, *Trails Illustrated*.
Jurisdiction: Cloud Peak Wilderness (Bighorn National Forest).

FINDING THE TRAILHEAD

Four-wheel drive is a requisite for reaching this trailhead. Follow US Highway 14 south from Burgess Junction to mile 42.6. Drive east on FR 26, a good trunk road that wends its way through the mountains for 24 miles to reach Little Goose Park. Turn right (south) on FR 293, a primitive road. After 3 miles, bear right at the unmarked junction. Turn left 0.4 mile farther on as the road follows the shore of Park Reservoir. Then bear left to reach the Spear-O Wigwam resort, 5.1 miles in. Just beyond the resort, bear right on FR 293, following signs for Coffeen Park. Traveling the last 3.1 miles to the Coffeen Park Trailhead/campground is a harrowing journey. GPS: 44.518912° N, 107.245332° W.

THE HIKE

This major trunk trail follows the wooded valley of the East Fork of Big Goose Creek. Along the way, it passes the ruins of a small village of log cabins, dating from gold prospecting days in the 1920s. The upper reaches of the trail run past the long and sinuous arm of Lake Geneva then climb high into the mountains, passing Crystal Lake in a high cirque en route to Geneva Pass. On the far side of the divide, the trail links up with the Cliff Lake Trail in an alpine lake basin. The Geneva Pass Trail is commonly combined with the Cliff Lake and Edelman Pass routes for a loop trip.

The trek begins by traveling up the valley of the East Fork of Big Goose Creek. Granite bluffs overlook the boggy meadows beside this stream. The trail, however, sticks to the pine-clad benches to the west of the creek and seldom offers views. After passing a junction with the trail to Rhinehart Lakes, the main path surmounts a hill and follows the terraces to reach the cutoff trail to Cross Creek. Continue straight ahead as the path skirts open meadows, then meets the Edelman Pass Trail.

Bear left at this junction as the Geneva Pass Trail climbs gently through the forest, passing among the ruins of log cabins and gold mines. After passing beneath a rugged face of granite, the trail climbs to intersect the spur path to Duncan Lake. This spur trail climbs gently northward, then turns east to cross a spruce-clad flat en route to the lake. This quiet mere is sheltered within a shallow, wooded basin, and marshes ring its shorelines.

Meanwhile, the main trail continues southward, passing several more ruins on its way to a calf-deep ford of the East Fork of Big Goose Creek. The pines now give way to pretty bottomland stands of ancient spruce interspersed with flower-strewn glades. The East Fork soon increases its gradient and the trail follows suit, climbing beside the miniature waterfalls and dark pools of the stream. The final pitch leads up a granite outcrop

marked with a dike of igneous rock, which flowed in liquid form into a crack in the much older bedrock.

At the top of the grade is Lake Geneva. From this point onward, campers will find it impossible to find a legal spot to build a fire. The slender and fjord-like lake is bordered by steep slopes robed in a spruce forest. Above its head loom massive, rounded peaks of granite. The trail fords the outlet of the lake, then follows the eastern shoreline. Near the head of the lake, it reveals a stunning waterfall on the far wall of the valley. Well-drained meadows border the head of Lake Geneva and a spur path crosses them, bearing for the base of the falls.

The main trail continues southward, climbing steeply to avoid the rocky gorge above the lake. The path soon zigzags up onto a steep, flower-strewn mountainside, rising to the timberline. It then levels off and enters the trees to cross the headwaters of the East Fork. Just beyond the crossing, a spur path glides down into the verdant meadows beside Crystal Lake. This beautiful alpine tarn sits at the base of sheer cliffs that bear slender waterfalls during the snowmelt season.

From the junction, the Geneva Pass Trail climbs steeply to surmount a wooded knoll, then descends into the luxuriant meadows at the head of the valley. Bluebell and mon-keyflower bloom along the watercourse, while paintbrush, bistort, and buttercup light the streamside swards. Great walls of granite enclose the basin on three sides, surrounding a narrow gap where the path will climb through Geneva Pass. The trail ascends steeply through this gap, which is choked with cabin-sized blocks of granite. It then rises into the gentle meadows of Geneva Pass, which faces southward over rolling country flanked by great massifs of stone.

The trail now descends into the meadows at the head of North Paint Rock Creek. It soon passes the shining mirror of Robin Lake and then threads its way among hillocks

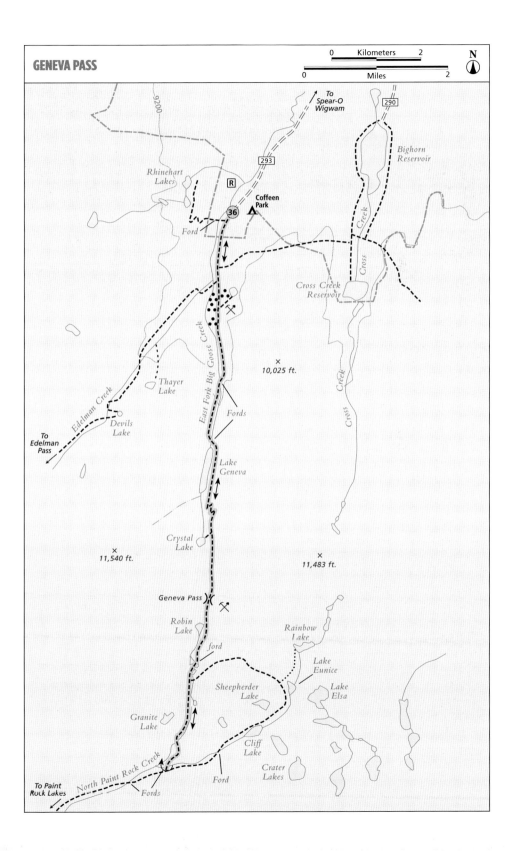

GENEVA PASS

To Spear-O Wigwam

290

Bighorn Reservoir

293

R

Rhinehart Lakes

Coffeen Park

36

Ford

Cross Creek

Cross Creek Reservoir

× 10,025 ft.

East Fork Big Goose Creek

Cross Creek

Thayer Lake

Edelman Creek

Devils Lake

To Edelman Pass

Fords

Lake Geneva

Crystal Lake

× 11,540 ft.

× 11,483 ft.

Geneva Pass

Robin Lake

Rainbow Lake

Lake Eunice

ford

Sheepherder Lake

Lake Elsa

Granite Lake

Cliff Lake

Crater Lakes

To Paint Rock Lakes

North Paint Rock Creek

Ford

Fords

9200

Kilometers   0   2

Miles   0   2

N

dotted with isolated groves of subalpine fir. The path rock-hops between two ponds on North Paint Rock Creek, then rises to meet the end of the Cliff Lake route. It then descends down wooded slopes and through odd, grassy finger ridges where the knobs of granite show through the soil. The trail bottoms out at the calf-deep fords of North Paint Rock Creek and the stream that issues from Cliff Lake. On the other side, it ends at an intersection with the Cliff Lake route. Cliff Lake lies just upstream, while the trail to the west leads to the Paint Rock Lakes.

MILES AND DIRECTIONS

0.0   Coffeen Park Trailhead.

0.2   Junction with Rhinehart Lakes Trail. Continue straight ahead.

0.9   Junction with cutoff trail from Cross Creek. Continue straight.

1.1   Junction with Edelman Pass Trail. Bear left.

1.6   Junction with trail to Duncan Lake (0.4 mile, easy). Continue straight ahead for Lake Geneva and Geneva Pass.

2.4   Trail fords East Fork of Big Goose Creek and follows west bank.

3.4   Foot of Lake Geneva. Trail fords the outlet.

4.1   Trail leaves head of Lake Geneva.

4.8   Junction with trail to Crystal Lake (0.1 mile, easy). Continue straight.

5.8   Geneva Pass. Trail descends into North Paint Rock drainage.

6.2   Robin Lake.

6.7   Trail fords North Paint Rock Creek.

6.8   Signpost marks end of Cliff Lake Trail. Continue straight ahead.

7.5   Gap to the west leads to Granite Lake.

8.0   Trail fords North Paint Rock Creek.

8.3   Trail fords outlet stream of Cliff Lake.

8.4   Trail ends at junction with Cliff Lake Trail.

37 RHINEHART LAKES

General description: A short day hike to Rhinehart Lakes, 0.7 mile one way.
Difficulty: Moderately strenuous.
Route finding: No problem.
Best season: Mid-July to mid-September.
Visitation: Moderate.

Elevation gain: 500 feet.
Maximum elevation: 9,000 feet.
Topo maps: Dome Lake, Park Reservoir (trail not shown), *Trails Illustrated*.
Jurisdiction: Cloud Peak Wilderness (Bighorn National Forest).

FINDING THE TRAILHEAD

The hike begins at the Coffeen Park Trailhead GPS: 44.518912° N, 107.245332° W ; page 119, Geneva Pass.

THE HIKE

This short trail makes a half-day hike to a pair of trout-filled lakes on a wooded shelf. It is a popular day trip for campers based out of Coffeen Park. The lakes lie just within the boundary of the Cloud Peak Wilderness.

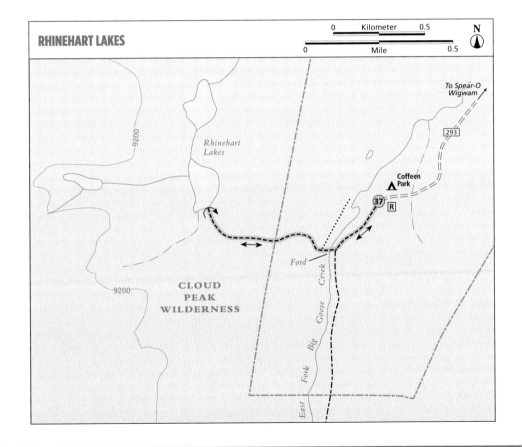

Upper Rinehart Lake.

To begin the hike, follow the Geneva Pass Trail to an unmarked intersection where a wide track descends to ford the East Fork of Big Goose Creek. Turn right at this intersection. After a calf-deep crossing, a footpath immediately climbs away to the south, entering a forest of lodgepole pines. The brief journey to the lakes is a constant and calf-burning ascent.

At the top of the grade is Upper Rhinehart Lake, surrounded by a mix of spruce, fir, and pine. A natural dam of boulders guards the eastern shore, representing a lateral moraine pushed up by the long-extinct Lighter Glacier. The lower lake lies to the northwest and can be reached via a short jaunt through the untracked forest. The lower lake receives lots of use, and both lakes are home to pan-sized rainbow trout.

MILES AND DIRECTIONS

- **0.0** Coffeen Park Trailhead. Follow Geneva Pass Trail south.
- **0.1** Junction with Rhinehart Lakes Trail. Turn right and ford East Fork of Big Goose Creek.
- **0.2** Trail enters Cloud Peak Wilderness.
- **0.7** Upper Rhinehart Lake.

General description: A backpack from Bighorn Reservoir to Highland Park, 7.2 miles.
Difficulty: Moderately strenuous.
Route finding: No problem.
Best season: Mid-July to mid-September.
Visitation: Light.

Elevation gain: 1,900 feet.
Elevation loss: 870 feet.
Maximum elevation: 10,350 feet (pass that leads into Highland Park).
Topo maps: Park Reservoir, Cloud Peak; *Trails Illustrated*.
Jurisdiction: Cloud Peak Wilderness (Bighorn National Forest).

FINDING THE TRAILHEAD

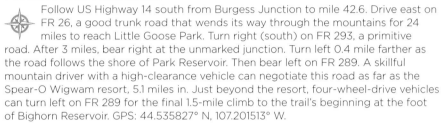

Follow US Highway 14 south from Burgess Junction to mile 42.6. Drive east on FR 26, a good trunk road that wends its way through the mountains for 24 miles to reach Little Goose Park. Turn right (south) on FR 293, a primitive road. After 3 miles, bear right at the unmarked junction. Turn left 0.4 mile farther as the road follows the shore of Park Reservoir. Then bear left on FR 289. A skillful mountain driver with a high-clearance vehicle can negotiate this road as far as the Spear-O Wigwam resort, 5.1 miles in. Just beyond the resort, four-wheel-drive vehicles can turn left on FR 289 for the final 1.5-mile climb to the trail's beginning at the foot of Bighorn Reservoir. GPS: 44.535827° N, 107.201513° W.

THE HIKE

Highland Park is a wild and grassy moor perched on a high shelf above Kearny Creek, with the most jagged peaks of the Cloud Peak massif for a backdrop. This trail offers a well-beaten route to the park, climbing from the forested benches near Bighorn Reservoir through the alpine slopes at the head of the East Fork of Little Goose Creek. The trail joins the Little Goose Trail along the way. Spear Lake and the Lake Winnie Loop make excellent day trips for backpackers based out of Highland Park.

The trail begins by following the eastern shore of Bighorn Reservoir, first atop a finger ridge and later along the shoreline. Elk Peak crowns the massif to the west, and to the south are the nameless summits that crowd the head of the Cross Creek drainage. At the head of the reservoir, the path enters the forest following the base of a stony ridge. At first, the trail is accompanied by grassy meadows and later by the rushing waters of Cross Creek. The path soon joins the Solitude Trail at a well-marked intersection. Continue straight ahead along a boggy trail closed to mechanized vehicles.

This path soon makes a stiff climb through the pines. At the top of the initial grade, the trail enters the Cloud Peak Wilderness and is joined by the West Fork Little Goose Trail. A gentler grade now leads the trail upward and the heavy timber soon gives way to young pines that grew in the wake of an old fire. The path ultimately crests a high, bald knob at the foot of a rocky summit. From here, you can take in superb views of the peaks that rise along the northern fringe of the Cloud Peak massif.

The path now dips into the subalpine basin beyond, where copses of fir are interspersed with lush glades. Watch for the blossoms of white paintbrush, elephant's head, and shooting star amid the more common meadow wildflowers. As the trail continues southward, it rises above the timberline. Here, mats of alpine plants like mountain avens and spreading phlox grow amid the frost-shattered stone. A few subalpine firs have managed

Black Tooth Mountain dominates the wet meadows of Highland Park.

to survive by adopting a growth form that hugs the ground, where they are sheltered from the wind by snowdrifts.

The path tops out as it passes through a high saddle, then contours above the next high basin to reach a second gap. Here, the Little Goose Trail rises to join the Highland Park route. A steep and rocky descent leads into the headwater basin of Little Goose Creek's East Fork. Copses of fir line the trail as it makes its way down to the stream crossing. The path then climbs steadily, making for a gap on the opposite wall of the valley. As it approaches this gap, the trail is joined by a primitive cutoff trail that rises from the valley below.

A final, steep pitch leads upward through the alpine tundra to reach a pass between outcrops of granite. The trail then glides down into Highland Park, a vast and boggy meadow a full square mile in area, occupying a shelf perched high above the Kearny Creek Valley. The mountain views from the park are magnificent, with Black Tooth Mountain rising dramatically to the south and a sawback ridge connecting its shoulders to the rounded summit of Penrose Peak. An abandoned path splits away to follow the western edge of Highland Park, while the main trail follows the cairns southeast across well-drained grasslands lit by the blossoms of lupine, forget-me-not, and buttercup. The trek ends at a signpost in a gap that occupies the southeastern corner of the park. From here, trails take off toward Lake Winnie to the southeast and Highland and Spear Lakes to the west.

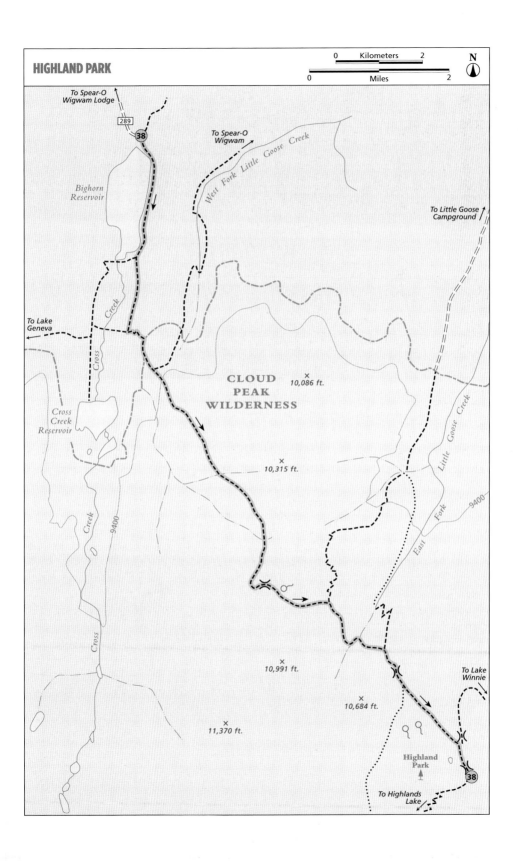

HIGHLAND PARK

0   Kilometers   2

0   Miles   2

N

To Spear-O
Wigwam Lodge

289
38

Bighorn
Reservoir

To Spear-O
Wigwam

West Fork Little Goose Creek

To Little Goose
Campground

To Lake
Geneva

Cross Creek

Cross
Creek
Reservoir

9400

Cross Creek

CLOUD
PEAK
WILDERNESS

×
10,086 ft.

×
10,315 ft.

Little Goose Creek

East Fork

9400

×
10,991 ft.

×
10,684 ft.

To Lake
Winnie

×
11,370 ft.

Highland
Park

38

To Highlands
Lake

Hiking through Highland Park.

MILES AND DIRECTIONS

0.0 Trailhead at foot of Bighorn Reservoir. Follow trail along eastern shore.

1.0 Trail leaves head of Bighorn Reservoir.

1.2 Junction with Cross Creek cutoff trail (a segment of the Solitude Trail). Turn left.

1.9 Trail enters Cloud Peak Wilderness.

2.1 Junction with trail to old Bishop Mine and West Fork Little Goose Creek. Stay right.

4.6 Trail crosses pass to enter watershed of East Fork Little Goose Creek.

5.2 Trail crosses second saddle. Junction with Little Goose Trail. Stay right for descent.

5.7 Trail crosses headwaters of East Fork Little Goose Creek and starts climbing.

6.2 Junction with cutoff to East Fork Little Goose Creek. Stay right.

6.3 Trail passes through saddle and enters Highland Park.

7.2 Signpost at southeast corner of Highland Park. Junction with Lake Winnie Loop and Spear Lake Trail.

39 THE LAKE WINNIE LOOP

General description: An extended loop trip from Highland Park, 6.7 miles total.
Difficulty: Moderate (clockwise); moderately strenuous (counterclockwise).
Route finding: Some challenges.
Best season: Mid-July to mid-September.
Visitation: Light.

Elevation gain: 995 feet.
Elevation loss: 995 feet.
Maximum elevation: 10,130 feet (Highland Park).
Topo maps: Cloud Peak, Willow Park Reservoir (not all trails are shown), *Trails Illustrated* (trail positions approximate).
Jurisdiction: Cloud Peak Wilderness (Bighorn National Forest).

FINDING THE TRAILHEAD

The beginning of the loop (the southeast corner of Highland Park) can be reached from the north via the Highland Park Trail (page 125, Highland Park). The southern corner of the loop (0.2 mile up FR 320 from the dam of Kearny Lake Reservoir) can be reached from the Hunter Trailhead by combining the Elk Lake and Reservoirs Trails (page 31, Elk Lake, and page 142, The Reservoirs).

THE HIKE

This loop route makes a good day trip for backpackers who base themselves out of Kearny Lake Reservoir or Highland Park. The trail can be accessed via the Highland Park or Little Goose Trails or from the south by combining the Elk Lake Trail with either the Reservoirs Trail or the Flatiron Lake route. The loop is described from Highland Park, and it descends past a pair of obscure lakes, then visits the foot of Kearny Lake Reservoir before returning to the heights of Highland Park. A side trip to Spear Lake (page 132, Spear Lake) can be tacked on for a longer trip.

From Highland Park, the trail passes eastward through a broad saddle, then runs northeast across rocky slopes. Snowdrifts often linger until late July in this locale. Alpine wildflowers are abundant as the path traverses around the meadows at the head of the basin that bears Lake Winnie and its smaller neighbor. You can see both lakes amid the trees at the lower edge of the basin. The path ultimately follows the cairns southward for a steady descent through an open woodland to reach them.

The trail approaches the shore of Lake Winnie twice as it turns eastward, yielding excellent views of conical Penrose Peak, the solitary pinnacle of Mount Woolsey, and the ragged summit of Black Tooth Mountain. These two lakes formed when a lateral moraine of the Kearny Glacier dammed this small valley, causing the water to back up. The lakes are slowly filling in with sediment. Both lakes are destined to become wet meadows and will later be overtaken by the forest.

The path crosses the boggy shelf bearing the lakes, then begins to descend along rocky ridges. Along the way, there are views of Kearny Lake Reservoir and the peaks that rise beyond it. A wet meadow awaits at the bottom of the grade. After crossing it, the path wanders amid boggy spruce flats to reach FR 320.

To complete the loop, turn right on the road and follow it to an overlook of Kearny Lake Reservoir. Here, a sign for Spear and Highland Park Lakes marks the next leg of the loop. Follow this path as it winds around a fenced-off meadow, then contours across

Penrose Peak and Black Tooth Mountain rise beyond Lake Winnie.

the rocky slopes above the reservoir. The trail climbs gently through a dense forest of pine, yielding views of the water only after it has climbed through a pair of switchbacks.

After a long upward journey, the trail crests a stony promontory and turns northward. From this point onward, there are superb views of the summits that ring the Kearny Creek Valley and the emerald meadows of upper Kearny Creek appear far below the trail. The route now leads around a steep-sided bowl, passing first through open woodland of spruce and later through aspen groves. Upon reaching a rounded hilltop, the path turns south, climbing as it spirals around the hill to reach a junction in the saddle behind it. Here, the Spear Lake Trail runs west toward Highland Lake, while the loop route turns northeast.

This final leg of the journey climbs gradually across open, rocky slopes that offer ever-improving views of Penrose Peak, Black Tooth Mountain, and the impressive waterfall that descends from the basin between them. The path ultimately climbs through bogs and among copses of fir to return to Highland Park. It now follows the cairns back to the signpost at the starting point.

MILES AND DIRECTIONS

0.0   Signpost in southeastern corner of Highland Park. Follow trail eastward.

1.4   Lake Winnie.

1.7   Trail leaves Cloud Peak Wilderness.

2.7   Trail emerges on FR 320. Follow road westward.

2.9   Trail departs from road, bound northwest. Turn right.

4.5   Trail returns to Cloud Peak Wilderness.

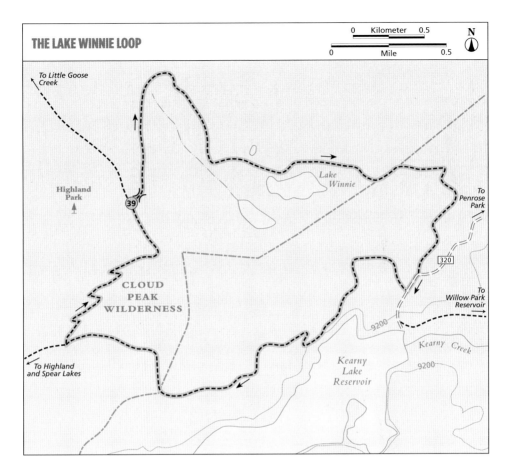

THE LAKE WINNIE LOOP

0   Kilometer   0.5

0   Mile   0.5

N

To Little Goose Creek

Highland Park

39

Lake Winnie

To Penrose Park

320

To Willow Park Reservoir

CLOUD PEAK WILDERNESS

9200

Kearny Creek

To Highland and Spear Lakes

Kearny Lake Reservoir

9200

5.2   Junction with trail to Spear Lake. Turn right to return to Highland Park.

6.7   Trail returns to signpost in Highland Park.

40 SPEAR LAKE

General description: An extended trip from Highland Park to Highland Lake (1.8 miles) or Spear Lake (4 miles).
Difficulty: Moderately strenuous.
Route finding: Some challenges.
Best season: Mid-July to mid-September.
Visitation: Moderate.

Elevation gain: 815 feet.
Elevation loss: 1,030 feet.
Maximum elevation: 10,150 feet (Highland Park).
Topo maps: Cloud Peak (trail shown incorrectly), *Trails Illustrated* (trail shown incorrectly).
Jurisdiction: Cloud Peak Wilderness (Bighorn National Forest).

FINDING THE TRAILHEAD

 The trail begins in the southeastern corner of Highland Park. Its midpoint can be accessed from Kearny Lake Reservoir via a leg of the Lake Winnie Loop.

THE HIKE

This spur trail follows Kearny Creek past a spectacular waterfall, then continues up to the head of the valley to access a turquoise tarn beneath jagged teeth of granite. The beginning of the trail is a long way from anywhere, which cuts down the traffic in this area. It can be reached from either Kearny Lake Reservoir (page 31, Elk Lake; page 142, The Reservoirs; and page 137, Flatiron Lake) or Highland Park (page 125, or page 134, The Little Goose Trail).

From the signpost at the southeastern corner of Highland Park, follow the large cairns southward along the edge of the clearing. At the far end of the meadow, the path turns west and begins a gentle descent through boggy glades. During the descent, you will see Penrose Peak, the more jagged summit of Black Tooth Mountain and then a spectacular waterfall plummeting from the basin between the peaks.

The open, rocky woodland found on these slopes is intermediate between the timberline groves of the subalpine zone and the lowland forest of the valley floor. Spruce and fir are intermixed freely with lodgepole and whitebark pine, and groves of aspen grow in the wetter spots. The path ultimately reaches a junction in the saddle behind a small hillock. Bear right as the trail climbs gently toward Highland Lake.

A short spur path leads to the wooded lakeshore. Highland Lake is guarded by nameless 11,000-foot peaks. Its crystalline waters are overpopulated with brook and rainbow trout.

Meanwhile, the main trail continues westward, making a knee-deep ford of the Highland Lake outlet stream. Before long, the trail undertakes a steep descent down an eastward-trending gully, then resumes its southwesterly course as the grade eases. The trail bears for the large waterfall seen from the Highland Park grade. There is an unmarked junction upon reaching the floor of the Kearny Creek Valley. The more heavily beaten path continues south to end at the base of the falls, while the Spear Lake Trail follows the cairns upward across granite balds for fine views of the cascade and the sawtooth ridges beyond it.

After a steady climb, the path descends to cross a substantial tributary stream. A great dome of granite divides this drainage from the Kearny Creek Valley, and the route follows mountain brooks as it climbs to pass behind this dome. Watch for the blossoms of pink monkeyflower along the way. After a long but moderate climb, the trail drops quickly

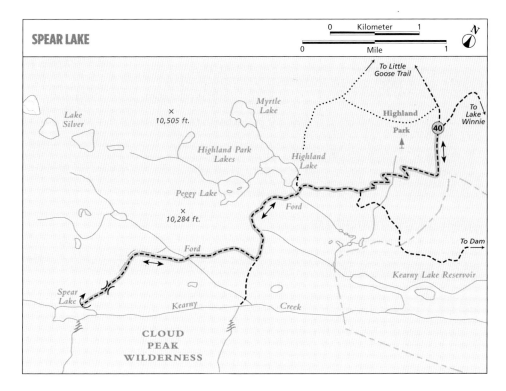

SPEAR LAKE

Myrtle Lake

Lake Silver

× 10,505 ft.

Highland Park Lakes

To Little Goose Trail

To Lake Winnie

Highland Park

40

Highland Lake

Peggy Lake

× 10,284 ft.

Ford

Ford

To Dam

Kearny Lake Reservoir

Spear Lake

Kearny

Creek

CLOUD PEAK WILDERNESS

through the forest to reach the lush meadows at the head of Spear Lake. Towering peaks rise above the turquoise water, highlighted by Black Tooth Mountain to the south and by dagger-shaped spires farther to the west.

MILES AND DIRECTIONS

0.0 Signpost in southeastern corner of Highland Park.

1.5 Junction with trail from Kearny Lake Reservoir. Stay right.

1.8 Highland Lake. Trail crosses outlet stream.

2.5 Junction with spur trail to base of waterfall (0.4 mile, moderate). Stay right.

3.1 Trail crosses tributary stream.

4.0 Spear Lake.

41 THE LITTLE GOOSE TRAIL

General description: A connecting trail from Hazel Park to the Highland Park section of the Solitude Trail, 4.6 miles.	**Visitation:** Very light.
	Elevation gain: 2,030 feet.
	Maximum elevation: 10,280 feet (at terminus).
Difficulty: Moderately strenuous.	**Topo maps:** Park Reservoir, Cloud Peak, *Trails Illustrated* (cutoff trail not shown).
Route finding: No problem on the Little Goose Trail; some challenges on the Highland Park cutoff.	
	Jurisdiction: Cloud Peak Wilderness (Bighorn National Forest).
Best season: Mid-July to mid-September.	

FINDING THE TRAILHEAD

The road to this trail involves a major ford of Little Goose Creek and is passable to four-wheel-drive vehicles only in late summer. From US Highway 14 south of Burgess Junction (or from the town of Big Horn), take FR 26 to FR 314, just east of the national forest boundary. Follow this bad jeep road for 2.5 miles of steep ups and downs to reach the ford of Little Goose Creek. After fording, drive onward 1 mile to an unmarked junction. Bear left and drive the remaining 2 miles to the grassy meadow of Hazel Park (GPS: 44.536986° N, 107.134962° W). Only a masochist would drive the road beyond this point.

THE HIKE

This remote trail provides the most direct access to Highland Park. The rough access road that leads to the trailhead winnows out all vehicles without four-wheel drive and high clearance. As a result, you can expect some solitude in this area. A pleasant day loop can be achieved by ascending the Little Goose Trail, turning south on the Highland Park segment of the Solitude Trail to visit spectacular Highland Park, and returning via the Highland Park cutoff trail.

From Hazel Park, follow the jeep trail southward as it climbs gently up a pine-clad ridgeline. The road ends at the wilderness boundary, and from here a good trail parallels the East Fork of Little Goose Creek as it continues the gradual ascent through the lodgepoles. As the path approaches the subalpine zone, gaps in the trees reveal the low but ragged peaks that guard the eastern side of the valley. The path soon encounters a substantial brook, which courses down through loose woodland of spruce and fir. A cairn marks a trail junction on the far bank; the Little Goose Trail veers to the right while the Highland Park cutoff (described below) descends to the left.

The main trail now climbs southwest into the watershed of the tributary stream, which is surrounded by stony foothills. The trees thin out as the trail gains altitude and before long the path rises into a rocky, timberline basin. Bear left as an abandoned trail splits away to the west. Now the main track climbs vigorously and a new set of summits rises at the head of the basin. The trail ultimately reaches a windswept pass behind a granite knob, reaching its end here at a junction with the Highland Park Trail. Look southward from this point to spot the jagged peaks of Black Tooth Mountain above the pale and frost-shattered granite of an intervening ridge.

Highland Park Cutoff. This rather faint and unmaintained trail runs along the riparian marshes beside the upper reaches of Little Goose Creek, then makes a stiff climb

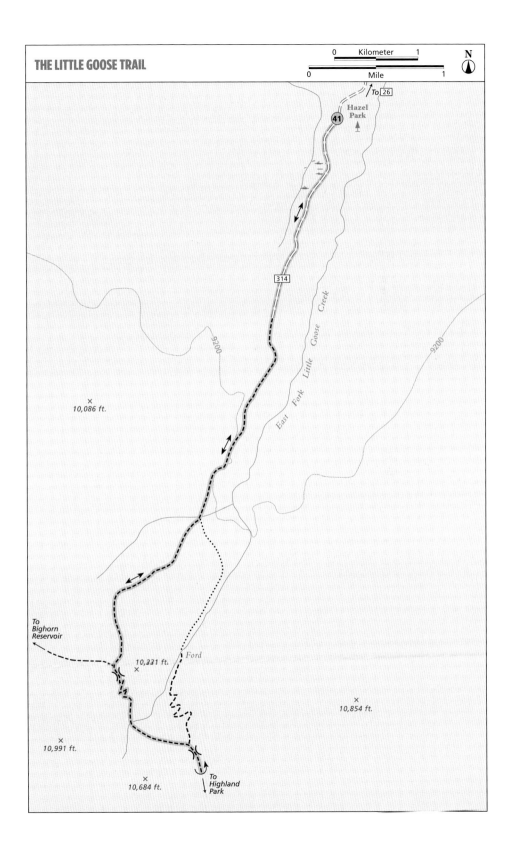

THE LITTLE GOOSE TRAIL

0   Kilometer   1

0   Mile   1

N

To 26

Hazel
Park

41

314

9200

East Fork Little Goose Creek

9200

×
10,086 ft.

To
Bighorn
Reservoir

Ford

×
10,331 ft.

×
10,854 ft.

×
10,991 ft.

To
Highland
Park

×
10,684 ft.

A nameless summit above the head of Little Goose Creek.

to meet the Highland Park Trail just north of Highland Park. From its junction with the Little Goose Trail, the path makes an initial dip and climbs steadily to reach a boggy shelf. This clearing offers the first good views of the peaks lining the head of the valley. The track then runs southward into open woodland, emerging again in the grassy parks beside the East Fork of Little Goose Creek.

The path now follows the stream closely as the surrounding forest takes on a subalpine character. The pathway becomes indistinct as it wanders beside bogs filled with sedges and willows. It finally crosses the creek, then climbs briskly up the eastern wall of the valley. Along the way, vistas open up to encompass the peaks of frost-shattered granite that guard the head of the valley. After zigzagging up through the subalpine firs, the trail reaches the timberline and meets the Highland Park Trail at a signpost just below the saddle that leads to Highland Park.

MILES AND DIRECTIONS

0.0   Hazel Park. Hike south on FR 314.

1.6   Road ends. Trail enters Cloud Peak Wilderness.

3.2   Trail crosses tributary stream to reach junction with old cutoff to Highland Park (2 miles, moderately strenuous). Stay right for the Little Goose Trail.

4.6   Little Goose Trail joins Highland Park Trail 2 miles north of Highland Park.

42 FLATIRON LAKE

General description: A wilderness route from Elk Lake to Kearny Creek, 8 miles. **Difficulty:** Moderate. **Route finding:** Some challenges. **Best season:** Mid-July to mid-September. **Visitation:** Moderate to Frying Pan Lake; otherwise very light.	**Elevation gain:** 610 feet. **Elevation loss:** 1,420 feet. **Maximum elevation:** 9,490 feet (near Penrose Creek). **Topo maps:** Willow Park Reservoir (trail not shown), *Trails Illustrated* (trail not shown). **Jurisdiction:** Cloud Peak Wilderness (Bighorn National Forest).

FINDING THE TRAILHEAD

The south end of the trail (marked with a sign that reads "Cloud Peak Reservoir") can be reached from Hunter Corrals via the Elk Lake Trail (8.5 miles) or the Ant Hill Trail (10.7 miles). The north end of the trail (at the outfitter's camp near Beaver Lakes) can be reached via a combination of the Highland Park, Lake Winnie, and Reservoirs Trails, 11.6 miles total.

THE HIKE

This trail links Elk Lake with Kearny Creek, providing a shortcut to the northern reaches of the Solitude Trail and avoiding the numerous ATVs that can be found along the Reservoirs route. Along the way, the trail visits a number of beautiful lakes where trout are abundant. The Forest Service does not officially maintain the trail at this time, so sharpen your route-finding skills before you attempt it. In places, the trail is marked with little more than old saw-work and blazes, and intersections will be for the most part unmarked. Several fords of deep (but slow-moving) water lend a real wilderness feel to the trek. The rewards are well worth the extra effort, though, as the route passes through some of the wildest and most remote country in the Bighorn Mountains.

From the western shore of Elk Lake, follow signs for Cloud Peak Reservoir as the trail runs northwest along a stringer of grassy meadows. The path soon enters a pleasant subalpine woodland of fir, spruce, and whitebark pine. After a gentle downhill stroll, the path meets the ATV road that links Willow Park and Cloud Peak reservoirs.

To take the 1.6-mile side trip to Cloud Peak Reservoir, turn left as the road drops briskly at first and then at a shallow grade, yielding aerial views of Flatiron Lake and terminating at the earth-fill dam of Cloud Peak Reservoir. Cloud Peak itself is hidden from view, but there are excellent views of Bomber Mountain, Penrose Peak, and the massive dome that rises between them.

To continue the trek, hike north on the ATV road from the original junction. After a distance of 0.2 mile, cairns mark a side trail that drops away to the left (west). Hike down this well-beaten path, which descends steadily toward the middle lakes of South Piney Creek. The path bottoms out beside a small tarn, its clear waters turning a brilliant sapphire in the depths. The path leads along the south shore of this pool to reach the edge of much larger Flatiron Lake, which offers superb views of the high peaks. Follow its shoreline to reach the outlet of the lake, where it will be necessary to hike through the midst of an outfitter's camp to reach a knee-deep ford of South Piney Creek.

Flatiron Lake.

On the far bank, a faint and neglected trail runs around the western shore of a smaller lake below Flatiron. Follow the occasional cairns as this track moves inland and passes through sparse timber. The trail roughly parallels South Piney Creek on its way to Frying Pan Lake. Here, the path emerges in a grassy meadow where there are fine camping spots. Frying Pan Lake is a broad and shallow pool that spreads its waters through the midst of grassy wetlands. From here, it is necessary to ford the knee-deep water of the narrows to reach the peninsula beyond.

Once on the peninsula, the trail is again well-beaten and obvious as it runs northeast through the lakeshore timber. A swampy opening choked with low-growing willow stretches northeast from the foot of Frying Pan Lake, and the trail follows the edge of this extensive bog. At its northernmost end is a trail junction marked only with a signpost advertising the distances to Elk Lake and Cloud Peak Reservoir.

The main trail seems to run southeast from this point, but our route follows the less-traveled path that makes a northward descent along the stream that drains the swamps. This narrow, boulder-choked vale leads down to a rock-hop across Elk Creek, after which the trail climbs to reach a neighboring ridgetop. It now drops northward along the ridgeline to reach a junction marked with a cairn. Here, a well-groomed trail drops eastward and then climbs to meet the Reservoirs section of the Solitude Trail. Our route follows the fainter path (marked by blazes) that continues down the ridgeline to reach a wooded saddle.

Turn left (west) at the unmarked junction in this saddle as our route runs along the edge of a broad boulder field and passes a woodland pond on its way to the confluence of Elk and South Piney Creeks. The path seems to dead-end at a large cairn beside a vast swamp. Ford the waist-deep but slow-moving waters of both streams to pick up the blazed trail as it departs from the north end of the swamp.

The path now descends gently along the timbered benches to the west of South Piney Creek. The path drops to the stream bank 0.7 mile beyond the confluence. This spot will look like a ford to southbound travelers, but it isn't. The trail continues down the west bank of the stream, passing through spruce bottomlands. As the watercourse steepens and the valley narrows, the track traverses onto the side of a ridge.

Upon rounding the toe of this ridge, the path turns west into a karst landscape of eskers, moraines, and kettle ponds left behind during the retreat of glacial ice. A ragged woodland now covers this rolling country and the trail wanders up and down through a confusing landscape of finger ridges. The path finally emerges above a swampy meadow beside Penrose Creek. The path now follows Penrose Creek upward, rising gently across wooded flats and then climbing steadily along the lower edges of talus slopes.

The trail flattens out upon reaching the upper basin of Penrose Creek. As the trail breaks out into grassy glades, a calf-deep ford of Penrose Creek leads to a large cairn where our route meets the Penrose Creek Trail. Turn left (west) on this trail to reach a second cairn where our route departs to the north once more. A short side trip west from this cairn leads to the vast subalpine meadow at the base of Penrose Peak.

Meanwhile, the Flatiron Lake route glides up through the forest to reach the edge of a steep escarpment, then starts a steady descent into the Kearny Creek Valley. The trail is easy to follow and you will enjoy some of the best-engineered switchbacks in the Bighorn National Forest along the way. There is an unmarked junction at the bottom of the grade. Just a short distance to the west lie the Beaver Lakes, a pair of rock-bound tarns set in the midst of the forest. They offer fine fishing and are well worth the side trip.

To complete the trek, turn right at the junction as the path emerges into a lush meadow along Kearny Creek. Follow the edge of the clearing eastward to reach a footlog that spans the stream beside a split-rail fence. The trail then follows the fence past the "Beaver Lakes Country Club," an outfitter's camp the Spear-O Wigwam resort leases from the Forest Service by special permit. The journey ends at a junction with the Reservoirs portion of the Solitude Trail, 1.3 miles below Kearny Lake Reservoir.

MILES AND DIRECTIONS

0.0   Trail leaves the western shore of Elk Lake.

0.5   Trail leaves Cloud Peak Wilderness.

0.6   Trail joins old road to Cloud Peak Reservoir (1.6 miles, moderate). Turn right on road.

0.7   Turn left (west) onto trail that descends toward Flatiron Lake.

1.0   Bottom of grade. Trail passes nameless lake.

1.2   Trail fords South Piney Creek at foot of Flatiron Lake and turns north.

1.3   Trail passes nameless lake below Flatiron Lake.

1.8   Trail fords arm of Frying Pan Lake.

2.5   Junction with Frying Pan Trail at edge of marsh. Turn left (north) as trail descends.

2.6   Trail crosses Elk Creek.

3.0   Junction with cutoff to Reservoirs route. Continue straight ahead.

3.2   Unmarked junction in low saddle. Turn left.

3.4   Trail makes fords of Elk and South Piney Creeks to follow west bank downstream.

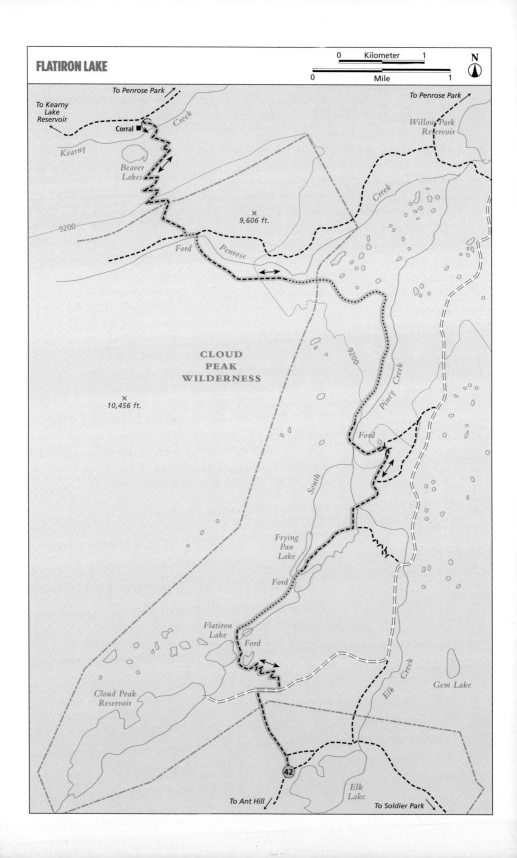

FLATIRON LAKE

0 Kilometer 1

0 Mile 1

N

To Penrose Park

To Kearny
Lake Reservoir

Corral ■

Kearny

Creek

Beaver
Lakes

9200

Ford   Penrose

×
9,606 ft.

To Penrose Park

Willow Park
Reservoir

Creek

CLOUD
PEAK
WILDERNESS

×
10,456 ft.

9200

Piney Creek

Ford

South

Frying
Pan
Lake

Ford

Flatiron
Lake

Ford

Elk Creek

Gem Lake

Cloud Peak
Reservoir

42

To Ant Hill

Elk
Lake

To Soldier Park

4.5 Trail leaves South Piney Creek.

5.2 Trail enters Cloud Peak Wilderness.

6.3 Trail fords Penrose Creek to join Penrose Creek Trail. Turn left.

6.5 Turn right at unmarked junction as Flatiron Lake Trail resumes.

6.7 Trail leaves Cloud Peak Wilderness.

7.8 Trail reaches meadows of Kearny Creek. Junction with Beaver Lakes spur (0.2 mile, easy). Turn right to complete trek.

7.9 Footbridge over Kearny Creek at east end of meadow.

8.0 Trail joins the Reservoirs segment of the Solitude Trail.

43 THE RESERVOIRS

General description: An extended trip from Elk Lake to Willow Park Reservoir (4.7 miles) or Kearny Lake Reservoir (11.7 miles).
Difficulty: Moderate.
Route finding: No problem.
Best season: Mid-July to mid-September.
Visitation: Heavy.

Elevation gain: 605 feet.
Elevation loss: 1,695 feet.
Maximum elevation: 9,885 feet (near Elk Lake).
Topo maps: Willow Park Reservoir, *Trails Illustrated*.
Jurisdiction: Bighorn National Forest (Tongue Ranger District).

FINDING THE TRAILHEAD

The south end of the trail (at the foot of Elk Lake) can be reached from the Hunter Trailhead via the Elk Lake Trail (7.9 miles) or the Ant Hill Trail (11.3 miles). The north end of the trail (the foot of Kearny Lake Reservoir) can be reached via a combination of the Highland Park and Lake Winnie trails, 10.3 miles total.

THE HIKE

Much of this portion of the original Solitude Trail was built as a gravel road to access Cloud Peak Reservoir. It remains open to motorized vehicles and is, in fact, quite popular with ATV riders. The route is not very scenic and is principally used as a link-up for hikers on extended trips in the northern part of the Cloud Peak Wilderness. Hikers who seek a more remote and pristine experience and who have strong wilderness skills should consider the Flatiron Lake route (page 137) as an alternative. Between the Kearny Creek Bridge and Kearny Lake Reservoir, the route follows a horse trail, offering more solitude and fine scenery along Kearny Creek.

From the foot of Elk Lake, follow the horse trail that runs northward along the marshy meadows lining Elk Creek. It soon swings into the trees, a loose assortment of spruce and whitebark pine. After 0.3 mile, the trail leaves the Cloud Peak Wilderness and runs into the heavily traveled ATV road that links Willow Park and Cloud Peak Reservoirs (also known as the Solitude Trail).

Follow this roadbed downward past a little-used spur to Gem Lake as the ATV road continues to parallel Elk Creek through the sparse timber. There is a short connecting trail to Frying Pan Lake beside the ford of Elk Creek. Hikers should be able to hop across this stream on the rocks. The ATV road now follows a low finger ridge to the east of Elk Creek and maintains its altitude as the valley falls away below. There are only occasional glimpses of the mountains to the west as the roadway descends through a woodland of pine and spruce. A cutoff trail to Frying Pan Lake ultimately drops into the valley below, while the main route makes a shallow descent toward the head of Willow Park Reservoir.

As it approaches the bottom of the grade, the road bends eastward and passes through a regenerating forest. There is a meeting of roadways near the head of Willow Park Reservoir. Turn left, following signs for "Trail 038" as the ATV track now descends through the trees to the western shore of the reservoir. Willow Park Reservoir is set on a pine-clad shelf, with little in the way of mountain views from its upper end.

At the head of the reservoir, a bridge leads across South Piney Creek. The original horse trail can still be followed around the north shore of the lake, but it has been abandoned and is hard to follow in places. The ATV track jogs upstream, following South Piney Creek upward for a time before it turns northward into the timber. It soon reaches the unmarked junction with the Penrose Creek Trail, which is not suitable for ATVs. The main trail crosses a swampy opening and approaches the north shore of the reservoir.

It now follows the shoreline, always in view of the water. There are a number of woodland pools to the north of the trail. At one point, the track swings out onto a retaining dike for a fine view of Penrose Peak. At the foot of the reservoir, the roadway angles down below an earth-fill dam and begins to descend through the forest. It passes several woodland meres early on in the descent, then winds downward through a monotonous forest of pines. At the bottom of the grade, the roadbed emerges on an open shelf above the bridge over Kearny Creek.

Turn left on the far bank as the Solitude Trail now follows Kearny Creek upward along a route seldom traveled by motorized vehicles. At first the traveling through the lodgepoles is tedious, but after 0.6 mile the path enters a spruce bottom where there are fine camping prospects beside the stream. The trail then returns to the lodgepole woodland for more steady climbing.

At mile 8.5, the trail reaches a splendid series of waterfalls cascading down between outcrops of granite. Watch for the water ouzel, a tiny gray bird that builds its nests behind

Kearny Lake Reservoir.

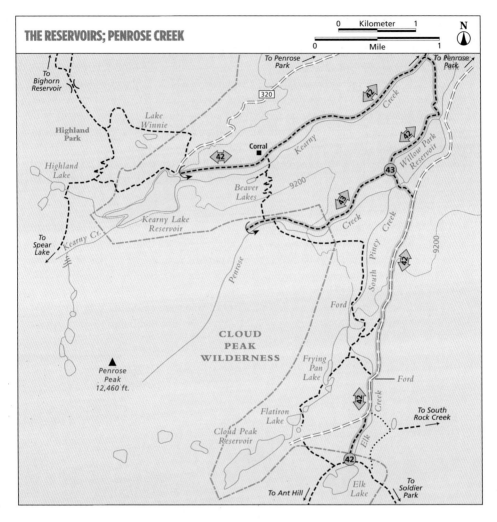

waterfalls and dives into rapids to walk on the bottom and pick at the aquatic insects that make up its diet.

After a hearty ascent beside the falls, the path climbs into a hanging valley. It soon crosses two extensive meadows before returning to the trees. The trail next emerges to cross a small boulder field. A short distance beyond is an outfitter's camp leased to the Spear-O Wigwam resort by special permit from the Forest Service. There is an unmarked junction in a pocket meadow beside this camp. From here, you can follow the split-rail fence across Kearny Creek and along the far edge of the meadows to reach the Beaver Lakes. These scenic, rockbound pools are filled with trout and are well worth the side trip. This junction also marks the terminus of the Flatiron Lake route.

Meanwhile, the main trail continues westward, climbing steadily through the timber to reach its end atop the earth-fill dam of Kearny Lakes Reservoir. Pikas live among the boulders here and there are views of the high peaks to the west. Another ATV road (FR 320) comes in from the northeast to reach the dam. Follow this road northeast for 0.2 mile to find the junction to link up with the next leg of the Solitude Trail.

MILES AND DIRECTIONS

0.0   Trail junction at foot of Elk Lake. Hike north.

0.3   Trail leaves Cloud Peak Wilderness.

0.5   Junction with jeep road to Cloud Peak Reservoir (1.6 miles, moderate). Turn right onto road.

0.7   Faint trail runs east to Gem Lake. Stay on road.

1.2   Trail descends westward to Frying Pan Lake. Stay on road.

1.3   Ford of Elk Creek.

2.1   Cutoff trail descends toward Frying Pan Lake. Stay on road.

4.4   Jeep road splits. Turn left.

4.7   Bridge over South Piney Creek at head of Willow Park Reservoir. Follow signs westward.

5.0   Unmarked junction with Penrose Creek Trail. Continue straight ahead.

6.2   Trail reaches dam at foot of Willow Park Reservoir. Beginning of descent.

7.2   Bridge over Kearny Creek.

7.3   Junction with trail that follows Kearny Creek. Turn left onto it.

8.5   Waterfalls on Kearny Creek.

10.4   Outfitter's camp. Junction with trail to Beaver Lakes (0.4 mile, easy) and Flatiron Lake route. Continue straight ahead.

11.7   Trail emerges atop dam at foot of Kearny Lake Reservoir and joins FR 320.

44 PENROSE CREEK

See map on page 144.

General description: A side trip from the head of Willow Park Reservoir to the meadows of upper Penrose Creek, 3 miles one way.

Difficulty: Moderate.

Route finding: Some challenges.

Best season: Mid-July to mid-September.

Visitation: Very light.

Elevation gain: 800 feet.

Maximum elevation: 9,470 feet.

Topo maps: Willow Park Reservoir (location approximate), *Trails Illustrated* (location approximate).

Jurisdiction: Cloud Peak Wilderness (Bighorn National Forest).

FINDING THE TRAILHEAD

From the Hunter Trailhead, this trail can be reached via the Elk Lake and Reservoirs trails (12.9 miles). From the north, it can be reached by combining the Highland Park, Lake Winnie, and Reservoirs trails (17 miles). The Flatiron Lake route also intersects the trail. The trail departs from the Reservoirs Trail at an unmarked junction between two marshy openings, 0.3 mile north of the bridge over South Piney Creek.

THE HIKE

This trail makes an ideal day trip for hikers who find themselves at Willow Park Reservoir and want to escape from the ATVs. It climbs into the Cloud Peak Wilderness to reach the high country at the foot of Penrose Peak, intersecting with the Flatiron Lake Trail along the way. The lower portion of the route is little more than an avenue worn into the grouse whortleberry and marked by blazed trees. Game trails crisscross the area, so good route-finding skills are a must.

The path departs from an unmarked junction on the Reservoirs portion of the Solitude Trail. The junction lies about midway between the two swampy clearings above the head of Willow Park Reservoir. The trail rises gently through the lodgepoles at first, ultimately turning north to cross an open bog. It then turns west again, continuing through the forest to reach the edge of a broad clearing. The path skirts through the timber on the north side of this opening, and now the rushing of Penrose Creek can be heard to the south.

The gradient increases as the trail makes a moderate ascent, alternately looping up through the forest and traversing along level terraces. The path ultimately reaches a talus slope that indicates the rather steep final pitch. The trail tops out near the crest of a finger ridge, then descends a bit to enter the upper basin of Penrose Creek.

The crystalline waters of this stream wander lazily between sandy banks carpeted with lush meadows. The trail makes its way through sunny glades and stands of young pine, with two cairns marking the two intersections with the Flatiron Lake Trail, which runs south to Frying Pan Lake and north to the Beaver Lakes. Before long, the trees draw back from Penrose Creek and a broad park leads up to the base of Penrose Peak. The path peters out at the edge of this meadow, which is guarded to the south by low pinnacles of shattered stone and to the west by the lofty summit of Penrose Peak.

Meadows at the head of Penrose Creek.

MILES AND DIRECTIONS

0.0 Unmarked junction with the Reservoirs segment of the Solitude Trail.

0.9 Trail enters Cloud Peak Wilderness.

1.8 Top of grade.

2.2 Trail approaches Penrose Creek.

2.3 First junction with Flatiron Trail. Continue straight ahead.

2.4 Second junction with Flatiron Trail. Continue straight ahead.

3.0 Trail peters out in vast meadow.

ADDITIONAL TRAILS

An old jeep trail runs from the Adelaide Lake area to **Porcupine Creek** and then on to the Shell Lakes. It is faint and unmarked in places and crosses trackless meadows where route finding is difficult.

The **Sawmill Pass** Trail occupies an old roadbed that runs from the West Fork of Big Goose Creek to Sawmill Pass. There are several ruins from the pioneer era along the way. The west end of the trail is not marked.

The routes that run along **Graves Creek** and the **West Fork of the South Tongue River** are marked as trails on the forest map, but in fact they are jeep roads open to vehicles.

Twin trails follow the banks of the South Tongue River downstream from **Tie Flume** Campground. Both trails are chiefly for fishing access and they peter out after a mile. Along the way are ruins of the old tie flume, a wooden aqueduct used to float railroad ties down from the high country at the turn of the 20th century.

The **Adelaide Lake** Trail runs from the Shell Creek Ranger Station to Adelaide Lake, which is a popular destination for ATV traffic. En route, the path crosses a portion of the Cloud Peak Wilderness, passing through a pretty valley where meadows are bordered with aspen and spruce, then makes a rocky ascent to reach its terminus.

A heavily used ATV track links Bighorn Reservoir with **Cross Creek Reservoir**.

A portion of the Solitude Trail runs between Cross Creek and the **East Fork of Big Goose Creek**, crossing a low and wooded ridge en route. The trail is closed to motorized traffic.

Trails over **Dutch Oven Pass** and into the high country beyond Geddes Lake have been abandoned by the Forest Service to restore pristine conditions to these areas; the trails have been swallowed up by the wilderness.

The **Frying Pan Lake** Trail runs from a ford of Elk Creek on the Reservoirs Trail to Frying Pan Lake, where it intersects the Flatiron Lake route. It is a well-beaten trail of 1.3 miles.

Looking back across the valley of Porcupine Creek.

THE PRAIRIE FOOTHILLS

The eastern front of the Bighorn Mountains is characterized by short but stunning canyons, tall reefs of sedimentary rock, and vast grasslands behind the first range of summits. This area receives some use by horse parties from the neighboring guest ranches, but it is relatively unknown to hikers. There are several expanses of roadless terrain in this area, offering excellent opportunities for long backpacks and mountain solitude. Cattle are grazed in several of the large parks during summer. In winter, these same areas become an important range for elk and deer.

Road access to this area is fairly easy, with good gravel roads leading up to most of the trailheads along the leading edge of the mountains. Be aware some roads that lead to established trails are not open to the public and respect "No Trespassing" signs. The Red Grade Road (FR 26) climbs from Big Horn to the top of the range. It is a steep and winding road and tends to be full of potholes. Travelers with low-clearance cars should

Along the West Fork of Big Goose Creek en route to Walker Prairie.

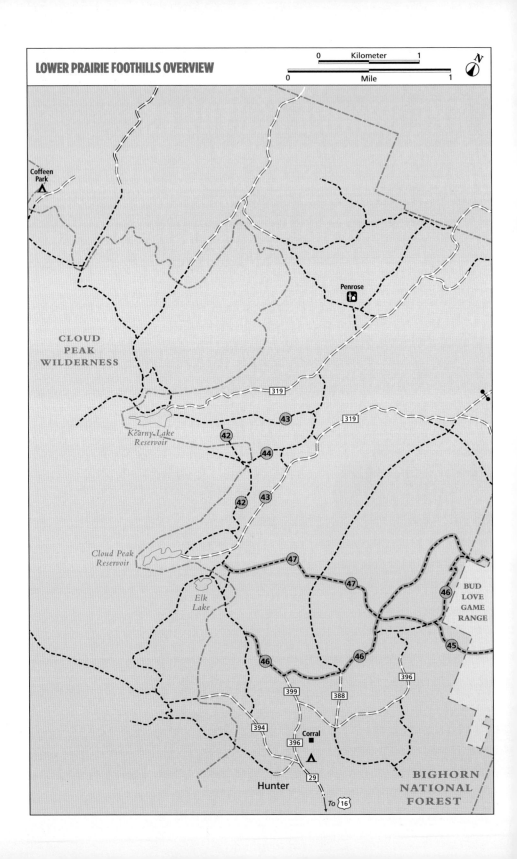

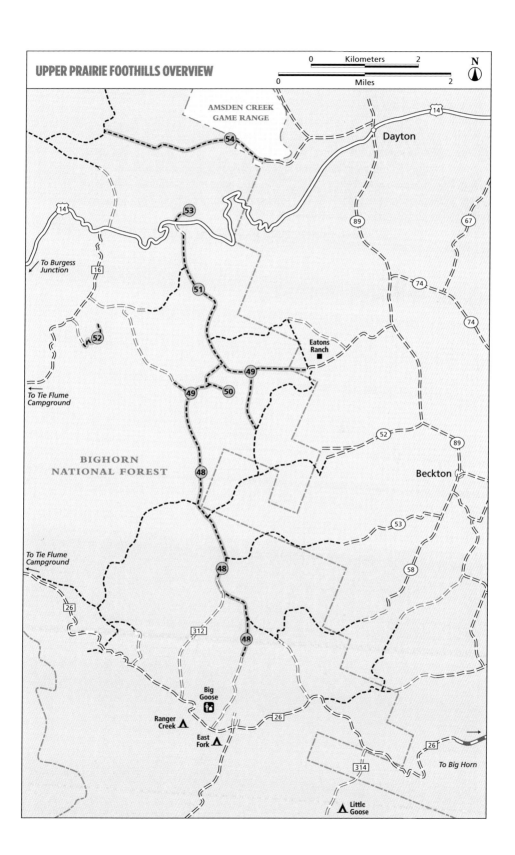

0   Kilometers   2

0   Miles   2

N

AMSDEN CREEK
GAME RANGE

54

Dayton

14

53

14

89

67

To Burgess
Junction

16

51

74

52

74

Eatons
Ranch

49

49   50

To Tie Flume
Campground

52

89

BIGHORN
NATIONAL FOREST

48

Beckton

To Tie Flume
Campground

53

26

58

312

48

Big
Goose

26

Ranger
Creek

East
Fork

26

314

To Big Horn

Little
Goose

approach this road along good-quality trunk roads that run east and south from US Highway 14. Access to the southern end of the prairie foothills is a bit more challenging. Roads that run north from Hunter Trailhead tend to be rocky and may have fords or wet-weather mud pits.

Camping areas along the foot of the mountains are scarce. There is a good campground in Tongue Canyon and the Bud Love Wildlife Management Unit has a parking pullout where camping is permitted. Most of the country falls within private lands. The Bighorn National Forest offers several developed campgrounds along the Red Grade Road. The communities of Dayton, Big Horn, and Ranchester offer gas, restaurants, and a limited range of supplies. You can find almost everything you need in the larger towns of Sheridan and Buffalo. Both of these small cities have Forest Service ranger stations where you can get current information on roads and trails.

45 FIREBOX PARK

General description: A day hike or connecting trail to Firebox Park, 2.8 miles one way.
Difficulty: Moderately strenuous.
Route finding: Some challenges.
Best season: Mid-May to early October.
Visitation: Very light.

Elevation gain: 840 feet.
Elevation loss: 180 feet.
Maximum elevation: 7,060 feet.
Topo map: Stone Mountain (trail not shown).
Jurisdiction: Bighorn National Forest (Buffalo Ranger District).

FINDING THE TRAILHEAD

From the west side of Buffalo, drive north on North De Smet Avenue, following signs for the Bud Love Wildlife Management Unit. After 2.3 miles, the road splits. Bear right. The pavement ends 6 miles beyond this point. Drive onward for 2.5 miles to reach a sign for the Bud Love Winter Range; turn left onto a dry-weather road. Follow this road 2.4 miles, bearing right at all junctions, to reach the trailhead at its end. GPS: 44.408650° N, 106.872511° W.

THE HIKE

This trail climbs through a steep canyon at the edge of the mountains, then ascends to the elevated grassland known as Firebox Park. For hikers bound on extended trips in

Firebox Park.

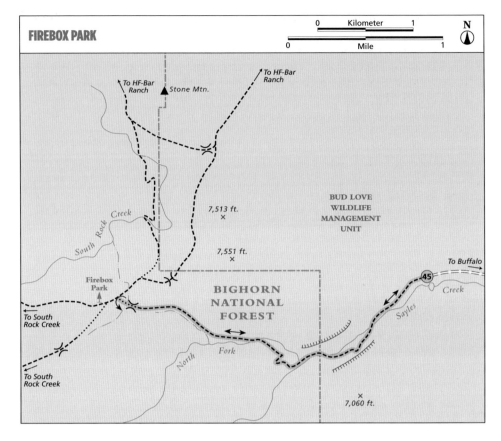

the Rock Creek watershed, the Firebox Park Trail makes an ideal starting point. From Firebox Park, trails radiate throughout the Rock Creek Valley.

The trek begins on the grassy plains of the Bud Love big-game winter range. Follow the footpath that descends to a gate in the fence of an abandoned homestead. The trail then glides up to the base of the mountains, following North Sayles Creek. The brushy riparian habitat along the stream banks makes excellent hiding cover for white-tailed deer, which are abundant in this area. Ahead is the mouth of a narrow canyon, flanked by upthrust strata of dolomite and sandstone that have been carved into eerie pillars and pinnacles by the forces of erosion.

Upon entering the canyon, the path makes three quick crossings of North Sayles Creek. It then begins an unbelievably steep ascent through a stand of Douglas fir, the gradient precipitous despite the switchbacks. At the top of the grade, the trail surmounts a near-vertical slab of sandstone, then dips and rises as it crosses other rock strata. Next it descends to cross the creek and follow the more open north bank. Here, North Sayles Creek pours down a series of waterfalls linked by quiet pools, and old spruce trees shade the watercourse.

At the national forest boundary, the canyon opens up at the confluence of two stream branches. The trail initially crosses the main branch and follows the more southerly stream, gliding upward across grassy slopes to reach a grove of aspen. It then doglegs sharply to the northeast, climbing to the top of a grassy rise. Here, one can look down through the canyon and out onto the High Plains. To the north, an imposing reef rises above high grasslands.

The path now runs northward through a spruce-aspen woodland beside North Sayles Creek. It soon makes a final crossing of the stream and climbs into the vast grasslands beyond. North Sayles Creek soon bends west into the mountains, but the path continues north through the grassy vale guarded by an imposing reef of sandstone. There is a low gap at the head of the drainage, but the trail bends northwest to pass through a higher saddle to the west of a rocky hillock.

The trail now descends into Firebox Park. This high and verdant meadow has a small brook running along its southern edge, providing a dependable supply of water. (Be sure to use a filter before drinking as cattle use this area as a summer pasture.) At the center of the park is a signpost, with paths running west to Johnson and South Rock Creeks and east to the HF-Bar Ranch. The rise at the center of the park offers superb vistas of the reefs and foothills in all directions.

MILES AND DIRECTIONS

0.0   Trailhead on Bud Love Wildlife Management Unit.

0.3   Trail enters canyon of North Sayles Creek.

0.5   Trail crosses North Sayles Creek to south bank.

1.0   Trail returns to north bank of North Sayles Creek.

1.1   Trail enters Bighorn National Forest.

1.2   Trail crosses to west bank of North Sayles Creek at stream confluence.

1.7   Final crossing of North Sayles Creek.

2.6   Trail crosses pass to enter South Rock Creek drainage.

2.8   Trail joins South Rock Creek Trail in Firebox Park.

46 SOUTH ROCK CREEK

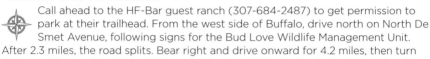

General description: A backpack from the HF-Bar Ranch to the Elk Lake Trail, 13.6 miles total.
Difficulty: Moderately strenuous.
Route finding: Some challenges in the Firebox Park area.
Best season: Mid-June to late September.
Visitation: Very light.

Elevation gain: 4,580 feet.
Elevation loss: 630 feet.
Maximum elevation: 9,420 feet.
Topo maps: Stone Mountain, Hunter Mesa, Lake Angeline, Willow Park Reservoir (location approximate).
Jurisdiction: Bighorn National Forest (Buffalo Ranger District).

FINDING THE TRAILHEAD

Call ahead to the HF-Bar guest ranch (307-684-2487) to get permission to park at their trailhead. From the west side of Buffalo, drive north on North De Smet Avenue, following signs for the Bud Love Wildlife Management Unit. After 2.3 miles, the road splits. Bear right and drive onward for 4.2 miles, then turn right on Johnson Creek Road. After 1.2 miles it will join the Rock Creek Road. Follow this road west as the pavement plays out. After 4 miles, you will meet the Shell Creek Road. Bear left and follow the Rock Creek Road for 2 miles to enter the HF-Bar Ranch. Drive another 2.2 miles on a good county road to reach the ranch complex. Ask the ranch hands where you should park. The hike begins on the jeep trail that leaves the guest ranch through a green gate between the main barn and the corrals. GPS: 44.457623° N, 106.899266° W.

THE HIKE

This trail is the main trunk route for travel through the Rock Creek watershed. It begins by traveling through a short but spectacular canyon, then follows South Rock Creek through timbered bottoms and extensive meadows. There are a number of fords along the way. Wait until after spring runoff to attempt the trail and be prepared to get your feet wet.

The jeep road that is an official Forest Service trail departs the HF-Bar Ranch on a southwesterly bearing, climbing gently across the open prairie to reach a grassy saddle. Follow the right fork as the road splits. This road descends to South Rock Creek and then turns west to reach the first of many fords. Just beyond this crossing, follow the horse trail that splits away to the right. Vertical slabs of sedimentary rock rise to the north of the stream as the trail winds through the final, grassy foothills to reach the base of the mountains.

Upon entering the canyon of South Rock Creek, the path makes several more knee-deep fords. Great, slanted strata of sedimentary rock rise skyward and South Rock Creek dances through a series of minor waterfalls and quiet pools at the foot of the cliffs. At one point, a full-fledged brook pours out of a solid face of rock, a geological oddity that attests to the porous nature of the limestone.

After passing through the canyon, the trail enters the Bighorn National Forest. The trail to Balm of Gilead and Spring creeks immediately splits away to the right, while the main trail continues westward to cross South Rock Creek a short distance upstream. It then switchbacks steadily upward through a forest of Douglas fir and ponderosa pine. After a steep initial grade, the climbing eases and soon you will see the stark spire that

The canyon of Rock Creek.

guards the mouth of Balm of Gilead Creek. The trail tops out on a spur of Stone Mountain. Broad grasslands stretch ahead, bordered by giant ponderosa pines. Immense reefs of sedimentary rock now rise above the grassy slopes of the valley.

The trail crosses a second high spur, then traverses for a time before descending through the huge boulders that have fallen from the face of Stone Mountain. At the bottom of the grade, a cutoff to the Stone Mountain Trail climbs southward, while the main trail fords South Rock Creek to reach a camp spot beside a pleasant meadow. The path then makes a steady climb to surmount a pine-clad hill. A brief jog to the north leads to a second ford. Just beyond the crossing, the trail switchbacks lazily up through the pines.

The path emerges in open grasslands and promptly disappears. Follow the northern edge of the meadows to meet the Stone Mountain Trail in a high and grassy saddle. Firebox Park stretches westward from this saddle, guarded by stony hillocks. The park is watered by an aspen-girt stream that courses down along its southern edge. The trail descends to cross this stream, then rises into the heart of the park. A signpost marks the departure of a connecting trail bound for Johnson Creek.

Bear right as the South Rock Creek Trail descends toward the valley floor once again. This is as pretty a landscape as any in the foothills, with Penrose Peak guarding the western skyline and a picturesque bottomland meadow stretching below, bordered by a rich forest of spruce and aspen. The path drops into the bottomland clearing, crosses several spring-fed rills, then turns west to follow South Rock Creek.

After a few small glades, the lodgepole pines take over. The unbroken forest lasts until the confluence with Middle Rock Creek. At the confluence, the trail crosses South Rock Creek and rises to the edge of a long and grassy clearing. A signpost to the north announces the departure of the Middle Rock Creek and Balm of Gilead Trails. The main path continues westward along the south fork and the meadows persist as far as the junction with trail #549, a cutoff to Firebox Park. A mixed woodland of aspen and spruce now fills the bottomlands, and the trail makes a ford to reach the south bank of the stream.

A pleasant glade lies at the junction with trail #084, and there are fine possibilities for camping here. Another trail leads southward at Keno Creek, bound for the broad and beautiful meadows at the end of FR 388. The main trail is now muddy and flood damaged as it continues to follow South Rock Creek upward. After several stream crossings, the path climbs briskly up a wooded vale to the south of the creek. It tops out in a ridgetop park at the end of FR 399. Looking west, Ant Hill is the prominent summit.

The route now adopts an old road grade for the steep descent to the final ford of South Rock Creek. On the far side, a good trail zigzags lazily up the wooded drainage to the north. It first passes through an unbroken stand of aspen, then through a vast woodland of lodgepole pine. The trees become sparse as a cutoff trail runs south toward Triangle Park. Bear right to finish the trek as the route leads up a rocky and washed-out track. A vigorous climb leads through the spruce forest to join the Elk Lake Trail 2.6 miles from the lake.

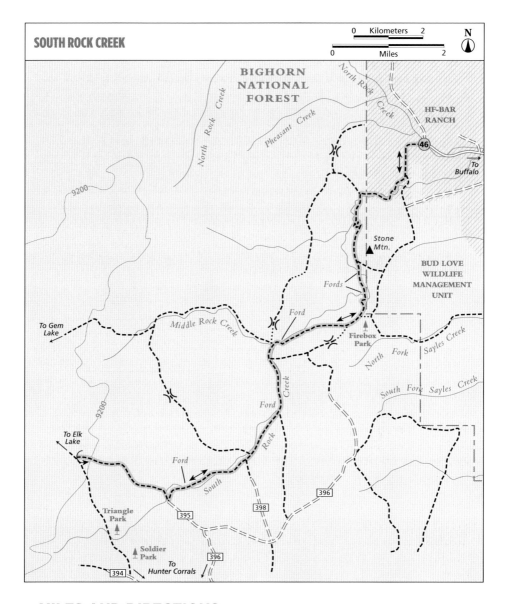

MILES AND DIRECTIONS

0.0 Trail leaves HF-Bar Ranch. Follow jeep trail southwest.

0.5 Jeep trail splits. Bear right.

1.0 First of seven fords of South Rock Creek. Trail enters canyon.

1.1 Junction with Red Canyon Trail. Continue straight ahead.

1.7 Trail enters Bighorn National Forest.

1.8 Junction with Balm of Gilead Trail. Main trail makes 7th ford of South Rock Creek.

3.6 Junction with cutoff to the Stone Mountain Trail. Bear right and descend.

3.8 Trail fords South Rock Creek and follows north bank.

5.0 Trail returns to south bank of South Rock Creek.

4.6 Trail emerges in high meadow. Follow the trees southwest.

4.8 Junction with the Stone Mountain Trail. Turn right as trail enters Firebox Park.

5.2 Junction with cutoff trail to upper reaches of South Rock Creek. Bear right.

6.6 Trail fords South Rock Creek to follow north bank.

6.7 Junction with Middle Rock Creek Trail. Continue straight ahead.

7.2 Junction with cutoff trail from Firebox Park. Continue straight ahead.

7.6 Trail fords South Rock Creek and follows south bank.

7.9 Junction with Johnson Creek Trail. Bear right.

8.9 Junction with Keno Creek Trail. Bear right.

9.1 Junction with cutoff trail to Middle Rock Creek. Continue straight ahead.

9.7 Trail fords South Rock Creek and follows north bank.

10.2 Trail returns to south bank of creek.

10.8 Junction with FR 399. Turn right and descend to ford creek.

13.6 Trail joins Elk Lake Trail 2.6 miles below lake.

47 MIDDLE ROCK CREEK

General description: An extended trip from South Rock Creek to Gem Lake, 6 miles.
Difficulty: Moderately strenuous.
Route finding: Some challenges.
Best season: Mid-June to late September.

Visitation: Very light.
Elevation gain: 2,870 feet.
Maximum elevation: 9,900 feet.
Topo maps: Stone Mountain, Willow Park Reservoir.
Jurisdiction: Bighorn National Forest (Buffalo Ranger District).

FINDING THE TRAILHEAD

Hike up the South Rock Trail 6.7 miles from the HF-Bar Ranch. GPS: 44.457623° N, 106.899266° W; see page 156, South Rock Creek, for directions to the HF-Bar Ranch.

THE HIKE

This obscure trail follows a minor branch of Rock Creek through a timbered valley guarded by slender pinnacles of rock. It ends up at Gem Lake, which occupies a high and timbered shelf within the Cloud Peak Wilderness. Route-finding skill is an asset here.

The trail begins by following Middle Rock Creek through a shady forest of spruce. Lodgepole pine forms a solid forest on the slopes to either side of the stream bottoms. The trail stays close to the water, making shallow fords at frequent intervals. A waterfall

Pinnacles above Middle Rock Creek.

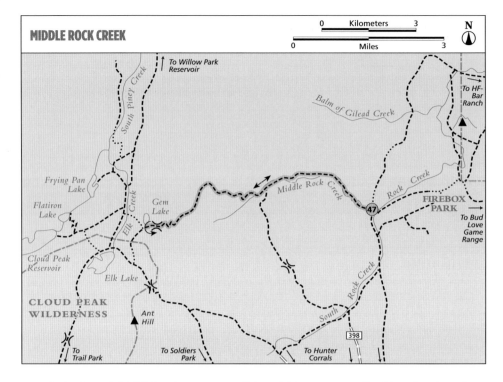

early in the trek highlights the scenic qualities of this pretty woodland brook. The valley soon bends west, entering a landscape of surreal spires and balanced rocks that have weathered out of the upthrust strata of granite.

The narrow valley ultimately opens up into a lodgepole pine flat, and then the trail is joined by the North Rock Creek Trail and later by a cutoff trail to Paradise Ranch and South Rock Creek. The main trail crosses an overgrown meadow to reach a final ford of Middle Rock Creek, then runs upstream to reach a major, northern tributary. Beyond this point, the trail undertakes a calf-burning climb, surmounting the rounded, pine-clad hill to the north. High on the ridge, the trail levels off as the lodgepoles give way to a loose woodland of spruce and fir. The path then drops onto the south slope of the ridge, turning westward.

Cairns mark the trail at frequent intervals, despite the fact that it is easy to follow here. The path grows faint, however, as it climbs the final pitch to reach an open meadow. Look back for views that stretch far out onto the plains.

At the top of the grade, follow the cairns through a loose parkland of subalpine fir. After a short distance, the path emerges in the lush meadows that lead down to the shore of Gem Lake. This small tarn occupies a wooded shelf above Elk Lake. The jagged summits that are visible in the distance belong to Bomber Mountain, an eastern buttress of Cloud Peak, and Penrose Peak. A well-beaten path leads south from a camp spot near Gem Lake to link up with the Elk Lake Trail in the high, open meadows above that lake. A faint track leads westward to meet the Reservoirs Trail, which links Elk Lake with Willow Park Reservoir.

MILES AND DIRECTIONS

0.0 South Rock Creek. Hike north on Middle Rock Creek Trail.

0.1 Junction with Balm of Gilead Creek Trail. Bear left.

2.9 Junction with cutoff trail to South Rock Creek and Paradise Ranch. Bear right.

3.1 Trail makes final ford of Middle Rock Creek.

5.7 Top of grade.

6.0 Gem Lake.

48 WALKER PRAIRIE

General description: A backpack to Walker Prairie, 11.1 miles one way.
Difficulty: Moderately strenuous.
Route finding: Some challenges.
Best season: Late June to early October.
Visitation: Very light.

Elevation gain: 2,155 feet.
Elevation loss: 2,155 feet.
Maximum elevation: 7,990 feet.
Topo maps: Beckton, Park Reservoir, Walker Mountain.
Jurisdiction: Bighorn National Forest (Tongue Ranger District).

FINDING THE TRAILHEAD

From US Highway 14 south of Burgess Junction (or from the town of Big Horn), follow FR 26 to Big Goose Park. Turn north on FR 296, following signs for the ranger station. Drive past the ranger station to reach a junction after 0.8 mile. Turn right and follow the primitive road (high clearance needed) for 1 mile. At the end of the road, drive across the pole bridge over Ranger Creek to reach the trailhead beside a cabin. GPS: 44.622270° N, 107.211173° W.

THE HIKE

Walker Prairie is the largest expanse of grassland within the eastern foothills of the Bighorn Mountains. The route described here is the most direct and accessible way to get there. There are grazing leases in parts of Walker Prairie; be prepared to meet cattle along the way. The Wolf Creek and Horseshoe Mountain Trails provide good access to the north end of Walker Prairie.

The trail begins with a short climb along a pine-clad hillside, then descends along the ridgeline and into the bottoms of the East Fork of Big Goose Creek. Here, the path follows the west bank through shady stands of spruce and across a few open glades bordered by lodgepole pine. After a while, the trail makes two knee-deep fords of the East Fork. (A steep path climbs the hillside west of the stream to avoid the crossings.) These trails rejoin after 0.1 mile, but soon there is a crossing that cannot be avoided. Be careful—the round boulders of the streambed are quite slippery.

The trail follows the far bank to reach a grassy meadow and trail #238 joins the Walker Prairie Trail at the far edge of this clearing. A second ford leads to more extensive grasslands bordered by bald hills. The trail now starts up the hillside, dipping into an aspen-girt draw before it rises to the top of the hillock. From here, views stretch northward up the East Fork to take in the crags of the Cloud Peak Wilderness. The trail now fades out. Hike westward along the edge of the trees, then bear for the saddle to the left (south) of the granite outcrop at the far edge of the meadows. Along the way, eastward views encompass the rugged canyon of Big Goose Creek.

After passing through the saddle, the path descends across a small meadow to join FR 312 (this "road" is really no more than an ATV trail). Follow the roadbed northwest as it climbs a bit, then plummets down the hillside to reach the West Fork of Big Goose Creek. Along the way, watch for northward views of Walker Prairie and, to the southwest, views of Dome Peak. Upon reaching the creek bottoms, turn downstream to reach a bridge that spans the West Fork just above a striking outcrop of granite.

On the far bank, a horse trail climbs steeply into the grasslands, surmounting an open saddle that leads into the Prairie Creek drainage. After passing through a fence, the path descends to cross this stream amid a loose grove of aspen. It then follows the far bank downward. As Prairie Creek empties into the much larger Walker Creek, the trail fords the latter stream and follows a steep and gullied track high into Walker Prairie. It meets the Big Goose Trail on the heights behind a granite knob. From here you can look south for superb views of Dome Peak.

The crags of Black Tooth Mountain rise on the southern skyline as the Walker Prairie Trail runs northwest. Across the grassy slopes, it charts a high course that stays above the granite knobs that guard Walker Creek. This vast prairie owes its existence to the bedrock beneath it. This thick layer of limestone is quite porous, and rainwater percolates quickly away from the surface of the soil through passageways in the rock. Conifers rely on long taproots to find groundwater at the bedrock level, but here the groundwater flows far beneath the bedrock. Grasses, on the other hand, have dense mats of shallow roots that quickly absorb the water from the brief summer rain squalls as it soaks into the upper layers of the soil. This strategy allows the grasses to thrive on the open slopes of Walker Prairie.

As the path continues across Walker Prairie, a shallow vale descends from the cleft between She Bear and Walker Mountains, bearing a small brook. The Soldier Creek Trail follows this stream eastward and, after passing its marked junction, the main trail wanders into the grassy bottoms beside Walker Creek. It passes a primitive cow camp, then crosses a fence line. Just beyond the fence, the Walker Prairie Trail veers northeast to climb vigorously up a grassy draw. Watch for posts that mark the way as the path climbs high beneath the sandstone edifice of Walker Mountain.

Big Mountain (at left) and Little Mountain rise above Walker Prairie.

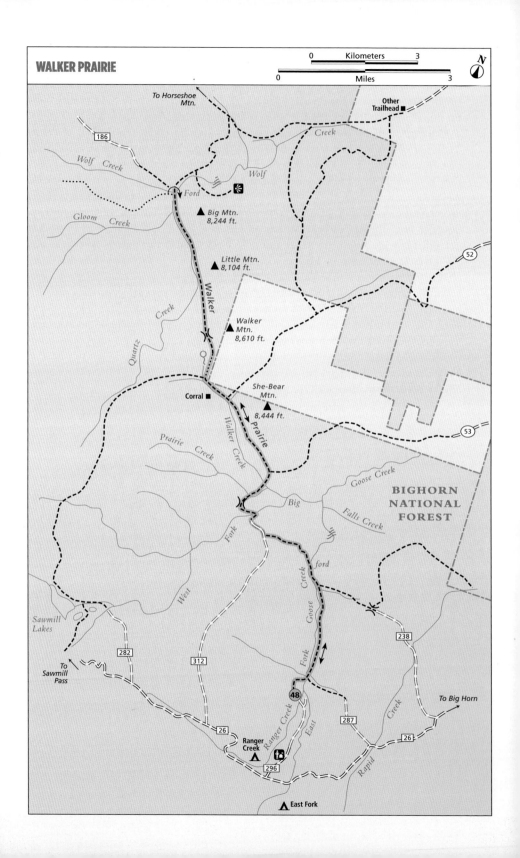

WALKER PRAIRIE

Kilometers

Miles

N

To Horseshoe Mtn.

Other Trailhead

186

Wolf Creek

Wolf Creek

Ford

Gloom Creek

▲ Big Mtn. 8,244 ft.

Walker Creek

52

▲ Little Mtn. 8,104 ft.

Quartz Creek

▲ Walker Mtn. 8,610 ft.

Corral ■

She-Bear Mtn.
▲ 8,444 ft.

53

Prairie Creek

Walker Creek

Prairie

Goose Creek

BIGHORN NATIONAL FOREST

Big

Falls Creek

West Fork

ford

Goose Creek Fork

238

Sawmill Lakes

282

312

To Sawmill Pass

48

To Big Horn

26

Ranger Creek

287

26

Ranger Creek

Rapid Creek

East Fork

296

East Fork

The trail stays above the trees as it crosses a drainage divide to enter the Quartz Creek watershed. A backward glance reveals the distant summits of the Cloud Peak massif, and ahead lie the sandstone reefs of Little and Big Mountains, with the wooded summit of Black Mountain rising to the northwest. The trail now splits in two. The upper path has the gentler gradient and superior scenery while the lower path offers better access to the grassy bottoms of Quartz Creek. The two trails rejoin near the valley floor, about halfway between Little Mountain and Big Mountain. The path now skirts the upper edge of several tall cutbanks, staying up in the grasslands until it reaches the confluence of Quartz and Wolf Creeks. Here, it fords Quartz Creek to meet the upper end of the Wolf Creek Trail.

MILES AND DIRECTIONS

0.0   Trailhead at end of FR 296.

1.2   First compulsory ford of East Fork of Big Goose Creek. Trail now follows east bank.

2.3   Junction with cutoff trail to Rapid Creek. Continue straight ahead.

2.5   Trail fords the East Fork, then climbs westward.

3.7   Trail joins FR 312. Turn right and follow road downward.

4.2   End of FR 312. Turn right and hike downstream to bridge.

4.3   Bridge over West Fork of Big Goose Creek.

4.6   Trail crosses divide into Prairie Creek drainage.

4.8   Trail crosses Prairie Creek.

5.0   Trail fords Walker Creek and starts climbing into Walker Prairie.

5.3   Junction with Big Goose Trail. Turn left.

6.9   Trail crosses Buck Creek to join Soldier Creek Trail. Bear left.

8.4   Trail crosses divide to enter Quartz Creek watershed.

11.0   Trail fords Quartz Creek.

11.1   End of Walker Prairie Trail. Wolf Creek Trail runs north.

49 WOLF CREEK

General description: A long day hike or short backpack to the north end of Walker Prairie, 6.2 miles one way.
Difficulty: Moderately strenuous.
Route finding: Some challenges.
Best season: Late June to late September.
Visitation: Light.

Elevation gain: 2,895 feet.
Elevation loss: 200 feet.
Maximum elevation: 7,460 feet.
Topo maps: Wolf, Dayton South, Walker Mountain.
Jurisdiction: Eatons' Ranch, Bighorn National Forest (Tongue District).

FINDING THE TRAILHEAD

Call ahead to the Eatons' Ranch to get permission to cross their private land and access this trail. From Sheridan, drive west on West Loucks Street, which becomes Wyoming 331. Follow it for 10 miles, then turn right on County Road 89, just east of Beckton. Follow this gravel trunk road north for 6 miles to the entrance of Eatons' Ranch then turn left to take the main road the last 3 miles to the ranch GPS: 44.771546° N, 107.238606° W. Ask the ranch hands where you should park. The trail begins on a jeep track behind the guest cabins.

Big Mountain from the Wolf Creek Trail.

Falls and pools on Wolf Creek.

THE HIKE

This trail runs from Eatons' Ranch into the foothills of the Bighorn Mountains. The guest ranch uses the trail heavily for horseback rides for its guests. Views of small waterfalls and massive reefs of sandstone accompany the trail, which makes a substantial climb to meet the Horseshoe Mountain and Walker Prairie Trails. The Wolf Falls Trail provides a spectacular side trip from the upper reaches of Wolf Creek.

From Eatons' Ranch, the trail runs westward through the ponderosa pine savannas beside Wolf Creek. Upon entering the mountains, you will notice that this canyon is not as rugged and spectacular as others along the Bighorn Mountain front. The creek makes up for this shortfall, cascading across ledges of bedrock into quiet emerald pools. The stream gradient increases as the trail enters national forest lands, and the trail switchbacks upward onto the open slopes to the north. Wolf Creek is now a constant chain of waterfalls coursing down among the enormous boulders fallen from the slopes above.

At the upper end of the canyon is a fine camp spot beside the creek. There is an unmarked junction just above the camp. Bear right for the Wolf Creek Trail. It zigzags lazily upward, crossing open grasslands sprinkled sparsely with ponderosa pines. Cattle drive trails render the trail difficult to follow as it snakes upward, yielding fine eastward views of the Wolf Creek Canyon. The path then traverses westward, climbing gently as it rounds a spur ridge. Across the valley, slanted cliffs and reefs tilt skyward.

After passing through a fence, the trail rounds a grassy hillside and ends up climbing atop a tilted stratum of limestone. After a steady climb, the route drops into a grassy vale and promptly disappears. Follow the streamcourse upward to reach the saddle at the head

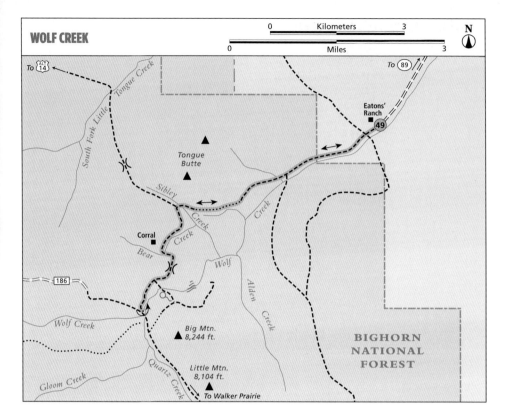

of this small vale. Entering the Sibley Creek watershed, the path crosses the meadows to reach a crossing of that stream. On the far bank is a junction with the Horseshoe Mountain Trail at a sign marked "Cow Camp."

Bear left as the Wolf Creek Trail heads straight up the hill, following the edge of aspen groves. The path soon swings south, climbing steadily as it traverses across the hillsides to reach the mouth of the Bear Creek Valley. Entering this valley, the path stays high above Bear Creek, which gurgles down a steep course shaded by aspens. Lodgepole pines robe the north-facing slopes beyond the stream, while the trail climbs heartily across the grassy slopes that face southward. The path ultimately reaches a meadowy basin guarded by pine-clad hills. There is an outfitter's camp at the head of this basin.

The trail crosses Bear Creek, then climbs southward to reach a low and grassy saddle in the hills. The path then breaks out onto a high, bald hilltop. As it begins to descend, a signpost marks the spot where the Wolf Falls spur trail drops away to the left. The main trail descends gradually across the hillsides to reach the Wolf Creek bottoms. After crossing the rather pathetic trickle that masquerades as upper Wolf Creek, the trek ends at the grassy flat known informally as the "River Bend." From here, the Walker Prairie Trail runs southward along the substantial flow of Quartz Creek, while a connecting trail climbs steeply to the northwest to reach FR 186.

MILES AND DIRECTIONS

0.0 Trailhead at Eatons' Ranch.

1.0 Trail enters Bighorn National Forest.

1.9 Junction with Alden Creek Trail. Stay right.

3.2 Trail reaches nameless stream. Turn right and hike up to saddle.

4.0 Junction with Horseshoe Mountain Trail. Bear left, crossing Sibley Creek.

4.7 Trail crosses Bear Creek below "Cow Camp."

5.2 Junction with Wolf Falls Trail. Bear right.

6.2 Trail crosses Wolf Creek to reach "River Bend" area. End of trail. Walker Prairie Trail crosses Quartz Creek and runs south.

50 WOLF FALLS

General description: An extended trip from the Wolf Creek Trail to waterfall overlook, 1.3 miles one way.
Difficulty: Moderately strenuous.
Route finding: Some challenges.
Best season: Late June to late September.
Visitation: Light.

Elevation gain: 400 feet.
Elevation loss: 695 feet.
Maximum elevation: 7,560 feet.
Topo map: Walker Mountain (trail not shown).
Jurisdiction: Bighorn National Forest (Tongue Ranger District).

FINDING THE TRAILHEAD

Follow the Wolf Creek Trail 1.0 mile north from Quartz Creek or 5.2 miles west from Eatons' Ranch to reach the marked junction with this spur trail. GPS: 44.771546° N, 107.238606° W; see page 168, Wolf Creek, for directions to Eatons' Ranch.

THE HIKE

This spur trail does not appear on the official maps. It came into being to access an overlook of the remote and spectacular falls on Wolf Creek, which occupy an impenetrable granite canyon. Backpackers can access this trail via Walker Prairie (12.1 miles), Wolf Creek (5.2 miles), or Horseshoe Mountain (6.1 miles).

The trail begins by making a steep descent from the top of a grassy bald to the bottoms of Wolf Creek. After a knee-deep ford, follow the grassy shelf downstream past a log corral. The trail departs from the lower end of the clearing, climbing steeply up the pine-clad slopes. After a vigorous ascent, the path meets the old Christmas Trail and turns east. It now traverses through the deep shade of a spruce forest.

Before long, the path attains the ridgeline that divides the valleys of Wolf and Alden creeks. Dropping sharply along the ridgetop, the path now yields fine views of the Alden Creek Valley and the rugged reef that rises beyond it. After a short descent, the path wanders northwest to end atop a granite outcrop. From here, you can view Wolf Falls tumbling hundreds of feet down a craggy cliff of granite, with a tall crag guarding its north flank.

Cloud Peak from the Wolf Falls Trail.

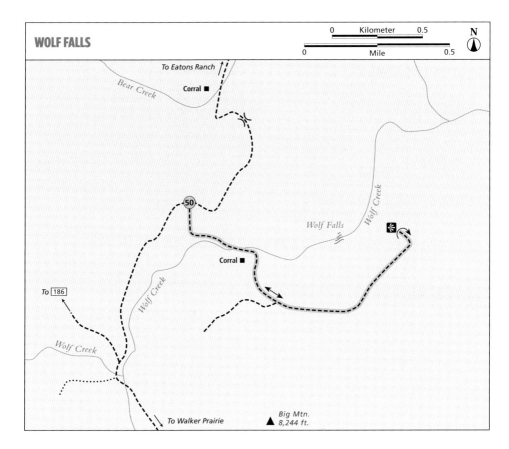

MILES AND DIRECTIONS

0.0 Junction with Wolf Creek Trail.

0.3 Trail fords Wolf Creek.

0.6 Junction with Christmas Trail. Turn left.

1.3 Wolf Falls overlook.

51 HORSESHOE MOUNTAIN

General description: A day hike or short backpack from the Little Tongue River to the Wolf Creek Trail, 5.4 miles one way.
Difficulty: Moderate.
Route finding: Some challenges.
Best season: Late June to mid-September.

Visitation: Light.
Elevation gain: 1,410 feet.
Elevation loss: 1,450 feet.
Maximum elevation: 7,500 feet.
Topo map: Dayton South.
Jurisdiction: Bighorn National Forest (Tongue Ranger District).

FINDING THE TRAILHEAD

 From Dayton, follow US Highway 14 west for 19 miles. Park at a pulloff on the north side of the highway GPS: 44.803657° N, 107.364674° W, just beyond an unmarked, two-rut road that descends to the valley floor. The hike begins across the highway.

THE HIKE

This trail crosses a series of grassy vales behind the front range of the Bighorn Mountains. It is used primarily as a cattle drive trail and can be faint in places. Expect to meet livestock in some of the grazing allotments along the way.

The trail begins with a half-mile jaunt down an old jeep trail, through the meadows to the Little Tongue River. A rickety footbridge (or a rock-hop) crosses the Little Tongue River. This waterway is really no more than a middling-sized creek, and it hurries eastward through shady riffles. On the far bank, follow the steep roadbed that leads upward through the trees to emerge in a grassy vale. A footpath crosses the rivulet that flows through this draw, then follows the west bank up to an open saddle. Look back for a fine view of Steamboat Point. To the west, knobs of granite rise from pine-clad slopes, while to the east the grassy hillsides lead up to the caprock.

After passing through a gate, the path enters a much longer valley that leads to the southeast. Soon it passes a brass boundary marker that dates from the original Bighorn Forest Reserve, circa 1902. The trail follows the east bank of a small brook as the open grasslands lead down to the South Fork of the Little Tongue. An impressive reef rises beyond this small river, and the bowed strata of Horseshoe Mountain tower above the trail as it approaches the water. The crossing of the South Fork is an easy rock-hop except during spring runoff.

Beyond the crossing, steep cattle trails lead up into a grassy depression. Ignore these trails and turn west along the South Fork to reach a shallow vale that enters from the left (south). The route follows this valley upward, with stands of lodgepole pine to the west and open slopes to the east. There is a high gap at the head of this drainage. Look east to view the lone pillar of Elephant Foot standing apart from the limestone cliffs of Tongue Butte.

The trail now drops into the valley of Sibley Creek, following the west bank of this incipient stream. The trail reaches its end at a marked junction with the Wolf Creek Trail about halfway down the valley. Watch for a sign marked "Cow Camp" at this intersection. From here, one might hike east down Wolf Creek to the Eatons' Ranch or southeast on the Wolf Creek Trail toward Walker Prairie and Wolf Falls.

Aspens in the valley of the South
Fork of the Little Tongue.

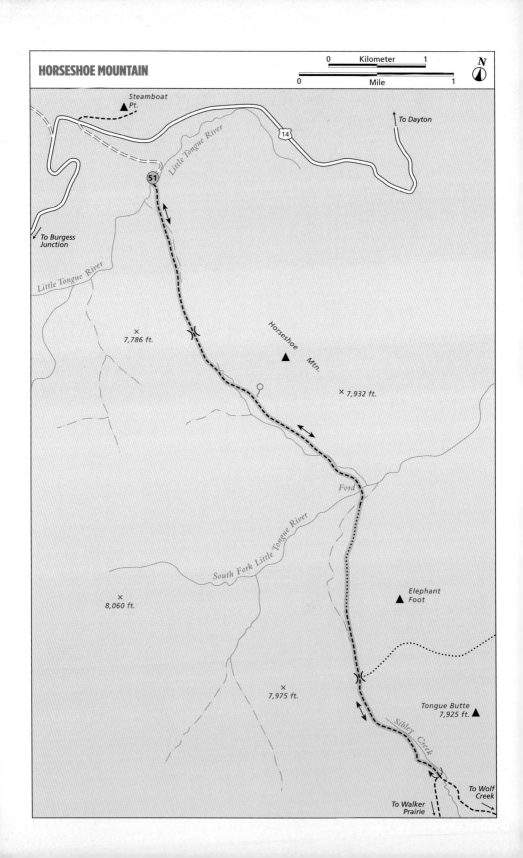

HORSESHOE MOUNTAIN

0 Kilometer 1

0 Mile 1

N

Steamboat Pt.

Little Tongue River

14

To Dayton

51

To Burgess Junction

Little Tongue River

× 7,786 ft.

Horseshoe Mtn.

× 7,932 ft.

Ford

South Fork Little Tongue River

× 8,060 ft.

Elephant Foot

× 7,975 ft.

Tongue Butte 7,925 ft.

Sibley Creek

To Wolf Creek

To Walker Prairie

MILES AND DIRECTIONS

0.0 Steamboat Point Trailhead. Cross the highway to acquire old jeep trail

0.5 Old jeep trail ends. Trail crosses Little Tongue River.

1.6 Trail crosses divide to enter South Fork of the Little Tongue drainage.

3.2 Trail fords the South Fork of the Little Tongue.

4.5 Trail crosses pass to enter Wolf Creek watershed.

5.4 Trail ends at junction with Wolf Creek Trail.

52 BLACK MOUNTAIN LOOKOUT

General description: A half-day hike to the old Black Mountain fire lookout, 1.2 miles one way.
Difficulty: Moderate.
Route finding: No problem.
Best season: Early July to mid-September.

Visitation: Light.
Elevation gain: 1,269 feet.
Maximum elevation: 9,849 feet.
Topo map: Woodrock.
Jurisdiction: Bighorn National Forest (Tongue Ranger District).

FINDING THE TRAILHEAD

From Dayton, follow US Highway 14 to the top of the range. Turn south on FR 16, a trunk road susceptible to potholes. Follow it for 3.5 miles to reach FR 222. Turn left on it. If you have two-wheel drive, park beside the stream at the bottom of the hill. Four-wheel-drive vehicles can make it the remaining 0.9 mile to the trailhead at the road's end. GPS: 44.738081° N, 107.387827° W.

THE HIKE

This trail makes a nice short hike to a historic fire lookout dating from the 1930s. From the trailhead, a footpath climbs steadily through a loose woodland of lodgepole pine. It

The rocky summit of Black Mountain.

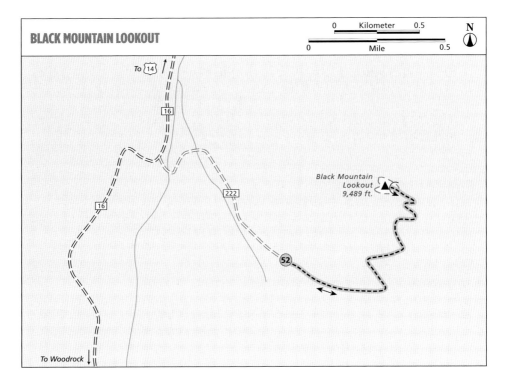

BLACK MOUNTAIN LOOKOUT

grew in the wake of an intense wildfire that once burned the slopes of Black Mountain. The trail zigzags upward at a steady pace. As it climbs there are several spots where the lookout can be seen far above. Great outcrops of granite loom ahead as the path nears the ridgetop. After cresting the divide, the route snakes upward among the towers of stone, visiting dizzying precipices along the way.

Black Mountain is a lofty prow of stone that juts high above the surrounding forests. Upon reaching the old fire lookout on its summit, you will be rewarded with panoramic views of rolling forests and meadows. To the east, the High Plains stretch away to the horizon. The distant summits of the Cloud Peak massif rise to the south.

MILES AND DIRECTIONS

0.0   Trailhead.

1.2   Black Mountain Lookout.

53 STEAMBOAT POINT

General description: A short day hike to the summit of Steamboat Point, 0.7 mile one way.
Difficulty: Moderately strenuous.
Route finding: No problem.
Best season: Mid-June to mid-September.

Visitation: Light.
Elevation gain: 666 feet.
Maximum elevation: 7,916 feet.
Topo map: Dayton South (trail shown incorrectly).
Jurisdiction: Bighorn National Forest (Tongue Ranger District).

FINDING THE TRAILHEAD

From Dayton, follow US Highway 14 west for 19 miles. Park at a pulloff on the north side of the highway, just beyond an unmarked, two-rut road that descends to the valley floor. GPS: 44.803657° N, 107.364674° W.

THE HIKE

This route makes an excellent short hike to the summit of a prominent reef, but only the locals seem to know that the trail exists. The hike begins on a closed jeep trail that makes an incredibly steep ascent up the grassy apron at the foot of Steamboat Point. Allow yourself a rest stop or two along the way and take in the pastoral landscape to the south. Here, the Little Tongue River flows down from grassy meadows and timbered reefs. The jeep track climbs all the way to the enormous boulders at the foot of Steamboat Point, where (none too soon) a well-engineered footpath takes over at a much shallower pitch.

This path passes along the foot of the massive limestone cliffs, and a scattering of ponderosa pines provide shady spots for a possible rest break. After traversing below the

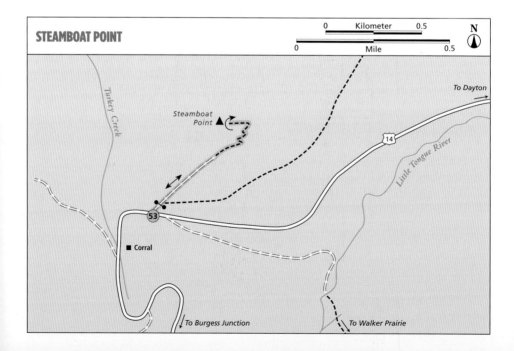

south face of Steamboat Point, the path climbs steadily through a steep couloir via a series of cunningly built switchbacks. The trail tops out on the tabletop surface of Steamboat Point, amid a loose woodland of whitebark and limber pine.

The path turns west now, dropping onto the south side of the hilltop for its final climb to the summit. Here, extremes of temperature, wind, and water deprivation have resulted in sparse vegetation of cinquefoil, mountain mahogany, and a few dwarfed limber pines. A hitchrail of sorts is all that stands between the trail's end and the rim of the 200-foot cliffs. From here, you can enjoy panoramic views of the surrounding country. To the north is the valley of the Tongue River, which emerges from the granite rift of Box Canyon into a broad and grassy basin. Eastward views from the back of the summit stretch far out onto the High Plains.

MILES AND DIRECTIONS

0.0   Trailhead. Follow closed jeep road upward.

0.2   Jeep track ends. Follow trail northeast.

0.7   Summit of Steamboat Point.

54 TONGUE CANYON

General description: A day hike through the rugged canyon of the Tongue River, 5.3 miles one way.
Difficulty: Moderate to Sheep Creek; moderately strenuous beyond.
Route finding: No problem to Horse Creek; some challenges beyond.
Best season: Early June to mid-October.

Visitation: Moderate.
Elevation gain: 3,215 feet.
Elevation loss: 185 feet.
Maximum elevation: 7,230 feet.
Topo maps: Dayton South, Skull Ridge.
Jurisdiction: Bighorn National Forest (Tongue Ranger District).

FINDING THE TRAILHEAD

From the east end of Dayton, follow River Road north and then west along the Tongue River. After 2.3 miles, the road splits. Bear left, following signs for Tongue Canyon. A potholed but passable gravel road leads the remaining 2.6 miles to the trailhead in the Amsden Creek Wildlife Management Unit. GPS: 44.846884° N, 107.330248° W.

THE HIKE

This trail runs through the towering walls of Tongue Canyon, then climbs across grassy slopes that are an important winter range for elk. The granite chasm of Box Canyon can be reached via a short cross-country walk from the trail. Once the trail reaches the top of the range, it meets a tangle of livestock trails and ATV roads.

The trail begins by following the north bank of the Tongue River as it passes through a deep and rugged gorge of limestone. Great pillars and crenelated cliffs soar overhead, and a keyhole arch can be seen to the east along the north wall of the canyon. Although the river bottoms are lush with such hardwoods as cottonwood, box elder, and ash, the slopes above the trail are arid and support only a sparse growth of sagebrush. After a short distance, a bridge leads across the river, providing access to Tongue River Cave.

The main trail stays with the north bank and the scenery remains inspiring as the route makes its way through Tongue Canyon. After some distance the walls open up. Here, the south-facing slopes are wooded with ponderosa pine, and yucca grows from the sandy soil below the trees. The path soon climbs into a grassy meadow filled with sego lily, harebell, and horse mint. It then descends to cross Sheep Creek, where a miniature waterfall splashes through an idyllic woodland.

The trail then ascends onto a broad, grassy hillside that slopes upward to the northwest. The path heads straight up the slope, climbing steeply at times. These slopes were burned intentionally during 1996 to wipe out the encroaching sagebrush and make way for the grasses that make superior winter forage for elk. Watch to the west for views of the impenetrable granite chasm of Box Canyon. It is possible to wander across the open slopes to the rim of this chasm and view the river churning among the boulders far below. But the main trail continues upward, away from this cleft, tracking the course of Horse Creek, which runs beside the western edge of the slope. Beyond Horse Creek lies a stretch of wild and broken country, with outcrops of bedrock and thickets of aspen, grassy glades and groves of wind-torn conifers.

Tongue Canyon.

There is a brief intermission as the trail crosses gentler terrain, but then it resumes its vigorous climb across grassy balds punctuated with great boulders of limestone. At the top of the grade is an enormous boulder pointing skyward like an accusing finger. Pay attention here, because there is a parting of the ways 50 yards beyond this rock. A well-beaten path now leads up the north bank of Horse Creek (see Horse Creek Option, below) while the official route glides down to a rock-hop crossing of the creek.

The trail then climbs the hillside beyond, sticking mainly to the open meadows as it wanders upward among hillocks crowned with stone menhirs. After gaining consider-able elevation, the trail swings north for a gentler jaunt across sparse grasslands. It tops out at a gate in a barbed-wire fence. Beyond lies one of the grazing allotments where cattle may be found in great numbers during the summer. The trail wanders down to Horse Creek and crosses it. The path then angles upward to reach a second fence gate, where the trail ends at an unmarked junction of old roads.

Horse Creek Option. This well-beaten path follows the cairns along the north bank of Horse Creek, crossing meadowy slopes beneath the cliffs of Horse Creek Ridge. The damp swales harbor extravagant quantities of lupine and blanketflower, which put on a colorful display during early summer. The path ultimately wanders through a draw grown up in aspen, then continues along the stream to reach a pair of springs used as mineral licks by cattle and elk. The trail ends here at a fence gate. It is possible to follow cattle trails south along the fence to intersect the Tongue Canyon Trail high on an open knoll beyond Horse Creek.

The inner gorge of the Tongue River.

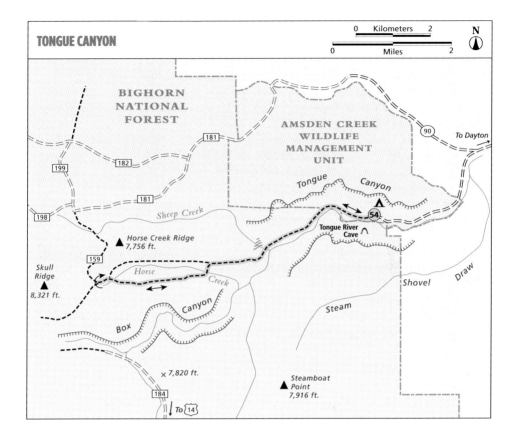

TONGUE CANYON

0　　Kilometers　　2

0　　Miles　　2

N

BIGHORN
NATIONAL
FOREST

AMSDEN CREEK
WILDLIFE
MANAGEMENT
UNIT

To Dayton

181

199

182

181

198

Sheep Creek

Tongue   Canyon

90

54

Horse Creek Ridge
7,756 ft.

Tongue River
Cave

Skull
Ridge

159

8,321 ft.

Horse   Creek

Shovel   Draw

Canyon

Steam

Box

× 7,820 ft.

184

To 14

Steamboat
Point
7,916 ft.

MILES AND DIRECTIONS

0.0　Tongue Canyon Trailhead.

0.2　Bridge leads to Tongue River Cave. Continue straight ahead.

2.2　Head of Tongue Canyon. Trail crosses Sheep Creek.

3.4　Unmarked trail junction. Turn left to cross Horse Creek.

5.0　Trail crosses Horse Creek and returns to east bank.

5.3　Junction with trail #159.

ADDITIONAL TRAILS

The **Quartz Creek** Trail runs from Sawmill Reservoir to Walker Prairie, passing a historic copper mine along the way. The route receives very little use. Consequently, you can expect a low level of maintenance and some route-finding challenges.

The **Gloom Creek** Trail runs down from FR 16 to disappear in a series of clearcuts.

The upper **Wolf Creek** Trail once linked FR 16 with Walker Prairie, but it has long since disappeared.

The **Soldier Creek** Trail is a good horse trail that runs over the front range south of Walker Mountain. Access to the trailhead is blocked by private land and you will need to get permission from the landowner before you attempt it.

The **Christmas Trail** runs from the Wolf Falls Trail to the north end of Walker Prairie. It has been abandoned and the grassland portions have been completely erased from the slopes.

The **North Rock Creek** Trail starts on private land with no public access and wanders through a viewless lodgepole forest to join the Middle Rock Creek Trail.

The **Middle Rock Creek cutoff** joins Middle and South Rock Creeks via a faint track through the lodgepole forest.

The **Penrose Park** Trail is an ATV road from Story, Wyoming, to Kearny Lakes Reservoir. It runs through the old Stockwell Fire and is often obstructed by blowdown.

The **Black Canyon** Trail runs through burned-over country dating from the Stockwell Fire.

THE BORDER COUNTRY

Extending across the Montana border, the northern tail of the Bighorn Mountains offers a wild and remote stretch of country where a sea of bald summits is carpeted with alpine meadows. Sandstone strata form small reefs that rise above the uplands, and bands of limestone weather into spires and hoodoos that rise from the hillsides. The North Tongue and Little Bighorn rivers offer superb trout fishing for folks of a piscatorial bent. A handful of maintained trails runs through this forgotten end of the Bighorns, and adventurous souls can try one of the primitive trails and cross-country routes that receive no maintenance from the Forest Service.

This high and windswept landscape is haunted by relics from a not-so-distant past: The mysterious Medicine Wheel is a prehistoric site with Stonehenge-like qualities; it was built by a forgotten band of indigenous hunters. The abandoned shacks of gold-crazed prospectors can be found at the site of Bald Mountain City. The line cabins left behind by frontier cattlemen and sheepherders are scattered throughout the backcountry.

Herder's shack near Bald Mountain.

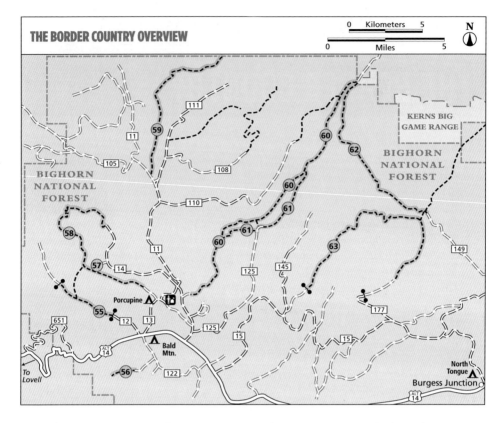

The primary access to this area is via US Alternate 14, a scenic highway known as the Medicine Wheel Passage. A network of forest trunk roads leads from the highway into the far corners of the mountains. Most of these roads are passable to low-clearance vehicles, but when the weather turns rainy, even four-wheel-drive trucks can't negotiate many of them. The primitive roads are similar: Significant obstacles are rare here, but the roadbeds turn into a sticky gumbo when they get wet. On the Montana side of the border, the mountains fall within the Crow Indian Reservation, a nation within a nation. Access to this area is restricted; visitors will need to get permission from the tribal government before venturing onto the reservation.

This is remote country, and services are far away. Burgess Junction has a small lodge that offers gas, a restaurant, and souvenirs. For supplies, the nearest towns are Greybull, Lovell, and Sheridan. The Forest Service has recently built a new visitor center just east of Burgess Junction; be aware that there is an entrance fee in effect here. Developed campgrounds can be found in the Bald Mountain area, north of Burgess Junction, and along the headwaters of the South Tongue River.

55 THE MEDICINE WHEEL

General description: A short day hike to the Medicine Wheel National Historic Site, 1.3 miles one way.
Difficulty: Easy.
Route finding: No problem.
Best season: Mid-July to mid-September.

Visitation: Moderate.
Elevation gain: 150 feet.
Elevation loss: 130 feet.
Maximum elevation: 9,640 feet.
Topo map: Medicine Wheel.
Jurisdiction: Bighorn National Forest (Medicine Wheel Ranger District).

FINDING THE TRAILHEAD

Follow US Alternate 14 to the top of the Bighorn uplift, where the Medicine Wheel Road (FR 12) runs north from a flat grassland at mile 35.6. Follow this road for 1.7 miles to reach the trailhead at its end. GPS: 44.819758° N, 107.898496° W.

THE HIKE

This short hike follows a closed road to the mysterious prehistoric site known as the Medicine Wheel. The road is closed to all access at the trailhead except to the handicapped, who are permitted to drive to the site. Built by indigenous people between 300 and 800 years ago, this rockwork ring with its cairns is viewed by experts as a sort of New World version of Stonehenge. The site is still considered sacred by many of the Plains tribes, who visit the site to make prayer offerings. Interpretive rangers are on hand to answer questions about the history and spiritual significance of this enigmatic structure.

The trek begins with a gradual climb across rounded slopes of alpine tundra. Initial views stretch northward across the valley of Porcupine Creek to take in the sandstone reefs that rise beyond. As the roadway approaches a low saddle, ragged breaks and

The Medicine Wheel.

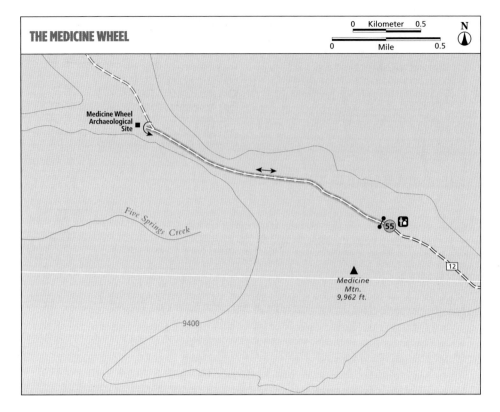

hoodoos of limestone rise ahead along the south face of a tabletop mountain. A brisk ascent leads to the summit, where the Medicine Wheel lies amid the tundra with views in all directions.

The limestone boulders of the Medicine Wheel are arranged in a circle 80 feet in diameter, with 28 "spokes" radiating out to the edge from a central cairn. There are six peripheral cairns sited around the edge of the circle. According to the oral traditions of the Plains tribes, the Medicine Wheel represents the architecture of the medicine lodge used in the Sun Dance ceremony. The 28 spokes represent the 28 roof poles of the medicine lodge, a number that reflects the days in a lunar cycle and also the number of ribs in a buffalo. Twenty-eight is also the product of the numbers 4 and 7, which are both sacred numbers in the Native American tradition.

The Sun Dance was undertaken by young braves to honor the sun and to fulfill vows that were made in the heat of battle. During the dance, the braves would have skewers punched through the skin and muscle of their chests, and a rawhide thong ran from the hooks to the top of the central pole in the medicine lodge. The braves would then dance around the pole, chanting and singing, all the while leaning back away from the pole until their weight tore the hooks from their bodies.

The builders of the Medicine Wheel oriented the structure so that it could serve as an astronomical observatory during significant days of the year. On the summer solstice, the longest day of the year, the central cairn lines up with one of the eastern cairns to mark the exact spot where the morning sun will rise from the horizon. Please respect the sanctity of this archaeological site, and do not take home souvenirs or disturb it in any way.

foot of the falls is bordered by a graded heap of old mine tailings; adventurous travelers can cross Porcupine Creek to explore the old mining camp just downstream from the falls. The camp dates from the early 1900s, when placer miners tried their hand at mining gold from the gravels in the pool below the falls. A diversion channel was blasted into the rock on the west side of the falls to carry water from the top of the falls down to a riffle box (used to separate the heavy gold from the lighter gravels). The spot where the diversion channel flows from the rock face into Porcupine Creek can be seen to the right of the falls.

58 BUCKING MULE FALLS— DEVIL CANYON

General description: A day hike to the Bucking Mule Falls overlook, 5.2 miles round trip; or a backpack across Devil Canyon and up Porcupine Creek, 14.3 miles.
Difficulty: Easy to Bucking Mule Falls; moderately strenuous beyond.
Route finding: No problem to Bucking Mule Falls; some challenges otherwise.
Best season: Mid-July to mid-September.

Visitation: Light to Bucking Mule overlook; otherwise very light.
Elevation gain: 295 feet (to overlook); 3,485 feet (overall).
Elevation loss: 345 feet (to overlook); 3,125 feet (overall).
Maximum elevation: 8,660 feet (southeast trailhead).
Topo maps: Mexican Hill, Bald Mountain, Medicine Wheel (location approximate).
Jurisdiction: Bighorn National Forest (Medicine Wheel Ranger District).

FINDING THE TRAILHEAD

Take US Alternate 14 west from Burgess Junction to reach FR 14, marked "Devil Canyon Road." Follow it for 3 miles, then bear left at the junction with FR 11 to stay on FR 14. Follow it another 8 miles to reach the Bucking Mule Falls Trailhead GPS: 44.884208° N, 107.906277° W. To reach the south trailhead, drive US Alternate 14 to its junction with FR 13, then drive north for 2.3 miles to reach Jaws Trailhead. GPS: 44.834182° N, 107.851358° W.

THE HIKE

This National Recreation Trail runs to an overlook above the 500-foot drop of Bucking Mule Falls, then crosses the upper end of Devil Canyon and follows the highlands to the west of Porcupine Creek. Most folks hike to the falls in an easy half-day and then turn around; the trail beyond the falls cutoff is rough and somewhat primitive, with some steep sections. Backpackers will find camp spots near the Porcupine Creek bridge and at Tillets Hole, and throughout the upper reaches of Porcupine Creek.

The trail begins by descending gently through a woodland of lodgepole pine that is interspersed with dry pocket meadows. It soon turns north, following a finger ridge down to a granite outcrop above Big Teepee Creek. From this point, views stretch across the valley of Porcupine Creek to the grassy dome of Mexican Hill. The forest takes on a subalpine character as the path turns east, gliding down to a bridge over Big Teepee Creek. A gentle incline now leads the path westward again, following the contours of a rounded promontory. Sagebrush balds soon yield eastward views of the bare summits along the crest of the range.

The path soon reaches a well-marked junction. The wide and level track that runs north from this point leads a hundred yards or so to the Bucking Mule Falls overlook. The overlook is perched atop a spur of granite that juts out over a yawning precipice; watch out for loose rocks and uneven footing en route to the overlook. This cliff-hanging aerie rises high above Bucking Mule Falls, which emerges between twin pillars of granite and plummets more than 500 feet over a sheer dropoff. There are also fine views of the Pryor Mountains along the northwest skyline, and glimpses of the sedimentary cliffs of

Devil Canyon. The path that runs east from the overlook soon joins a network of old logging roads that leads back to the trailhead.

Meanwhile, the more primitive trail to Devil Canyon descends steeply from the junction to gain the next level shelf on the ridgetop. The forest type found here is determined by soil moisture: Douglas fir and grassy meadows on the drier sites, subalpine fir and spruce where moisture is plentiful. After a level trek, the trail seems to roll off the end of the world as it drops steeply down the nose of the ridge. Eventually, the descent eases as the path makes its way to a saddle where whitebark pines block out the views.

The trail now drops onto a south-facing slope, zigzagging downward at a steady pace. The arid slopes seem better suited to the junipers that grow in the understory than the sparse Douglas firs. After a long descent, the path bottoms out on a brushy bench beside Porcupine Creek. There are camp spots here, and a short distance to the north is a sturdy bridge.

After crossing it, the trail continues downstream, traversing higher onto the slopes so it can pass through a small gap in the granite outcrops. The great sedimentary cliffs of Devil Canyon stretch northwest from this point, but views are limited at this stage of the trek. The path soon adopts a finger ridge to the south of Railroad Springs Creek and follows it upward on a westward bearing. Most of the Douglas firs found here died in an outbreak of parasitic insects. Now the understory is crowded with thickets of ninebark and an occasional mat of juniper.

The trail ultimately begins a long series of switchbacks that lead to the very top of Railroad Ridge. Turn left at the marked junction with the Railroad Ridge and Mexican Hill Trails. The Bucking Mule Trail first traverses southward through a healthy coniferous forest, then plummets downhill at an insane rate. At the bottom of the grade, the trail crosses several boggy brooks, then rises into a sagebrush meadow for superb views into Devil Canyon. The route then continues up the valley, passing through a forest of Douglas fir and pine as it stays high above Porcupine Creek. From time to time, it wanders to the edge of the canyon for views of forested slopes, steep slabs of granite, and waterfalls in the drainages across the valley.

The path ultimately turns westward, descending into a side drainage called Tillets Hole. It passes several lush meadows along the way, and one of them has an ice-cold spring with good camp spots nearby. The path then reaches a signpost; the Tillets Hole Trail continues up the drainage into sagebrush meadows, while the Bucking Mule Trail crosses the small stream and then climbs into the forest. At the top of the grade are several level meadows situated behind a wooded hillock. After passing through them, the path descends to the bank of Porcupine Creek, which is now shaded by a mature growth of conifers.

A stock bridge soon leads to the far bank. The upper basin of Porcupine Creek is crisscrossed with unmarked trails, and the first one of these is met just beyond the bridge. Our route follows the northern bank of the stream, climbing gently through a bottomland forest of Englemann spruce. The forest opens up at a grassy meadow where Long Park Creek enters from the west. Unmarked trails run east and west, while the main trail continues up the north bank of Porcupine Creek and soon enters the trees. The path then reaches a knee-deep ford and begins to follow the south bank, becoming faint near its marked junction with the Long Park Creek Trail.

Not far upstream, a footbridge leads back to the northern side of Porcupine Creek, where the trail will remain for the balance of the trek. The country is now characterized

Looking into Devil Canyon from the ridges above Porcupine Creek.

by sagebrush parks separated by stands of lodgepole pine, and twin outcrops of sandstone arise periodically on either side of the creek like giant stone gates. The trail ultimately reaches the end of FR 137; hike along the road, past two privately leased cabins, and follow it eastward, passing through a portal of rocky bluffs. Just beyond this point, the road crosses a stream to reach a complex junction. Bear southeast (straight ahead, and watch for a footpath splitting away to the left, which leads upward across the meadows for the final half-mile to Jaws Trailhead.

MILES AND DIRECTIONS

0.0 Bucking Mule Falls Trailhead.

1.2 Trail crosses Big Teepee Creek.

2.4 Junction with spur trail to falls overlook (0.2 mile, easy); bear left for Devil Canyon.

3.6 Saddle above Devil Canyon.

4.8 Bridge over Porcupine Creek.

5.9 Junction with Railroad Ridge Trail at top of grade. Bear left.

6.4 Devil Canyon viewpoint.

8.9 Trail passes spring and enters Tillets Hole.

9.3 Junction with Tillets Hole Trail. Turn left.

10.5 Bridge leads to east bank of Porcupine Creek.

10.9 Trail passes mouth of Long Park Creek. Continue up north bank.

11.4 Ford of Porcupine Creek.

11.9 Junction with Long Park Creek Trail. Continue straight ahead.

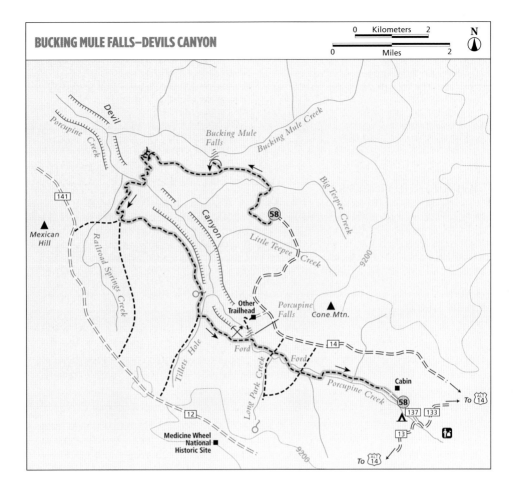

0   Kilometers   2

0   Miles   2

N

12.1 Footbridge leads back to north bank of creek.

12.7 Trail passes privately leased cabins.

13.3 Trail reaches old FR 137. Follow the road southeast.

13.8 Footpath runs eastward from road. Bear left.

14.3 Trail reaches Jaws Trailhead.

59 LODGE GRASS CREEK

General description: A backpack down the valley of Lodge Grass Creek, 9.3 miles.
Difficulty: Moderately strenuous.
Route finding: Some challenges.
Best season: Mid-July to mid-September.

Visitation: Extremely light.
Elevation gain: 435 feet.
Elevation loss: 3,365 feet.
Maximum elevation: 9,300 feet.
Topo maps: Boyd Ridge.
Jurisdiction: Bighorn National Forest (Medicine Wheel Ranger District).

FINDING THE TRAILHEAD

Take US Alternate 14 west from Burgess Junction to reach FR 14, marked "Devil Canyon Road." Follow it for 3 miles, then turn right on FR 11, a steep, winding trunk road (trailers not recommended). Follow it for 6.7 miles along the crest of the range to meet FR 110. Turn left at this junction, staying on the lesser road, which is FR 11. Follow it down to the first saddle, where a sign marks the hike's starting point. GPS: 44.916459° N, 107.857655° W.

THE HIKE

This old stock trail follows one of the major drainages in the remote northern Bighorns. Lodge Grass Creek is bordered by broad grasslands along much of its length, and striking cliffs guard the rims of the valley. Cattle graze heavily in this entire valley; treat all water sources as if they are known to be contaminated. The myriad livestock paths that braid away from the main trail make route finding a challenge; the lowermost pathway is typically the right one. Anglers who are willing to battle the brush will find the lower reaches of the creek to be populated with rainbow and cutthroat trout.

From the windswept heights of the Bighorn divide, the hike begins by following an old two-rut track down into an open vale. Alpine tundra soon grades into sagebrush meadows, and tors and cliffs of Bighorn limestone guard the waterless drainage. Sheep Mountain is the rounded summit to the north, and soon the headwaters of Lodge Grass Creek come trickling down from its heights. The Lodge Grass Trail leaves the old road here, slanting down to a crossing of the stream.

The path now follows the west bank of Lodge Grass Creek as the waters run past sagebrush bluffs, and a number of natural springs augment the creek's flow. The east side of the valley is robed in subalpine forest, and soon there are copses of spruce and fir on the west side as well. Soon after entering a dense stand of timber, the trail makes a steep descent. It then levels off to traverse across lush meadows that are a favorite summer range of elk.

The trail ultimately reaches the ruins of a log cabin beside a substantial stream. The trail disappears in the meadow beyond; stay close to Lodge Grass Creek to pick up the path on the far side of the clearing. It follows the stream through a steep defile, then wanders inland and drops into a meadowy pocket. The route is faint here as well; climb over the grassy rise to strike the trail as it descends through the timber to reach a meandering brook. The cliff bands and tors on the far wall of the valley now rise to form an imposing wall, and the trail offers unobstructed views as it climbs steeply across a grassy slope to reach a fence gate in a ridgetop saddle.

After passing through the gate, the path descends out of the subalpine zone, bending northwest to cross the next stream. Another sheer face of cliffs rises ahead as the route

follows stock trails toward Lodge Grass Creek. Here, the stream enters a broad, grassy basin dotted with aspen groves. Stay close to the creek as the route continues northward, then crosses a meadowy rise strewn with enormous boulders. On the far side of the rise, the path makes a shallow ford of Line Creek and follows it downstream, passing through another fence along the way.

As the main valley bends to the east, it is dominated by stone pillars and small fragments of cliff that rise from the valley walls. On the far side of the stream is the Pumpkin Creek Burn, caused by careless forest visitors. It consumed 4,500 acres of timber in 1970. As a sheer slope rises from the north bank of Lodge Grass Creek, the trail makes a shallow ford to reach gentler country, then quickly returns to the north bank after passing the obstacle. The trail now traverses across arid, grassy slopes above the brush-choked bottomlands. The slopes support only the occasional limber pine, a specialist at colonizing dry and windswept locales.

As a major tributary arrives from the south, the trail passes above a broad and inviting bottom that offers fine camp spots in a sparse woodland of cottonwood and Douglas fir. The main trail continues to sidehill to the base of a rocky promontory, where a drift fence has been built amid the massive boulders. Beyond the fence, the trail makes a final ford of Lodge Grass Creek, then climbs to a high and open shoulder that commands views of the lower canyon that stretch eastward onto the High Plains.

The trail now wanders out across rolling prairies above the south side of the creek, with a stark summit of limestone rising above and sedimentary cliffs guarding the south side of the valley. The trek ends at the next fence, which delineates the Montana state line. The national forest lands end at the fence; to the north lies the reservation of the Crow Tribe.

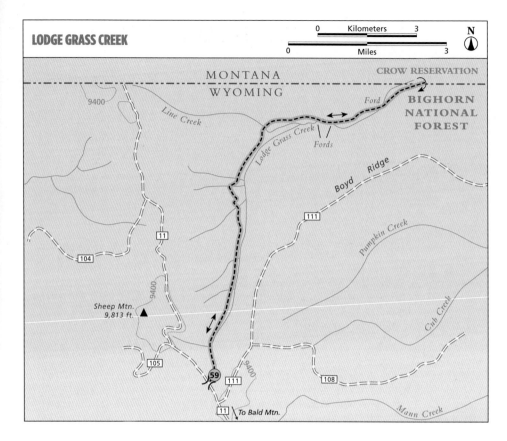

MILES AND DIRECTIONS

0.0 Trail leaves FR 11.

0.8 Trail crosses headwaters of Lodge Grass Creek.

1.9 Trail crosses small stream.

2.5 Ruins of old cabin. Trail crosses tributary stream.

3.7 Trail crosses small stream.

4.5 Trail crosses small stream to enter large basin.

5.6 Trail fords Line Creek.

6.7 Trail fords Lodge Grass Creek to south bank.

7.0 Trail returns to north bank of Lodge Grass Creek.

8.0 Trail makes final ford of Lodge Grass Creek.

9.3 Trail ends at fence at Montana border.

60 **THE LITTLE HORN TRAIL**

General description: A backpack from the mouth of the Little Bighorn Canyon to the crest of the Bighorn Mountains, 16.3 miles one way.
Difficulty: Moderately strenuous (north to south); moderate (south to north).
Route finding: Some challenges.
Best season: Mid-July to mid-September.

Visitation: Very light.
Elevation gain: 4,870 feet.
Elevation loss: 440 feet.
Maximum elevation: 8,960 feet (trail's end).
Topo maps: Bull Elk Park, Boyd Ridge; Bald Mountain (trail not shown).
Jurisdiction: Bighorn National Forest (Medicine Wheel Ranger District).

FINDING THE TRAILHEAD

Drive northwest from Ranchester on Wyoming 343 (old US Highway 89). After 12 miles, turn left (west) on County Road 144, a gravel highway, and follow it for 16.5 miles. Upon reaching the bottoms of the Little Bighorn River, the county road bends eastward. (This spot can also be reached from Wyola, Montana, via CR 418.) Turn left onto a primitive road that is marked "public access through private lands." This road is rough with some fords, and high clearance is required. Follow it for 2.8 miles, crossing the bridge and parking at the trailhead on the Kerns Wildlife Management Unit GPS: 44.980106° N, 107.646319° W. Hike the road to reach the beginning of the trail.

To reach the upper trailhead, take US Alternate 14 west from Burgess Junction to reach FR 14, marked "Devil Canyon Road." Follow it for 2.4 miles to reach FR 135. Turn right and park near the end of this dead-end road. The trail begins at the lower (east) end of the meadow. GPS: 44.836475° N, 107.827735° W.

THE HIKE

The valley of the Little Bighorn River is one of the largest roadless areas in the Bighorn National Forest. The Little Bighorn is considered a blue-ribbon fishery for trout, and because of its remoteness, it receives little angling pressure. It is also under consideration for "Wild and Scenic River" status. The Little Horn Trail is a major stock trail that begins in Little Bighorn Canyon and follows the river into the grasslands at the interior of the range. Expect to see cattle here, as this area is a summer pasture for livestock. The trail then follows lesser valleys up to the summit of the range. Along the way, the trail passes Leaky Mountain, an unusual feature where a large waterfall pours from the face of a blank cliff of limestone.

The hike begins by passing several summer cabins in the Douglas fir and ponderosa pine bottoms of the Little Bighorn. Here, the river churns through a long series of rapids punctuated with enormous boulders. The path soon turns a corner, and the soaring, sedimentary cliffs of Fisher Mountain rise above it. The path continues to follow the river along the base of the cliffs, then makes a short climb to surmount a washout.

It emerges on a shelf above the valley floor, crossing open country that is populated by thickets of chokecherry and serviceberry. Soon, the Boyd Ridge Trail departs through a gate in the barbed-wire fence that parallels the main path. The Little Horn Trail continues up the broad valley. The imposing reef that can now be seen to the east represents the north end of Dry Fork Ridge.

Leaky Mountain.

The path soon returns to the riverbank, following it into an inner gorge of ancient granite. Here, a small sand beach lies at the foot of a pretty waterfall. After passing this spot, the trail zigzags up to the base of the cliffs. It charts an improbable course across the high cliff ledges, then descends to reach the bottomlands beyond the gorge.

After following the river for a short distance, the trail arcs upward across an open grassland dotted with ponderosa pines. This area burned many years ago; more intensely burned slopes to the south are populated by a dense growth of young Douglas fir. The trail soon enters this shady woodland, staying high on the steep slopes that now rise above the river. The forest canopy shuts off the views as the trail passes the cliff-lined portal of the Dry Fork of the Little Bighorn.

The path emerges from the heavy timber just below the confluence with Taylor Creek, and now great walls and pinnacles rise to the west of the river. Steep slopes and cutbanks continue to render access to the river a difficult and dangerous proposition. A signpost soon announces the "Taylor Creek Stock Driveway," but the trail crosses an arid draw and approaches an old fence before this trail (page 207, The Fuller Trail) descends to ford the river.

The main trail continues southwest through grassy meadows and brushfields. The sedimentary walls of Boyd Ridge tower overhead, and soon the gushing waterfalls of Leaky Mountain can be seen ahead. The falls spring from the foot of limestone cliffs, not following any particular drainage pattern but instead flowing from subterranean passageways in the stone. After crossing the stream that issues from Leaky Mountain, the trail begins a steady climb across rolling country. Each saddle that you attain will yield views of another, still higher pass to be climbed. Look backward along the way for final views of the Little Bighorn Canyon.

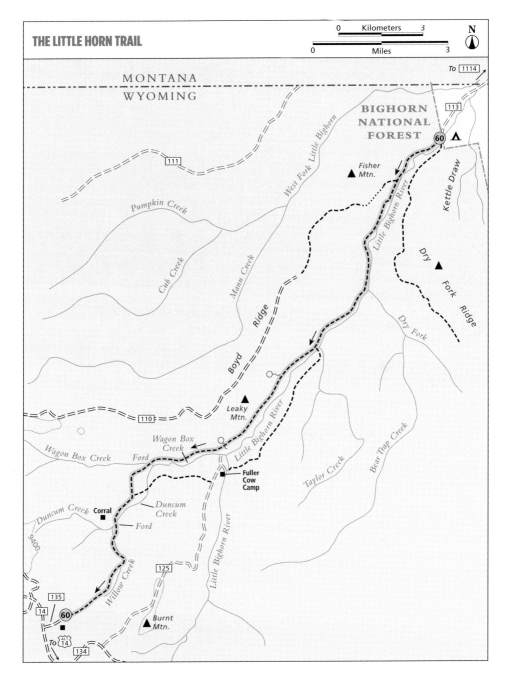

0   Kilometers   3

0   Miles   3

N

MONTANA
WYOMING

BIGHORN
NATIONAL
FOREST

To 1114

113

111

West Fork Little Bighorn

Fisher
Mtn.

60

Kettle Draw

Pumpkin Creek

Cub Creek

Mann Creek

Boyd Ridge

Little Bighorn River

Dry Fork Ridge

Dry Fork

110

Leaky
Mtn.

Wagon Box
Creek

Little Bighorn River

Wagon Box Creek   Ford

Fuller
Cow
Camp

Taylor Creek

Bear Trap Creek

Duncum Creek   Corral

Duncum
Creek

Ford

9400

Willow Creek

125

Little Bighorn River

135

14

60

To ALT 14

134

Burnt
Mtn.

At the top of the grade is a sagebrush flat, high above the confluence of Wagon Box Creek and the Little Bighorn River. Wagon Box Creek occupies the main valley, which bends westward here, while the Little Bighorn descends from the rolling country to the south. A big, rolling prairie stretches ahead, dotted here and there with aspen groves and copses of spruce. The Littlehorn Road (FR 125) can be seen descending the far slopes of the valley; it is possible to follow stock trails down to a footbridge across Wagon Box Creek to reach the end of the road.

The main trail stays high on the grassy balds to the north of Wagon Box Creek. It yields fine views of Boyd Ridge, where the cliff bands are now bordered by stands of timber. Duncum Creek soon pours in from the south, and the trail fords Wagon Box just above the confluence. The path now climbs stiffly through the sagebrush, heading westward. It ultimately reaches a washed-out roadbed and turns south, leveling off as it passes through a large grove of old aspens.

On the far side of the grove, the trail resumes its climb and soon joins the Little Bighorn Bench route. It now rises through spruce and lodgepole to gain a rocky saddle above a bottleneck on Duncum Creek. The official trail then fords Duncum Creek, while the more well-beaten track visits an outfitter's camp before rejoining the main trail just below the confluence with Willow Creek.

After a brisk climb through a shady grove of spruce, the trail crosses Willow Creek and follows it southward through broad meadows. The bald top of Burnt Mountain rises to the east, crowned with pillars of limestone that look like old, broken teeth. Before long, the Half Ounce burn of 1978 can be seen, and the trail soon enters it, crossing Willow Creek several times. Beyond the far edge of the burn, the meadows get smaller and soon the trail turns west for the final ascent to the upper trailhead. At the top of the grade, the path emerges into an open meadow; follow the telephone poles southwest to reach the end of FR 135.

MILES AND DIRECTIONS

0.0   Trailhead in Kerns Wildlife Management Unit. Hike west along road.

0.2   Road ends. Bear right as trail follows north bank of Little Bighorn River.

1.7   Junction with Boyd Ridge Trail. Continue straight ahead.

2.1   Granite inner gorge of Little Bighorn Canyon.

6.2   Junction with Fuller Trail ("Taylor Creek Stock Driveway"). Continue straight ahead.

7.4   Trail crosses stream that issues from Leaky Mountain.

9.7   Confluence of Little Bighorn and Wagon Box Creek. Trail continues southwest along Wagon Box.

11.4   Trail fords Wagon Box Creek.

12.2   Upper junction with Fuller Trail. Bear right.

13.2   Trail fords Duncum Creek.

13.6   First of "Willow Creek" fords.

14.5   Final ford of "Willow Creek." Trail begins final ascent.

16.3   Trail reaches end of FR 135.

61 THE FULLER TRAIL

General description: An extended trip along the Little Bighorn River from Taylor Creek to the confluence of Wagon Box and Duncum Creeks, 6 miles.
Difficulty: Moderate.
Route finding: Some challenges.
Best season: Mid-July to mid-September.

Visitation: Very light.
Elevation gain: 2,430 feet.
Elevation loss: 650 feet.
Maximum elevation: 7,560 feet.
Topo maps: Boyd Ridge, Bull Elk Park (trail not shown entirely).
Jurisdiction: Bighorn National Forest (Medicine Wheel Ranger District).

FINDING THE TRAILHEAD

The trek begins at mile 6.2 on the Little Horn Trail, at a signpost marked "Taylor Creek Stock Driveway." Continue straight ahead, across a draw and up to an old barbed-wire fence. The bench trail splits away to the left just beyond this fence. The Fuller Trail rejoins the Little Horn Trail just beyond the confluence of Wagon Box and Duncum Creeks, at mile 12.2.

THE HIKE

This trail runs along the southeast side of the Little Bighorn River, visiting elevated meadows above the valley floor. There are views of Leaky Mountain's waterfalls at several points along the route. Originally built as a cattle drive trail, this track is still used for trailing beef into summer pasture along Wagon Box Creek. The trail can be accessed from the Little Horn Trail at the mouth of Taylor Creek, at the confluence of Wagon Box Creek and the Little Bighorn, and just above the confluence of Wagon Box and Duncum Creeks.

The trek begins with a scramble down the steep bluffs beside the Little Bighorn. A knee-deep ford leads across the river a short distance above its confluence with Taylor Creek. On the far bank, the wide cattle trail climbs through heavy timber, making an extremely steep and sometimes slippery ascent.

At the top of the grade, a gate leads into a long, meadowy vale that parallels the river. The stone towers that guard the mouth of Taylor Creek rise from the timber to the south as the path begins its journey along the meadow. Watch for the purple blossoms of horse mint as the trail climbs modestly through the grassland. A dry draw ultimately enters from the east, and here several side paths join the main trail. A spur path descends from an outfitter's camp in the hanging meadow to the northeast, and just beyond this junction a second path swings westward toward the river.

The main trail continues southwest, climbing steadily up an open slope as the barren cliffs of Boyd Ridge reveal themselves across the valley. The trail ultimately reaches the top of a vast, meadowy shelf. Look westward to view the waterfalls that spring from the face of Leaky Mountain. The trail now charts a course through the heart of the high parkland, beneath the towers and buttresses that project from the rimrock above.

At the far side of the meadow, a brief descent leads to an improved spring, beyond which the path traverses timbered slopes. It soon reaches a much smaller hanging meadow. After crossing the clearing, another brief jaunt through the trees leads to the open slope above the point where the Little Bighorn River enters the valley from the

Grassy benches high above the Little Bighorn River.

south. After a faint stretch across a grassy bald, the path descends steeply to a knee-deep ford beside the Fuller Cow Camp.

Pass unobtrusively through the buildings of the camp, leaving the gates as you found them, and proceed up FR 125. This road runs west to meet a faint jeep track that descends to a footbridge over Wagon Box Creek. Bear left and follow the main road as it swings south and climbs through open grasslands.

Posts mark the point where the trail splits away from the road. It runs westward across rolling pastures, with fine views of the cliffs of Boyd Ridge. The path sticks to the uplands as it parallels Wagon Box Creek. This area is grazed heavily by cattle during the summer months. The trail passes a handful of seeps and ponds as it makes its way toward the mouth of Duncum Creek. The path crosses this stream 0.5 mile above its confluence with Wagon Box, then climbs heartily across sagebrush slopes bordered by great groves of aspen. The path meets the much fainter Little Horn Trail high on this slope, at an unmarked spot where cairn posts march away to the north.

MILES AND DIRECTIONS

0.0   Lower junction with Little Horn Trail.

0.1   Trail fords Little Bighorn River and climbs steeply.

0.3   Trail enters long meadow.

1.5   Side trails lead to grassy shelf to east and to lower benches above river.

2.7   Trail leaves long meadow.

2.9   Improved spring.

3.1   Trail crosses second meadow.

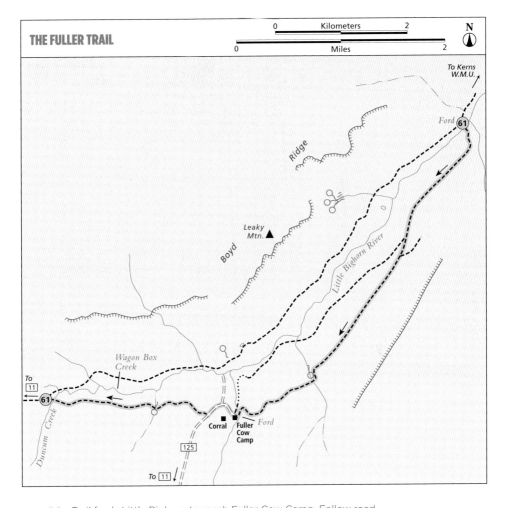

THE FULLER TRAIL

0 — Kilometers — 2

0 — Miles — 2

N

To Kerns W.M.U.

Ford 61

Ridge

Boyd

Leaky Mtn. ▲

Little Bighorn River

Wagon Box Creek

To 11

61

Duncum Creek

Corral Fuller Cow Camp

Ford

125

To 11

3.9 Trail fords Little Bighorn to reach Fuller Cow Camp. Follow road.

4.1 Trail departs from road. Follow it westward.

4.8 Trail crosses spring-fed rivulet.

5.8 Trail fords Duncum Creek.

6.0 Trail rejoins Little Horn Trail.

62 DRY FORK RIDGE

General description: A backpack from the Little Bighorn canyon, following a ridge above the Dry Fork, 10.4 miles.
Difficulty: Strenuous (north to south); moderate (south to north).
Route finding: No problem.
Best season: Mid-July to mid-September.

Visitation: Very light.
Elevation gain: 3,200 feet.
Elevation loss: 1,370 feet.
Maximum elevation: 7,020 feet.
Topo maps: Bull Elk Park, West Pass.
Jurisdiction: Bighorn National Forest (Medicine Wheel Ranger District).

FINDING THE TRAILHEAD

Drive northwest from Ranchester on Wyoming 343 (old US Highway 89). After 12 miles, turn left (west) on County Road 144, a gravel highway, and follow it for 16.5 miles. Upon reaching the bottoms of the Little Bighorn River, the county road bends eastward. (This spot can also be reached from Wyola, Montana, via CR 418.) Turn left onto a primitive road that is marked "public access through private lands." This road is rough with some fords, and high clearance is required. Follow it for 2.8 miles, crossing the bridge and parking at the trailhead on the Kerns Wildlife Management Unit GPS: 44.980106° N, 107.646319° W. Hike the road to reach the beginning of the trail.

THE HIKE

This trail climbs from the Little Bighorn River to the base of Dry Fork Ridge, then follows the ridge southeast to the headwaters of the Dry Fork of the Little Bighorn. Along the way are views of the virgin forests that stretch south from the river, and the possibility of sighting elk or moose during the twilight hours. Water is scarce on some parts of this trail; plan your hike accordingly.

The hike begins by crossing a sturdy bridge over the Little Bighorn River. The trail then climbs steeply, reaching the top of a cutbank high above the boulder-filled rapids. The cliffs that rise on the far side of the river belong to Fisher Mountain. The path then wanders inland, passing through hidden vales and up slopes timbered in Douglas fir. It soon climbs to a rounded rise, where ponderosa pines grow sparsely amid a grassy savannah. The trees fall away as the trail ascends into rolling country where there are copses of aspen and beaver ponds in the damp swales, and thickets of brush on the drier hillocks. Examine the shrubs for signs of elk browsing; this area is a major winter range for these animals.

The trail climbs high into a level basin rimmed with aspens, then follows an arid finger ridge even higher. Dry Fork Ridge rises to impressive heights above the rolling prairies, and the trail climbs toward it after reaching the spine of the ridge. After a brutal climb, it finally levels off and traverses across open slopes of sagebrush and arrowleaf balsamroot. It soon rounds a corner and sags across a narrow vale where a trickle of a stream drains northward toward the Little Bighorn.

The path now swings steadily southwest, rising ever higher as it surmounts a series of high gaps. (There always seems to be a higher saddle, and beyond that, a loftier ridge to cross.) The trail braids into several paths as it visits a high, waterless camp. It then passes through a sagebrush saddle to enter the valley of the Dry Fork of the Little Bighorn.

Still climbing through loose timber, the path surmounts several more spur ridges. It reaches its high point opposite the mouth of Bear Trap Creek. A series of broad and rolling sagebrush meadows stretches away to the southwest, while gentle scarps of virgin timber stretch southward from the Dry Fork. The lone clearing amid this forest is Bull Elk Park, on a high shelf atop the far wall of the valley. The trail descends across the rolling sagebrush country, which is dotted with copses of aspen and guarded by the cliff bands of Dry Fork Ridge. There are several spring-fed brooks coursing through this open country.

On the far side of the first clearing, the trail crosses the first of many rounded promontories that extend toward the Dry Fork from the base of the ridge. Each initially appears to be densely clothed in timber, but the southwestern exposures beyond the ridgelines support sage grasslands. There is an improved spring on the timbered slope of one such spur ridge, opposite Bull Elk Park. The trail descends gradually, and the cliffs recede. There are several broad ridgetops that are completely bare of trees, and one watercourse shelters an extensive grove of aspen. A short distance beyond this watercourse, there is a second improved spring in a stand of Douglas fir. The trail then makes a steep climb through shady timber to reach an open ridgetop beside a grove of aspen.

The trail now wanders across broad, sage grasslands above the Dry Fork. Soon the rocky crest of Riley Point can be seen to the east. The path wanders across an open basin that offers sweeping views, then passes through a fence and descends into a major valley

Forested ridges stretch to the horizon beyond the Dry Fork of the Little Bighorn River.

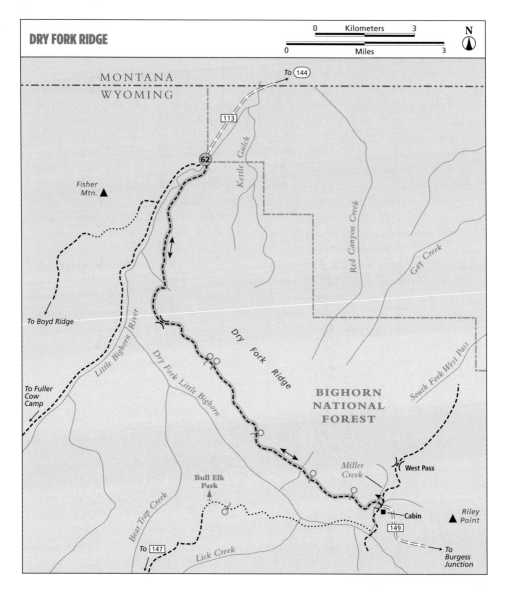

0   Kilometers   3

0   Miles   3

N

MONTANA
WYOMING

To 144

113

62

Fisher
Mtn.

Kettle Gulch

Red Canyon Creek

Gay Creek

To Boyd Ridge

Little Bighorn River

Dry Fork Ridge

South Fork West Pass

To Fuller
Cow
Camp

Dry Fork Little Bighorn

BIGHORN
NATIONAL
FOREST

Bear Trap Creek

Bull Elk
Park

Miller
Creek

West Pass

Cabin

Riley
Point

149

To 147

Lick Creek

To
Burgess
Junction

that enters from the northeast. The grassy divide of West Pass can be seen at the head of this valley. The trail, meanwhile, descends to reach its end at an old cabin just beyond Miller Creek. From here, the West Pass Trail runs northeast, the Lake Creek Ridge Trail descends along the watercourse, and FR 149 wanders southwest toward Burgess Junction.

MILES AND DIRECTIONS

0.0   Trailhead on Kerns Wildlife Management Unit. Follow road.

0.2   Road ends. Turn left, crossing bridge over Little Bighorn River.

3.1   Top of initial grade.

3.8 Junction with spur to cow camp. Bear right.

4.0 Trail crosses pass to enter Dry Fork watershed.

5.5 Trail crosses springs and small rivulets.

6.5 Improved spring.

8.2 Improved spring.

9.7 Improved spring.

10.3 Miller Creek.

10.4 Trail ends at Lower Dry Fork Road (FR 149). Miller Creek cow camp. West Pass Trail runs north; Lake Creek Ridge Trail runs south.

63 BULL ELK PARK

General description: A day hike to Bull Elk Park, 10.4 miles round trip, or a primitive route to Miller Creek cow camp, 10 miles overall.
Difficulty: Moderate to Bull Elk Park; moderately strenuous beyond.
Route finding: No problem to Bull Elk Park; map and compass beyond.
Best season: Mid-July to mid-September.

Visitation: Very light.
Elevation gain: 652 feet.
Elevation loss: 3,232 feet (to Miller Creek cow camp).
Maximum elevation: 9,420 feet (trailhead).
Topo maps: Bull Elk Park, Ice Creek (trail not shown entirely).
Jurisdiction: Bighorn National Forest (Medicine Wheel Ranger District).

FINDING THE TRAILHEAD

From US Alternate 14 west of Burgess Junction, follow the Dayton Gulch Road (FR 15) northward. After 7.2 miles, turn right (north) on FR 145, then make an immediate right on FR 147. This primitive road climbs through a saddle and continues up a steep ridge for 1.4 miles to reach a closure gate on the ridgetop GPS: 44.831891° N, 107.713109° W. The hike starts on the closed road.

THE HIKE

This trek follows a closed jeep trail down the ridgetop to reach the vast meadows of Bull Elk Park, then becomes a primitive track as it continues eastward to the Dry Fork of the Little Bighorn. Bull Elk Park is a *disjunct* of the Palouse Prairie of eastern Washington, an isolated patch of Idaho fescue and bluebunch wheatgrass that is hundreds of miles east of the nearest grassland community of its type. Its existence indicates that the Palouse Prairie grassland was once much more widespread, but following the glaciation that occurred along the Rocky Mountains during the Pleistocene epoch, short-grass prairie from the High Plains invaded the Bighorn Basin and, aided by drier conditions, replaced the Palouse community. In recognition of the ecological uniqueness of Bull Elk Park, the Forest Service has designated it a Research Natural Area, and livestock do not graze here.

At its outset, the route follows a logging road that has been used for recent salvage-cuts of the wind-thrown subalpine forest. The road passes the last of the logging activity after about a mile, and the ridgetop beyond is robed in pleasant glades and stands of subalpine fir. Periodic openings in the trees reveal the valleys of Lick Creek to the southeast and Bear Trap Creek to the northwest. The trail ultimately reaches a large, ridgetop meadow, and at this point the subalpine fir begins to give way to spruce. As the ridge loses altitude, these trees in turn are replaced by lodgepole pine and then Douglas fir.

After topping a lofty point of limestone, the path makes a hearty descent. It levels off as the trail enters the Bull Elk Park Research Natural Area. The trees soon open out into the broad grasslands of Bull Elk Park, and the trail vanishes as it enters the meadow. The cliff-girt mountain to the northeast is Dry Fork Ridge, while the bare summit of Fisher Mountain rises to the north.

To continue the trek, follow the treeline along the southeast edge of Bull Elk Park. The route descends gradually along the trees until it reaches a grassy cove. In the corner of this cove, a well-beaten trail leads through the doghair lodgepole to reach the small

Looking across Bull Elk Park at Fisher Mountain.

clearing beyond. There is an outfitter's camp and a pipe-fed spring at the far edge of this meadow.

From the camp, the trail passes through a fence and traverses eastward, maintaining its altitude as it stays near the ridgetops. It rounds the first, wooded finger ridge and turns south onto a grassy slope. The path disappears here; traverse southward across the top of the clearing, then follow the edge of the trees downward to pick up the trail. The path is now no better than a game trail with scattered blazes. It crosses a dry vale and then runs northeast to the top of the next finger ridge. After passing through a lodgepole stand that is full of blowdowns, it emerges on the ridgetop and becomes an obvious ribbon in the sandy soil. It soon turns east again, wandering through a spruce woodland.

The third finger ridge is wooded sparsely with Douglas fir. Descend northward along the grassy ridgeline to reach the lower edge of the clearing. The track now bails off of the eastern side of the ridge, plummeting through the Douglas firs at an insanely steep rate. Gaps in the forest canopy reveal the blocky cliffs that guard the Dry Fork of the Little Bighorn. The path bottoms out at the confluence of Lick Creek and the Dry Fork.

After a shallow ford of Lick Creek, there are several faint trails leading in different directions. The recommended route leads up the south bank of the river, following old blazes and saw-work on an otherwise abandoned trail. Cross to the north bank when steep slopes encroach on the river's edge. Just beyond the ford, a major valley enters from the south. The trail now runs upstream through the floodplain forest to reach the confluence of the Dry Fork with Lake Creek. These two streams carry similar flows of water. The trail makes two crossings of the Dry Fork, then continues up its north bank to reach Miller Creek, a small tributary brook. After crossing it, the trail ends at an unmarked junction with the Lake Creek Ridge Trail, just south of the terminus of the Dry Fork Ridge route and the Miller Creek cow camp.

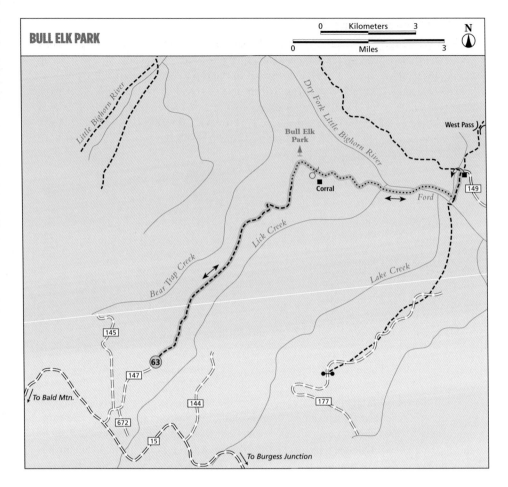

BULL ELK PARK

MILES AND DIRECTIONS

0.0 Trailhead. Hike down closed road.

4.7 Trail enters Bull Elk Park Research Natural Area.

5.2 Trail enters Bull Elk Park. Hike along southeast edge of trees.

6.0 Trail leaves Bull Elk Park.

6.2 Camp spot at spring.

7.3 Trail begins descent to Lick Creek.

7.7 Trail fords Lick Creek and follows Dry Fork of Little Bighorn.

8.4 Trail fords Dry Fork and follows north bank.

9.2 Trail crosses Miller Creek.

9.3 Trail joins Lake Creek Ridge Trail. Turn left for cow camp.

10.0 Miller Creek cow camp.

ADDITIONAL TRAILS

The **Boyd Ridge** Trail is a stockman's path that climbs moderately across an open slope above the Little Bighorn. The path ends at a spring on a timbered ridgetop and picks up again much higher up the ridgeline to ascend to the top of Boyd Ridge.

The trail that follows **Lake Creek Ridge** makes a tedious trek on a logging road, passing through recent clearcuts. Near the toe of the ridge, a path departs from the road and follows the ridgeline down to the Dry Fork of the Little Bighorn. On the far bank it meets the trail from Bull Elk Park, and just to the north is the end of the Dry Fork Ridge Trail.

THE WESTERN CANYONS AND BADLANDS

Along the western edge of the Bighorn Mountains, the arid badlands of the Bighorn Basin rise into steep and grassy hills that are dissected by a number of deep chasms. This is a landscape of rugged beauty, where geological wonders are the main attractions: wind-carved hoodoos of sandstone, painted desert scenery, and soaring canyon walls can be found here. Many of the routes described in this chapter will remain accessible through most of the autumn and spring months; the desert wildflowers bloom in great profusion from mid-May to early June, depending on rainfall. Expect blistering temperatures during the height of the summer, and carry a good supply of water at all times. The larger streams that issue from the Bighorn Mountains offer excellent trout fishing, and nature lovers can watch for birds in the canyons and elk and deer at the higher elevations. Rattlesnakes are abundant throughout this part of the Bighorns, particularly in the arid canyons.

The three highways that breach the mountains provide superb access to some of the hikes described here. These highways make excellent scenic drives in and of themselves, visiting points of interest like the Medicine Wheel, the ghost town of Bald Mountain City, Shell Falls, Shell Canyon, and Tensleep Canyon. Other hikes are reached via gravel thoroughfares that turn to slippery mud when it rains. Most of the hikes described in this chapter fall within BLM lands; some of the access roads cross private lands, and the landowner's permission may be required to drive them.

There are four developed campgrounds at low elevations along the western edge of the mountains: the Five Springs Campground, along US Alternate 14, run by the BLM; the state-run campground at the Medicine Lodge Archaeological Site (no fee is charged here); and the Tensleep and Leigh Creek campgrounds, administered by the Forest Service. You can seek current information at the BLM office in Worland or at the Forest Service ranger station in Lovell. The settlements of Tensleep and Shell offer gas and restaurants, while Hyattville has a small café. A wider range of goods and services can be found in Worland, Basin, Greybull, or Lovell.

Cedar Creek, along the Beef Trail.

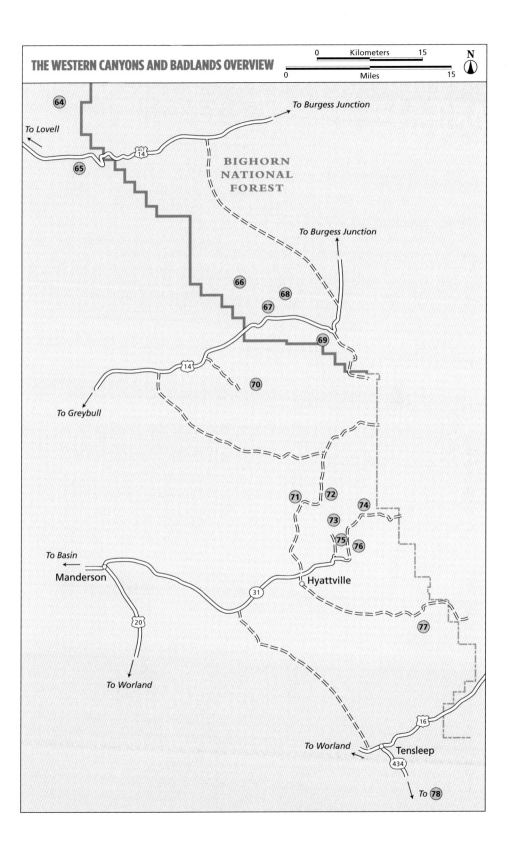

0   Kilometers   15

0   Miles   15

N

64

To Lovell

ALT 14

65

BIGHORN
NATIONAL
FOREST

To Burgess Junction

To Burgess Junction

66

68

67

69

14

70

To Greybull

71   72

74

73

75   76

To Basin

Manderson

31   Hyattville

20

77

To Worland

16

To Worland   Tensleep

434

To 78

64 **COTTONWOOD CANYON**

General description: A day hike up a deep canyon in the northern Bighorns, 2.5 miles one way.
Difficulty: Moderately strenuous.
Route finding: No problem.
Best season: Late March to early June; mid-September to mid-November.

Visitation: Light.
Elevation gain: 1,700 feet.
Maximum elevation: 6,750 feet.
Topo map: Cottonwood Canyon.
Jurisdiction: BLM (Cody Resource Area).

FINDING THE TRAILHEAD

Before setting off, obtain permission to cross the private lands en route to the trailhead by contacting Phil Schaelling at the Super 8 Motel in Lovell. Take US Alternate 14 west from Lovell. After crossing Bighorn Lake, turn left on the John Blue Road. Take an immediate right on a primitive road (once graded but now neglected) that leads east for 6 miles to the mouth of Cottonwood Canyon. Park next to the second gravel pit on the left. GPS: 44.867811° N, 108.071473° W.

THE HIKE

Cottonwood Creek has carved a deep chasm into the steep country of the northern Bighorns, and a good trail runs the length of the resulting canyon. It occupies a remote corner of the range, seldom visited by any save the occasional cattleman. Cottonwood

Deep in the heart of Cottonwood Canyon.

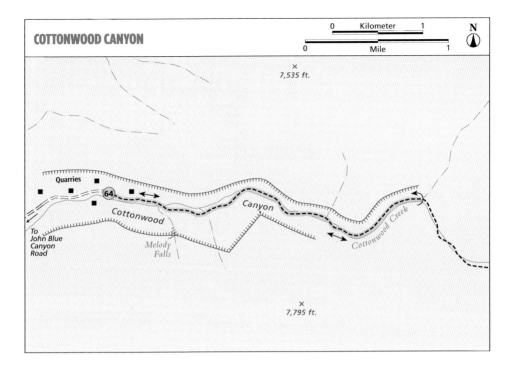

Canyon is an excellent place to seek solitude amid desert scrub and towering walls. This area gets quite hot during the height of summer, so carry plenty of water. Cattle range through this area in summer; purify all surface water thoroughly before drinking it.

The trek begins on a jeep road that runs between soaring walls of limestone capped by jagged pinnacles. Soon, the walls open up to reveal a broad, natural amphitheater that is guarded by sheer cliffs. The jeep track crosses the stream and charts a steep course across the amphitheater. The vegetation here is dominated by mountain mahogany, a desert plant with small, leathery leaves that help it retain moisture. A few cottonwoods straggle along the watercourse of Cottonwood Creek, sustained by the abundant groundwater found there. To the south, a small tributary plummets from a cleft in the cliffs, forming Melody Falls.

As the cliffs close in again, the jeep track becomes a pack trail used principally by cattle. Douglas firs now grow abundantly on the north-facing wall of the canyon, favored by the cooler temperatures and greater moisture found there. The trail makes numerous rock-hop crossings of Cottonwood Creek as it follows the steep watercourse upward. Watch for small waterfalls in this area.

Ultimately, the path climbs into a gentler section of the canyon where sagebrush slopes lead up to the base of the cliffs and aspens crowd the streamcourse. Expect several tricky fords as the route crosses the creek in the midst of deep pools. The canyon soon jogs north, still guarded on one side by rugged walls and buttes. After a stretch of easy traveling, a tributary enters from the north and the main canyon bends eastward again. The trail now devolves into a tangle of livestock paths, marking the end of the hike.

MILES AND DIRECTIONS

0.0   Parking area near gravel pits. Hike up jeep track.

0.5   Jeep track fords Cottonwood Creek and enters large basin.

1.2   Canyon narrows. First of many stream fords.

2.5   Hike ends at confluence of drainages.

65 RAINBOW CANYON

General description: An off-trail route down a painted-desert canyon, 4.8 miles one way.	**Visitation:** Light.
	Elevation gain: 60 feet.
	Elevation loss: 1,620 feet.
Difficulty: Moderate.	**Maximum elevation:** 5,760 feet.
Route finding: Map and compass.	**Topo maps:** Cottonwood Canyon,
Best season: Late March to mid-June; mid-September to mid-November.	Medicine Wheel, Alkali Creek.
	Jurisdiction: BLM (Cody Resource Area).

FINDING THE TRAILHEAD

 Take US Alternate 14 east from Bighorn Lake to the turnoff for Five Springs Campground. Turn right (south) on a primitive road across the highway from the campground access road. This road splits after 0.2 mile; turn right and follow the road another 0.2 mile to its end. GPS: 44.794256° N, 107.987697° W.

THE HIKE

This hike leads down a painted-desert canyon that runs through the arid badlands to the west of the Bighorns. In the heart of the canyon, the deeply eroded walls are banded with the brilliant hues of the Cloverly formation.

From the road's end, cross the small gulch and proceed down the old highway grade to an intersection of abandoned roadbeds. Turn left as the route follows an old jeep trail southward into the sagebrush hills. After cresting a rise, the track crosses the barren gulch that will ultimately become Rainbow Canyon. Cross to the south side of the wash and turn right, following the benches above the watercourse as you make your way downstream. The intermittent stream has carved a deep channel in the soft, black sediments of the Colorado formation. A sparse cover of saltbush and prickly pear cactus adds to the desert aspect of this barren landscape.

As a tributary wash enters from the north, cross the main wash and follow the rolling country above its north side. Badland hills now rise to the south of the watercourse, eroded by wind and water into rounded domes and beehives. Ahead, a lush growth of cottonwoods rises along Five Springs Creek, and our wash swings toward it. The gully soon deepens into an imposing canyon, and the route runs atop its ochre-colored caprock. The canyon walls now take on the brilliant hues of a painted desert, with bands of purple, red, and pink alternating with layers of black and white.

An old jeep trail soon drifts in from the north, bound for an overlook point on the canyon rim. Do not follow it; instead, turn northwest to round the head of a deeply incised gully that descends into the main canyon. As erosion deepens this gulch, it carves its way northward. If it maintains its present course, this small wash will undercut the valley of Five Springs Creek and "capture" that stream. The waters of Five Springs Creek will then flow through Rainbow Canyon to join Crystal Creek, and the entire drainage pattern of this arid region will have changed dramatically.

Our route continues to follow the caprock above Rainbow Canyon, offering views up and down the canyon. A vegetated slope soon leads downward from the rims, and our route follows it down to the canyon floor. The colors play out as the canyon walls sink lower, and the dry wash offers easy downstream traveling. Before long, the canyon

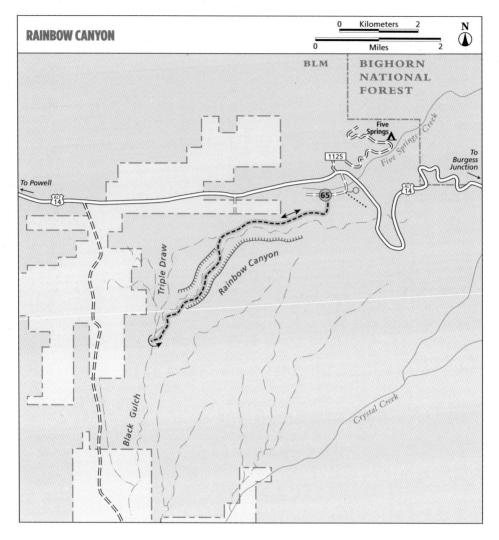

0   Kilometers   2

0   Miles   2

N

BLM

BIGHORN NATIONAL FOREST

Five Springs

Five Springs Creek

1125

To Powell

65

To Burgess Junction

Triple Draw

Rainbow Canyon

Black Gulch

Crystal Creek

dwindles away into sage-covered hills. Low, dun-colored walls soon rise around the watercourse, as it enters a series of *incised meanders*. Before the most recent uplift, this watercourse flowed lazily across a level plain, looping back on itself to form oxbow bends. When the landscape rose, the stream increased in gradient and gained new vigor. It cut downward rapidly along the sinuous channel that it occupied when the waters were sluggish. Thus, the meanders became entrenched in the bedrock, and the wash may never return to a straight course.

As the incised meanders end, the wash empties out into Black Gulch, a broad, barren valley guarded to the west by a long escarpment. This is a good turn-around point.

Looking down into Rainbow Canyon.

MILES AND DIRECTIONS

0.0 Parking area beside small stream. Cross stream and hike down old roadbed.

0.1 Junction of old roads. Turn left (south) on jeep track.

0.4 Old road strikes wash. Hike down south side of wash.

1.1 Route crosses wash and continues down north side.

2.2 Route crosses jeep trail to overlook point on Rainbow Canyon.

2.7 Route descends to floor of Rainbow Canyon.

4.8 Wash emerges into Black Gulch. Turn around here.

66 THE HORSE CREEK CANYONS

General description: A long day loop or short backpack down one rugged canyon and up another, 11.5 miles overall.
Difficulty: Moderately strenuous (clockwise); strenuous (counterclockwise).
Route finding: Some challenges (clockwise); map and compass (counterclockwise).

Best season: Mid-July to late September.
Visitation: Extremely light.
Elevation gain: 3,905 feet.
Elevation loss: 3,595 feet.
Maximum elevation: 8,770 feet.
Topo maps: Hidden Teepee Creek, Shell, Black Mountain.
Jurisdiction: Bighorn National Forest (Medicine Wheel Ranger District).

FINDING THE TRAILHEAD

Take US Highway 14 south from Burgess Junction to FR 10, just north of Granite Pass. Follow this trunk road (fair weather only!) for 12.6 miles. Turn left (south) on FR 207, the Sunlight Mesa Road. Bear left at the first junction as this four-wheel-drive road descends to reach the Horse Creek Cow Camp cabin after 1.7 miles. Drive around the back of the cabin and continue on FR 207, bearing right at the next junction and left at the junction with FR 208. One mile beyond this point, a two-rut track descends southwest toward Deer Spring. The hike begins on this track GPS: 44.640868° N, 107.684752° W. It emerges on FR 207 some 1.6 miles north of the starting point GPS: 44.663475° N, 107.679619° W.

THE HIKE

This primitive route follows a pair of forgotten trails through a remote corner of Sunlight Mesa. It runs from the grassy highlands all the way down to the arid country of the Bighorn Basin before making a vigorous climb on the return leg. Be sure to hike *down* the Dry Fork and up the main fork of Horse Canyon; the route-finding challenges are extreme when the route is approached from a counterclockwise direction.

At the outset, hike down through the sage to reach a clump of aspen where Deer Spring wells up from a fold in the hills. Follow the incipient flow of Horse Creek's Dry Fork downward from the spring. As the clearing narrows, wander to the south edge of the meadow to pick up a cattle trail that runs along the edge of the spruce. This path soon adopts an old roadbed that enters the shady forest, traversing across the hillside while maintaining its altitude. The spruce grove ultimately gives way to open slopes of sage, and the old road runs below a ridgetop grove of aspen to meet FR 243.

From this point, a shallow draw descends westward toward the Dry Fork of Horse Creek. There is no trail here, but the hiking is easy as the route glides down along a sagebrush bench to the north of a dry streamcourse. As the Douglas firs close in, a good path emerges from out of thin air, descending along the steepening draw. It crosses to the south bank at a spot where a spring emerges from beneath a limestone sill. It then traverses above limestone walls before returning to the dry wash. The path ultimately swings beneath a blade of stone that marks the confluence of the dry wash with the Dry Fork of Horse Creek.

On the far bank of the Dry Fork, the trail joins a faint track that descends from the east. The route now follows the streamcourse downward, crossing the stream frequently as imposing cliffs rise above its north bank. Before long, tall pillars of limestone soar

The mouth of Horse Creek Canyon.

skyward, independent of the cliffs. The trail works its way beneath them, and soon the forest of Douglas fir gives way to arid slopes of sage and mountain mahogany. A few cottonwoods and junipers are strung out along the watercourse.

It seems as if the path may reach the canyon mouth at any moment, but the Dry Fork drops ever more steeply toward the Bighorn Basin, and the cliff walls tower on either side. This is some of the steepest country in the Bighorn Mountains. The path snakes downward, a swath of loose rock that the streamcourse appropriates as a channel in some places. At the bottom of the grade, the trail emerges from the mouth of the canyon onto low hills of juniper scrub.

The route now enters state land. Ignore the cattle trail that rises into the hills to the south, and instead follow the north bank of the Dry Fork. Soon you will strike a jeep trail that will carry you down toward the confluence of Horse Creek and the Dry Fork. As the hill dividing the drainages sinks into the flats, hike around its toe to strike a similar jeep trail that follows the south bank of Horse Creek.

Turn east on this track as it passes badland hills of brilliant crimson en route to the jagged maw of the Horse Creek Canyon. Inside the mouth of the gorge, a footpath crosses to the north bank of the stream. It then traverses the skirts of arid, south-facing slopes, climbing in spurts. Across the stream are jagged, deeply incised strata and chimney rocks. The north side of the canyon is guarded by the gabled cliffs of the Horse Creek Mesa. Horse Creek itself flows through a narrow ribbon of cottonwood, sometimes at the surface, sometimes beneath the gravels of the streambed.

As the trail climbs higher, the north-facing slopes beyond the streamcourse gain a mantle of Douglas firs, and a backward glance yields fine views down the canyon. The views close in as the Douglas firs encroach on the south-facing slopes as well, and the

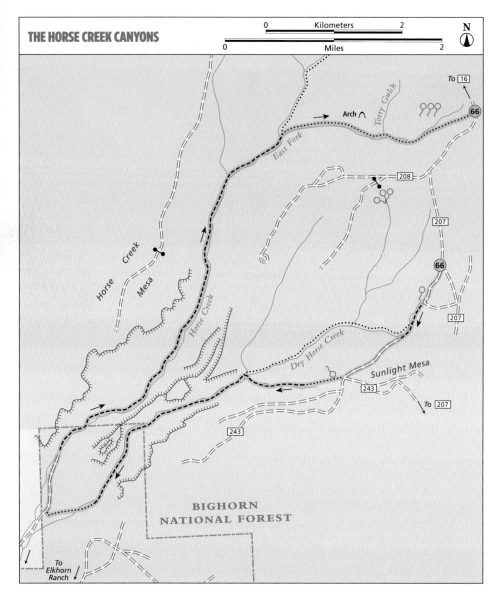

path now becomes more primitive. It crosses the creek many times, passing through grassy glades as it makes its way up to the confluence of the East and West Forks of Horse Creek. This is a tricky spot, since the East Fork is dry here and the trail that once followed it has been abandoned. Stay as far south as possible, following game trails up the dry wash of the East Fork.

After a difficult passage up the steep-sided valley, the tangle of undergrowth gives way to an old burn. The old trail can now be followed as it climbs steeply across the slopes to the north of the streambed. Before long, low-slung buttes of sandstone rise to the north of the valley, and one of them sports a natural arch. Just beyond the arch lies the mouth of Torry Gulch; once again, stay right as the old trailbed follows the East Fork. There is

Along Dry Horse Creek.

now some surface water running in the wash. Sagebrush slopes flank the stream, but the easiest traveling is along its bottoms.

Before long, a few old spruces appear beside the East Fork, and good cattle trails materialize to bear the traveler the remaining distance through rolling hills. After passing a water trough, watch for a path that veers away to the right (south). This is a shortcut to the end of the trek. It emerges in a meadow to meet FR 207, just 1.6 miles north of the starting point.

MILES AND DIRECTIONS

- 0.0 Starting point. Hike down jeep trail toward spring.
- 0.4 Deer Spring. Road veers left. Continue down valley on trail.
- 0.8 Trail picks up old roadbed at south edge of clearing. Follow it west.
- 1.5 Junction with FR 243. Hike northwest down shallow draw.
- 2.5 Draw empties into Dry Horse Creek. Follow trail downward.
- 3.2 Upper end of Dry Horse Creek canyon.
- 4.2 Mouth of canyon. Follow wash to trail on north bank.
- 5.0 Trail strikes jeep road along Horse Creek. Follow it northeast.
- 5.5 Jeep road ends at mouth of Horse Creek Canyon. Follow trail.
- 9.4 East Fork joins Horse Creek. Hike east up its valley.
- 10.4 Mouth of Torry Gulch.
- 11.0 Trail leaves East Fork, bound east.
- 11.5 Trail reaches FR 207.

67 **THE BEEF TRAIL**

General description: A day hike down Shell Canyon, 5.9 miles one way.
Difficulty: Moderate (east to west); Moderately strenuous (west to east).
Route finding: Some challenges.
Best season: Late June to early October.

Visitation: Very light.
Elevation gain: 235 feet.
Elevation loss: 1,940 feet.
Maximum elevation: 6,370 feet.
Topo maps: Shell Falls, Black Mountain (location approximate).
Jurisdiction: Bighorn National Forest (Medicine Wheel Ranger District).

FINDING THE TRAILHEAD

Drive east from Shell on US Highway 14 to mile 27.6. Turn north on FR 264 (high clearance a must; four-wheel drive recommended), which climbs onto grassy benches, then makes a steep descent to reach Brindle Creek after 2 miles. The hike begins on the closed road on the far bank GPS: 44.591408° N, 107.620837° W. The hike ends at an unmarked pulloff across from a footbridge at mile 20.6 on US 14 GPS: 44.574765° N, 107.698305° W.

THE HIKE

This trail is one of the best-kept secrets of the Bighorn Mountains. It follows the opposite wall of Shell Canyon from the highway, allowing visitors to experience the grandeur of the scenery in an atmosphere of solitude. The trail is first, last, and foremost a cattle drive trail, and stockmen still use it to drive their herds up into the summer pastures at the crest of the range. Travelers who hike here in early July and late September may meet oncoming bands of cattle on the trail. The lower stretches of the trail are renowned for their abundance of rattlesnakes; exercise caution, especially in morning and evening.

The trek begins by crossing Brindle Creek in a shady bottomland stand of Douglas fir. On the far bank, follow the closed road onto an arid, sage-clad bench. The old road splits here; to the right is the Cedar Creek Trail, while the Beef Trail runs straight ahead on a roadway blocked by boulders.

The old road winds across open benches and slopes of sagebrush, offering superb views of Shell Canyon. Copmans Tomb rises above the trail to the north, flanked by smaller wing cliffs. To the west are the cliffs of Pyramid Mountain and Sunlight Mesa. The latter landform shows a fault where the Tensleep caprock has bent, and just above the fault is a formation known as Elephant Head Rock. Across the valley are cooler, north-facing slopes that are robed in timber. The large fire scar originated in 1984 when visitors using illegal fireworks ignited the slopes.

After a gentle downhill journey, the trail swings north toward Cedar Creek. Along the way it crosses Fender Creek, a crystal-clear brook that offers fine camping opportunities. The trail soon splits, with a spur climbing away to the northeast toward higher pastures. Meanwhile, the Beef Trail arcs down across steep slopes above the gorge of Cedar Creek. This steep chasm is made up of the same granite that forms Shell Falls, with all of the grandeur of that site and no crowds to contend with. A sturdy bridge spans Cedar Creek above the head of the gorge, in an idyllic little glen shaded by juniper, Douglas fir, and cottonwood. This bridge not only helps hikers make the crossing with dry feet, but it also protects the stream from being fouled and muddied by crossing cattle.

The old road ends on the far bank, to be replaced by a tangled skein of stock trails. Follow the broadest trail, which runs south along the very rim of the gorge. The arid rimrock offers a foothold to mountain mahogany, a desert shrub that is similar to sagebrush in appearance but with a blackish coloring. It is a favorite winter forage of mule deer. The path ultimately turns westward to cross gentler slopes, allowing glimpses into the inner chasm of Shell Creek to the east. As the path jogs north to cross Cottonwood Creek, Pyramid Peak rises in all its imposing grandeur to the north. After a brief climb, the path leads across grassy flats where yucca and prickly pear grow.

The trail now runs toward the towering walls of Sunlight Mesa. Upon reaching the base of the cliffs, the trail becomes a cliff-hanging track high above the rapids of Shell Creek. Some of the most spectacular scenery of the trek is unveiled as the path enters the lower stretch of Shell Canyon, where a reddish caprock of Tensleep sandstone forms the upper stratum of sheer cliffs.

The path ultimately makes a sharp descent to reach the bottoms of Shell Creek, where tall cottonwoods are strung out along the watercourse. The track follows the bottoms with brief excursions onto the lower slopes for the remaining 0.6 mile of the trek. The hike ends at a stout bridge that leads across Shell Creek to reach the lower trailhead on US 14.

MILES AND DIRECTIONS

0.0   Brindle Creek Trailhead.

0.2   Junction with Cedar Creek Trail. Stay left.

0.3   Road splits. Bear left on road blocked by boulders.

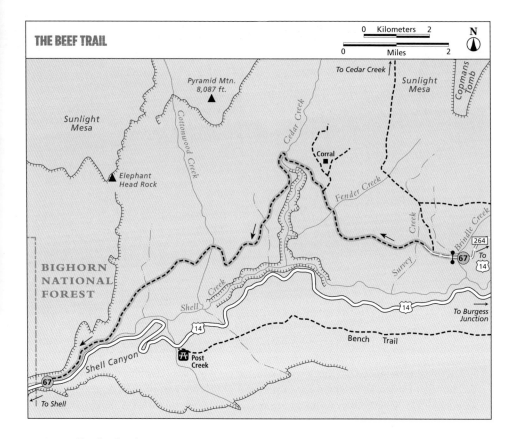

THE BEEF TRAIL

1.5   Fender Creek.

2.2   Bridge over Cedar Creek.

3.8   Cottonwood Creek.

4.8   Trail begins final descent.

5.3   Trail reaches floor of Shell Canyon.

5.9   Bridge over Shell Creek leads to lower trailhead.

68 CEDAR CREEK

General description: A day hike across mid-elevation meadows to Cedar Creek, 4 miles one way.
Difficulty: Moderately strenuous.
Route finding: Some challenges.
Best season: Early June to mid-October.
Visitation: Extremely light.

Elevation gain: 1,095 feet.
Elevation loss: 540 feet.
Maximum elevation: 7,240 feet.
Topo maps: Shell Falls, Black Mountain, Hidden Teepee Creek.
Jurisdiction: Bighorn National Forest (Medicine Wheel Ranger District).

FINDING THE TRAILHEAD

Drive east from Shell on US Highway 14 to mile 27.6. Turn left (north) on FR 264 (high clearance a must; four-wheel drive recommended), which climbs onto grassy benches and then makes a steep descent to reach Brindle Creek after 2 miles. The hike begins on the closed road on the far bank. GPS: 44.591408° N, 107.620837° W.

THE HIKE

This dead-end trail visits the lush meadows at the foot of Copmans Tomb before descending to Cedar Creek. From the trailhead, cross Brindle Creek on the rocks and follow the closed road westward. It soon emerges from the Douglas firs onto arid slopes of sagebrush and juniper. After a short distance, a jeep track climbs away to the right. Follow it to a stagnant pond (which, believe it or not, has fish in it). At the western edge of the pond, you will strike a faint horse trail that climbs straight up an open ridgeline to meet a second roadbed.

Follow this road upward as it makes a hearty ascent. At first, the open country reveals fine westward views of Sunlight Mesa, with Elephant Head Rock at its southern tip. (The lone pinnacle represents the trunk of the elephant). The south face of Copmans Tomb rises above the trail. This singular butte was named in honor of Wolfgang Copeman, a local cattleman who was so enamored with the spot that he wanted to be buried atop it. His last wishes were not honored. Across the valley of Shell Creek, the large burn in the timber dates from 1984.

The track ultimately climbs into a stand of Douglas fir, which shades the ascent to a high saddle on the shoulders of Copmans Tomb. This saddle leads into a broad meadow where sego lily and purple fleabane bloom amid the tall grass. The path glides down across the meadow, and at its far edge is Fender Creek. This tiny stream offers a seasonal supply of water. The trail soon runs northward, charting a fairly level course across the high shoulders of Copmans Tomb. Loose woodlands of Douglas fir alternate with old burns where wildfire has cleared away the trees and sagebrush to renew the grasslands. After 2.3 miles, the path reaches a second meadow, much larger than the first and lit by an even more diverse assemblage of wildflowers. The forested slopes of the mesas loom all around, broken here and there by sheer faces of sandstone and limestone.

At the far edge of the meadow, the trail drops steeply into a grassy gulch that bears you down toward the Cedar Creek bottoms. Near the valley floor, the path crosses the watercourse of the gulch and leads over rolling meadows that offer magnificent views of Copmans Tomb's west face. The path then drops steeply to enter the deep shade of the

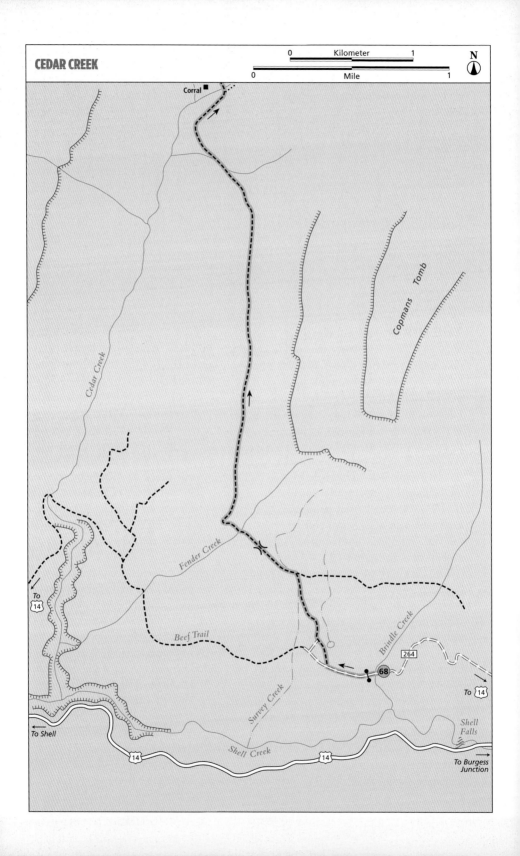

CEDAR CREEK

Kilometer

Mile

N

Corral

Copmans Tomb

Cedar Creek

Fender Creek

To 14

Beef Trail

Brindle Creek

264

68

To 14

Survey Creek

To Shell

Shell Falls

Shell Creek

14

14

To Burgess Junction

Copman's Tomb rises above flower-splashed meadows.

bottomland forest of Cedar Creek. An ankle-deep ford leads to a corral and camping spot on the far bank, and trail maintenance ends at this point. Trails running eastward along Cedar Creek and northward to the tops of the mesas have been abandoned.

MILES AND DIRECTIONS

0.0 Brindle Creek Trailhead.

0.2 Trail splits away from old road. Turn right.

0.3 Trail passes a stagnant pond.

0.4 Trail joins second roadbed and resumes climbing.

0.8 Unmarked trail joins in from the east.

0.9 Trail crosses dry wash of Survey Creek.

1.0 Trail crosses high saddle and enters first meadow.

1.2 Trail crosses Fender Creek and leaves first meadow.

2.3 Trail enters second meadow.

2.8 Trail starts to descend from second meadow.

4.0 Trail fords Cedar Creek and peters out.

69 THE BENCH TRAIL

General description: A long day hike through forest and clearcuts along the south wall of Shell Canyon, 10 miles.
Difficulty: Moderate (east to west); moderately strenuous (west to east).
Route finding: No problem.
Best season: Mid-June to mid-October.

Visitation: Light.
Elevation gain: 460 feet.
Elevation loss: 3,140 feet.
Maximum elevation: 7,720 feet.
Topo maps: Shell Falls, Black Mountain.
Jurisdiction: Bighorn National Forest (Medicine Wheel Ranger District).

FINDING THE TRAILHEAD

Drive east from Shell on US Highway 14 to mile 31.3. Turn right on FR 17 and follow this trunk road 2.8 miles to the Ranger Creek Campground. Drive into the campground and take the first left to reach the trailhead GPS: 44.545504° N, 107.500548° W. The trail ends at the Post Creek day-use area at mile 22.8 on US 14 GPS 44.579046° N, 107.675237° W.

THE HIKE

This trail offers a day trip down the shady north-facing wall of Shell Canyon. The climax forest of Douglas fir and spruce blocks out the distant views over parts of the trail's length, although there are two major logging cuts along the way that offer canyon vistas. The trail is popular with the mountain biking set; be prepared to meet them along the way. Surface water is hard to find here, so you will need to bring a plentiful supply.

The hike begins in a shady woodland of spruce and lodgepole pine, staying below a closed road and close to the bottoms of Shell Creek. A mountain pine beetle outbreak in the 2000s claimed a number of the lodgepole pines here, accelerating forest succession toward late-successional spruce and fir, which tends to be less fire-prone than lodgepole. A spur trail joins in at the Shell Creek campground, and just beyond the junction the path crosses through a sun-dappled woodland of aspen. A rail fence soon delineates a leased parcel of land, and the trail passes a summer cabin before entering the first of two vast clearcuts. Here all but a few commercially useless trees have been cut down and carried away, a "selective cut" that is better than a clearcut from an ecological standpoint, but not by much. The result of this salvage logging of beetle-killed pines has been to set back forest recovery to a much greater extent than if the beetle-thinned forest had been left alone.

The trail continues its gentle descent, but now the valley floor falls away and the trail traverses steep slopes. It works its way along terraces and through wooded pockets as the descent quickens. The lodgepole pines are gradually replaced by Douglas fir, more tolerant of shade and resistant to drought. As the path draws even with Granite Creek, it crosses an open hillside where the timber was swept aside by a devastating tornado in 1959. The tornado roared down from the ridge above, wreaking a path of destruction all the way to Granite Creek. From here, an interpretive sign points out that the slopes to the west of Granite Creek were burned by sheep men in 1897 or 1898 to create more pasture for their flocks.

The trail soon returns to the timber, descending at a steady clip. It emerges in an arid meadow that occupies a protected pocket, then drops along the crest of a finger ridge

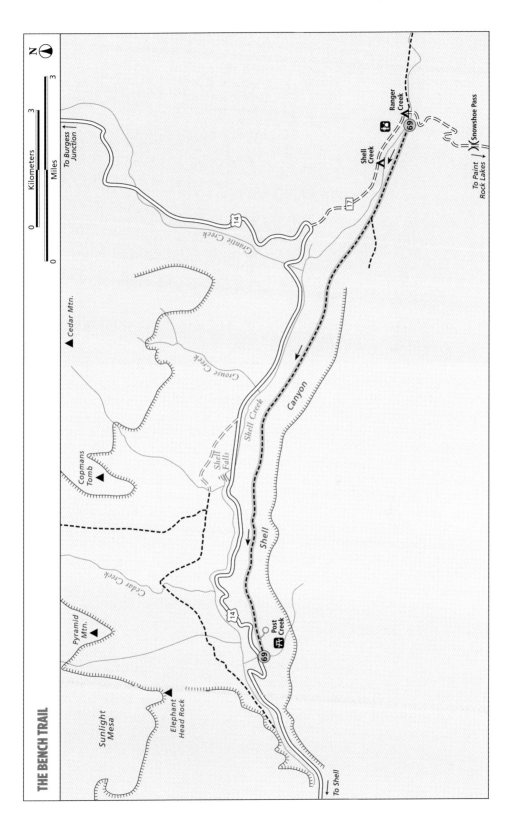

THE BENCH TRAIL

N

Kilometers
0   3

Miles
0   3

To Burgess
Junction

Cedar Mtn.

Granite Creek

14

Grouse Creek

Copmans
Tomb

Shell
Falls

Shell Creek

Shell

Canyon

Cedar Creek

Pyramid
Mtn.

Sunlight
Mesa

Elephant
Head Rock

14

Post
Creek

69

To Shell

17

Shell
Creek

Ranger
Creek

69

To Paint
Rock Lakes

Snowshoe Pass

Copmans Tomb.

that allows glimpses of Copmans Tomb across the valley. Watch for enormous boulders of limestone that have fallen into the forest from the cliffs above. The path next emerges from the timber on a grassy bald, cleared of trees by a fire in 1984. The fire was ignited by irresponsible visitors who were setting off illegal fireworks; the blaze quickly spread upslope from the highway to reach the ridgetop. Views across the valley now include the pale cliffs of Copmans Tomb, with the rugged façade of Pyramid Peak to the left of it and Sunlight Mesa farthest west.

The trail climbs and falls as it crosses the burn, then descends onto arid slopes where a steppe grassland is studded with sagebrush and juniper. Views now encompass the rugged lower reaches of Shell Canyon and the granite inner gorge below. A broad sweep of the Bighorn Basin stretches to the west with the jagged jawbone of the Absaroka Range rising from the western horizon. The trail drops steadily across open country, finally reaching the highway at a brilliant green oasis where the springs of Post Creek feed lush grasses and tall cottonwoods.

MILES AND DIRECTIONS

- **0.0** Trailhead in Ranger Creek campground.
- **1.0** Trail passes Shell Creek campground.
- **1.5** Trail passes privately leased cabin and enters first major logging area.
- **2.3** Junction with spur to the top of Lake Ridge. Stay right.
- **6.0** Tornado site.
- **8.0** Trail crosses 1984 fire site.
- **10.0** Trail emerges at Post Creek day-use area.

70 TRAPPER CANYON

General description: A challenging wilderness route down a remote canyon, 9.1 miles one way.
Difficulty: Strenuous.
Route finding: Map and compass.
Best season: Early September to late October.
Visitation: Very light.

Elevation loss: 2,730 feet.
Maximum elevation: 7,330 feet.
Topo maps: Black Mountain, Bush Butte, White Sulphur Spring.
Jurisdiction: Trapper Canyon Wilderness Study Area (BLM, Worland District).

FINDING THE TRAILHEAD

From the south end of Shell, follow the paved Trapper Creek Road. The pavement ends after 3 miles; bear right at the split and follow a primitive road around the irrigated fields of the Hunter Ranch. Turn left atop the next rise, and either park here and walk or drive the primitive, steep, and rocky track that runs eastward, climbing to reach a gate above the Dry Trapper watershed about 9 miles above the junction GPS: 44.496359° N, 107.711332° W. Upper GPS: 44.447913° N, 107.564759° W.

THE HIKE

Trapper Canyon is the wildest and most remote of the major canyons at the western edge of the Bighorn Mountains. Here, the thousand-foot walls stretch for 10 miles or more, guarding a seldom-breached fastness that harbors one of the most rich and diverse riparian communities in Wyoming. However, for the lure of the solitude, wildlife, grandeur, and burgeoning populations of native trout, there is a stiff price to be paid: The canyon is guarded by choking vines and brambles, rockfalls, rattlesnakes, stinging nettles, loose talus, and countless other obstacles. Not only is this wilderness travel, it is travel through a hostile wilderness, and all the skills and experience in the world won't make it an easy trip. Plan on at least two days to hike down through the canyon, plus a third day if you park at the lower end and hike up the road to start the trip. Visitors must obtain prior permission from the Hunter Ranch to cross private lands at the mouth of the canyon.

For those who hike the access road, the crossing of the Bush Creek wash leads to a steep climb through a desert scrub of rabbitbrush and prickly pear. The ascent eases as the road reaches the rolling grasslands of the uplands. The first canyon views are at mile 4.0, as the road crosses a parcel of private land. The track then passes behind the tree-clad summit of Bush Butte before ascending the ridgeline behind it. Follow the road for 9.2 miles total to reach a fence gate on the ridgetop. This marks the drop-in point to a valley known locally as "Dry Trapper Creek" and the beginning of the wilderness route.

Angle downstream as you descend into this tributary canyon, descending through the Douglas firs to avoid a beetle-killed and brushy area farther east. Upon reaching the bottomlands, you can either hike the streamcourse or try the wooded slopes that face north or the grassy, south-facing exposures. Whatever your choice, it will eventually become necessary to descend to the streambed to avoid the cliffs that guard the lower reaches of the valley. Here, you must tangle with the thorny brush and stinging nettles wherever boulders block the way. Take time to notice the astonishing diversity of butterflies and birds that call this canyon home.

Natural arch in Trapper Canyon.

After a difficult slog, Dry Trapper joins the much larger declivity of Trapper Canyon itself. There is a camp spot at the confluence; good camping spots will be found wherever tributary canyons join the main chasm. The slopes to the south of Trapper Creek are timbered in Douglas fir, while those to the north are open and arid. The stream is clogged with a tangle of brush, featuring thorns and stinging nettles. Pick your poison: cliffs and downed logs on the timbered slopes, rattlesnakes and rockfalls on the open exposures. Changing your mind is expensive here, with each trip through the riparian wall of thorn scrub a tedious and time-consuming battle.

In the initial stretch of Trapper Canyon, you can see a small arch up Dry Trapper as well as a much larger span down the main canyon. The big walls appear as you reach the first major side canyon on the north. In the heart of Trapper Canyon, the Douglas firs dwindle away, giving way to a scattered growth of mountain mahogany and other desert plants. A second, lower tier of cliffs now appears beside the creek, forcing additional stream crossings. After a short distance, the cliffs sink back into the valley floor, and for a time you will enjoy hassle-free traveling along grassy flats beside the creek.

Once you reach Spring Creek, a trail of sorts starts on the north side of the canyon floor and leads down past an overhanging cave. The neck-stretching walls run all the way to the mouth of the canyon. Here, they sink abruptly into the earth, and the bottoms are filled with a jungle-like growth of hardwoods and vines. The best course here is to splash down the shallow riffles until you reach the irrigation headgate, where you can pick up a dirt road for faster traveling across private land. Follow it to an intersection, then turn left and hike the jeep track up the wash of Bush Creek to intercept the original access road.

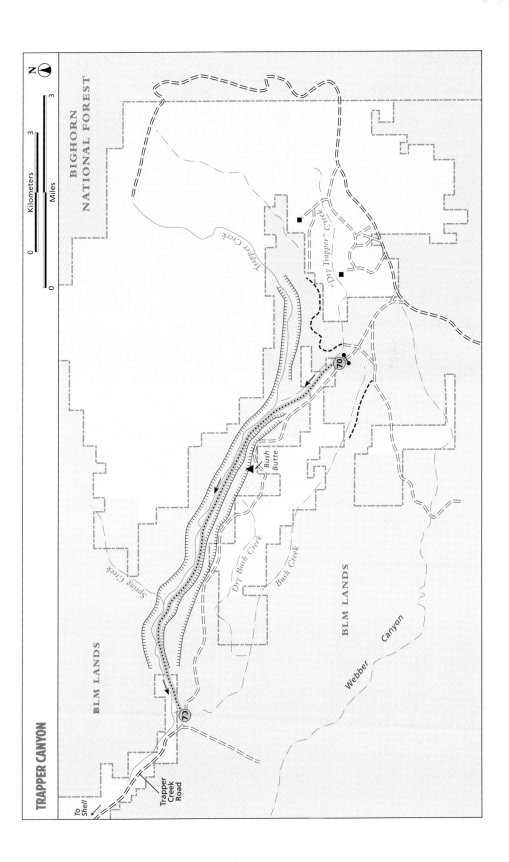

TRAPPER CANYON

BIGHORN NATIONAL FOREST

BLM LANDS

BLM LANDS

Trapper Creek

"Dry Trapper" Creek

Spring Creek

Dry Bush Creek

Bush Creek

Bush Butte

Webber Canyon

Trapper Creek Road

To Shell

N

Kilometers

0   3

Miles

0   3

70

73

Looking into Trapper Canyon from the south rim.

MILES AND DIRECTIONS

0.0 Route leaves jeep trail at fence gate. Angle west as you descend into "Dry Trapper" valley.

0.4 Route reaches bottoms of "Dry Trapper Creek."

1.2 Dry Trapper joins Trapper Creek in Trapper Canyon.

8.5 Irrigation headgate at mouth of Trapper Canyon. Hike west on road.

8.7 Turn left on jeep track heading south.

9.1 Jeep track meets Trapper Canyon road beside wash of Bush Creek.

71 ALKALI CREEK CANYON

General description: A wilderness route into a sandstone canyon, 1.7 miles.
Difficulty: Moderate.
Route finding: Map and compass.
Best season: Mid-April to late June; mid-September to early October.

Visitation: Light.
Elevation gain: 550 feet.
Maximum elevation: 5,500 feet.
Topo maps: Bush Butte, Hyatt Ranch.
Jurisdiction: Alkali Creek Wilderness Study Area (BLM, Worland District).

FINDING THE TRAILHEAD

Take Wyoming 31 to the Alkali Road, just west of Hyattville. This road is only paved for the first 0.2 mile, beyond which it becomes a fair-weather trunk road. Follow it 8 miles to Alkali Flats, then turn left onto a jeep road that runs northwest. After 0.3 mile, the jeep trail forks; park here and hike up the right-hand fork. GPS: 44.346383° N, 107.603751° W.

THE HIKE

The headwaters of Alkali Creek are made up of a maze of finger canyons and slickrock badlands carved into an upthrust layer of Tensleep sandstone. The desert scrub community, combined with the beauty of the slickrock canyons, create a landscape that is reminiscent of the Grand Staircase country of southern Utah. The route described here

The slickrock canyons of Alkali Creek.

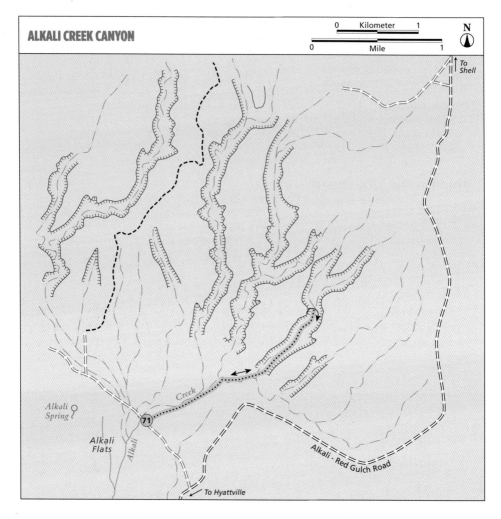

0   Kilometer   1

0   Mile   1

N

To
Shell

Alkali
Spring

71

Alkali
Flats

Creek

Alkali

Alkali - Red Gulch Road

To Hyattville

is only one of countless possible routes that follow canyons or ledges through this BLM Wilderness Study Area.

To begin the hike, follow the unsanctioned jeep trail northward through the sage and rabbitbrush of Alkali Flats. This low basin is rimmed to the south and west by red buttes of Chugwater sandstone. Straight ahead, the many branches of Alkali Creek have carved deep canyons into the upthrust strata of the Tensleep formation. The flats narrow to level benches beside the wash as the route enters the folds of the hills. Ignore the side canyons as the main streamcourse trends north-northeast into the heart of the hills.

Sedimentary walls soon slant upward beside the streamcourse, ranged in three tiers that form the canyon. Above it all are massive *klippes* of Tensleep sandstone, carved into eerie shapes by wind and rain. Initially, game trails provide easy traveling beside the wash, but as the walls close in, it becomes necessary to drop into the dry streamcourse.

After a brief journey across the slickrock streambed, the route encounters a stretch of stream where water is often found at the surface. Lush swards of grass grow on the sandy bars beside the water. Elsewhere in the bottoms, a growth of tall cottonwoods

and broadleaf shrubs create in this hidden garden a cool and protected woodland. Near the head of the canyon is a major confluence; travel becomes quite difficult beyond this point. Turn around and retrace your steps to complete the hike.

MILES AND DIRECTIONS

0.0   Starting point. Hike north on unsanctioned jeep track.

0.7   Route enters mouth of canyon.

1.7   Hike ends at forks in canyon.

72 MEYERS SPRING DRAW

General description: A wilderness loop route through sandstone badlands, 2.5 miles overall.
Difficulty: Moderate.
Route finding: Map and compass.
Best season: Early May to late June; early September to early October.

Visitation: Light.
Elevation gain: 400 feet.
Elevation loss: 400 feet.
Maximum elevation: 6,100 feet (starting point).
Topo map: Hyatt Ranch.
Jurisdiction: BLM (Worland District).

FINDING THE TRAILHEAD

Take Wyoming 31 to the Alkali Road, just west of Hyattville. This road is only paved for the first 0.2 mile, beyond which it becomes a fair-weather trunk road. Follow it 8 miles to Alkali Flats, after which it starts to climb. As the road bends north, a jeep track leads eastward. Park 0.2 mile beyond the jeep track on the main road. GPS: 44.366637° N, 107.561494° W.

THE HIKE

Meyers Spring Draw is a shallow valley in the midst of a surreal landscape of low cliffs and hoodoos. The route described here makes a short loop trip through the heart of the badlands, and it can easily be navigated in half a day of hiking.

To begin the trek, follow a faint jeep track down to the rim of the sagebrush escarpment. From this point, views extend across the first basin to the low, cross-bedded cliffs

Meyers Spring Draw

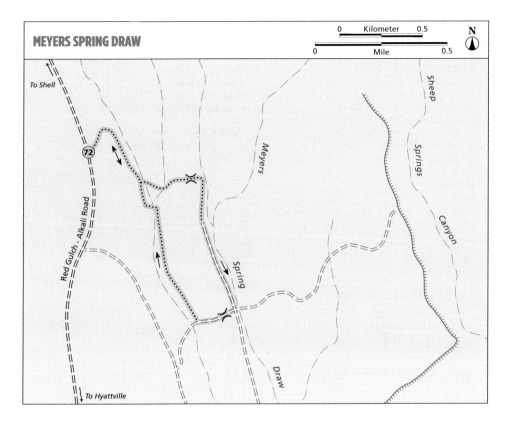

and hoodoos beyond. Follow a game trail down through the rock strata to reach the floor of the basin. Here, the juniper scrub was burned in 1997. Follow the watercourse downward, past the first rock mesa to the east. As you round the lower end of this mesa, look to the southeast to identify a low gap in the next line of cliffs. Make for this gap and seek out the passageway through the slickrock that leads to the narrow valley known as Meyers Spring Draw.

Hike down the draw through burned-over scrub and tortured rock to reach a jeep trail. Follow the jeep track southward as it climbs lazily to reach a saddle to the west of Meyers Spring Draw. Several jeep trails converge at this spot; to complete the trek, follow the one that leads westward. It crosses the sagebrush flats that fill the lower end of the first draw, then climbs to reach the top of the escarpment 0.7 mile south of the starting point. At the top of the grade, abandon the jeep road and hike along the edge of the escarpment for a spectacular aerial perspective on the badlands of Meyers Spring Draw.

MILES AND DIRECTIONS

0.0   Starting point. Hike to edge of escarpment and descend eastward.

0.2   Floor of gulch. Follow it downward.

0.5   Confluence of two washes. Hike east into saddle.

0.7   Route crosses saddle to enter Meyers Spring Draw. Hike downstream.

0.9   Route strikes jeep track. Follow it south.

Looking down into the grassy bottoms of Meyers Spring Draw.

1.2 Road junction in low saddle. Follow road westward.

1.6 Trail begins ascent of escarpment.

1.8 Top of grade. Hike north along top of escarpment.

2.5 Route returns to starting point.

73 DRY MEDICINE LODGE CREEK

General description: A wilderness day trip up an abandoned road that follows Dry Medicine Lodge Canyon, 5.6 miles one way.
Difficulty: Moderately strenuous.
Route finding: Some challenges.

Best season: Mid-June to mid-November.
Visitation: Light.
Elevation gain: 1,730 feet.
Maximum elevation: 6,950 feet.
Topo maps: Allen Draw, Hyatt Ranch.
Jurisdiction: BLM (Worland District).

FINDING THE TRAILHEAD

Drive east from Manderson on Wyoming 31. After 22 miles, turn left on the Alkali-Cold Springs Road. Turn right after 0.3 mile on Cold Springs Road. Follow the signs for the Medicine Lodge Archaeological Site, following farm roads through hayfields and then through the campground to reach the pictograph site GPS: 44.298221° N, 107.541823° W. From here, drive north up the jeep track that runs through the parking lot and up the canyon for 3 miles. Park at the spot where the road begins its climb out of the canyon GPS: 44.338717° N, 107.544816° W. End of hike GPS: 44.402619° N, 107.498371° W.

THE HIKE

This route follows an abandoned roadbed through the bottoms of a spectacular canyon. All of the bridges have long since washed out, and the roadbed is choked with fallen rocks in some places and thickets of brush and brambles in others. All in all, though, the old road provides speedy traveling through an otherwise wild and remote stretch of country.

At the outset, the old roadway follows the course of Dry Medicine Lodge Creek between low walls of brittle rock. Early on, a lush growth of cottonwood, box elder, and other canyon hardwoods crowds the dry wash of the creek. The walls soon rise to impressive heights as the canyon cuts into the western slope of the Bighorns. Just below the mouth of Sheep Springs Canyon, watch for the Arch, an enormous natural bridge that graces the western wall of the canyon. The Sheep Springs wash then enters the main canyon through a narrow rift flanked by vertical spires of stone.

Above this point, the canyon offers grassy traveling accompanied by orderly ranks of cliffs rising to either side. As the walls devolve into a series of solitary spires, the traveling gets rougher, with a greater number of thickets and brambles to negotiate. Before long, the unbroken cliffs return. Watch the side canyons to the east, where the first Douglas firs break the tawny monotony of the desert scrub. The arid lower slopes of the canyon continue to bear a growth of mountain mahogany, although the waters of Dry Medicine Lodge Creek flow at the surface here. A number of shallow stream crossings bear the old road from one side of the creek to the other.

The Douglas fir forest ultimately extends all the way down to the canyon floor, and ahead the walls recede to reveal open sky. The traveling is easy once more as the roadbed rises to reach a grassy wide spot in the canyon where a substantial valley enters from the west. This meadow is a good turn-around point for day hikers. The roadbed continues to provide grassy walking as it continues up the canyon. Timbered slopes now rise to the right (east), while to the left are receding battlements of limestone. The trek ends at a

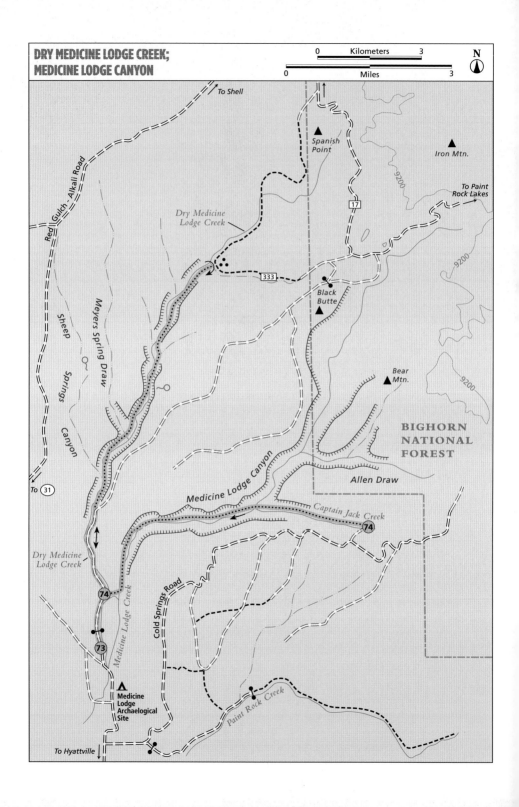

DRY MEDICINE LODGE CREEK;
MEDICINE LODGE CANYON

Kilometers   0   3
Miles   0   3

N

To Shell

Spanish
Point

Iron Mtn.

To Paint
Rock Lakes

9200

Red Gulch - Alkali Road

Dry Medicine
Lodge Creek

17

333

Black
Butte

9200

Sheep

Meyers Spring Draw

Springs

Bear
Mtn.

Canyon

BIGHORN
NATIONAL
FOREST

Allen Draw

9200

To 31

Medicine Lodge Canyon

Captain Jack Creek

74

Dry Medicine
Lodge Creek

74

Cold Springs Road

Medicine Lodge Creek

73

Medicine
Lodge
Archaeological
Site

Paint Rock Creek

To Hyattville

Natural bridge in the canyon of Dry Medicine Lodge Creek.

crude cabin on a tributary stream that enters the canyon from the east; the grassy roadbed that stretches ahead is now an extension of the Spanish Point Road (FR 333).

MILES AND DIRECTIONS

0.0   Start of hike. Follow old roadbed up canyon bottoms.

0.1   Roadbed crosses to west side of streambed.

1.3   The Arch.

1.5   Sheep Springs Canyon.

2.4   First of many stream crossings.

5.6   Hike ends at old shack. Junction with FR 333.

74 MEDICINE LODGE CANYON

See map on page 250.
General description: A wilderness route down Medicine Lodge Canyon, 6.4 miles.
Difficulty: Moderately strenuous.
Route finding: Map and compass.
Best season: Mid-June to mid-October.

Visitation: Very light.
Elevation gain: 150 feet.
Elevation loss: 2,850 feet.
Maximum elevation: 7,700 feet.
Topo maps: Allen Draw, Hyatt Ranch.
Jurisdiction: Medicine Lodge Wilderness Study Area (BLM, Worland District).

FINDING THE TRAILHEAD

Drive east from Manderson on Wyoming 31. After 22 miles, turn left on the Alkali-Cold Springs Road. Turn right after 0.3 mile on Cold Springs Road. The pavement ends just beyond the cutoff to the Medicine Lodge Archaeological Site. Follow the main road, which climbs into the hills for 9.6 miles to reach a jeep road that runs north just before the main road makes a major swing to the south. This jeep road marks the hike's beginning GPS: 44.329104° N, 107.447854° W. The trek ends 1 mile up the Dry Medicine Lodge Road from the Medicine Lodge pictograph site GPS: 44.298221° N, 107.541823° W; page 266, *Dry Medicine Lodge Creek.*

THE HIKE

This route penetrates one of the major western canyons in the Bighorn Mountains, traversing an area so wild and remote that the BLM has designated it a Wilderness Study Area. The canyon is a critical winter range for elk, and mule deer and even moose are occasionally sighted in the area. The canyon walls extend upstream to Black Butte, but the route described here covers only the more accessible lower reaches of the chasm in a convenient through-hike that can readily be completed in a single day.

From the starting point, follow the jeep trail north to the edge of the valley of Captain Jack Creek. The road soon descends gently toward the floor of this vale. After passing through a fence, follow the livestock trail that leads westward to the bottomlands. Here, lush swards of grass provide easy traveling, with slopes of Douglas fir to the south and outcrops of limestone to the north.

After 1.3 miles of easy traveling, the descent steepens and the route leads around a small, overhanging pour-off. Here, the cattle paths are replaced by elk trails. The cliffs rise in several tiers above Captain Jack Creek, which now flows at the surface. The creek bottoms are choked with brush and brambles, making for a laborious passage down the steep streamcourse. As the walls rise higher on both sides, the canyon of Captain Jack Creek joins with Medicine Lodge Canyon, and spectacular scenery unfolds ahead. Drift onto the slopes of mountain mahogany to the north of Captain Jack Creek, then work your way down the divide to reach the floor of Medicine Lodge Canyon.

The limestone walls of the canyon rise to staggering heights, and below them are steep slopes. Elk trails crisscross these slopes and can be followed for long stretches. Hike along the north-facing slopes of mountain mahogany or the south-facing slopes, which bear a sparse growth of grasses. The streamcourse is also a potential corridor for travel, but it is bordered by a dense tangle of brush and vines that is practically impenetrable. Select

a route and follow the canyon downward. Eventually the walls begin to dwindle, and it becomes possible to follow game trails along the grassy benches beside the stream.

As the canyon bends southward, watch for a rounded gap in the cliffs on the right (west) side of the canyon. Climb through this gap, which leads into the canyon of Dry Medicine Lodge Creek. Next, descend to the canyon floor to reach the jeep road on the far side of the wash. This road leads to the Medicine Lodge pictograph site after 1.3 miles.

MILES AND DIRECTIONS

0.0   Start of hike. Follow jeep track toward Captain Jack Creek.

0.3   Route leaves road at fence. Hike down to creek and follow it downward.

1.6   Streamcourse steepens markedly.

2.5   Route enters Medicine Lodge Canyon. Hike down the canyon.

6.0   Route begins ascent to saddle.

6.2   Route crosses saddle and enters canyon of Dry Medicine Lodge Creek.

6.4   Route intersects Dry Medicine Lodge Road.

THE PAINT ROCK BADLANDS

General description: A wilderness loop route through the sandstone badlands east of Medicine Lodge Creek, 2.7 miles overall.
Difficulty: Moderate.
Route finding: Map and compass.
Best season: Late March to mid-June; early September to mid-November.

Visitation: Light.
Elevation gain: 510 feet.
Elevation loss: 510 feet.
Maximum elevation: 5,380 feet.
Topo map: Hyatt Ranch.
Jurisdiction: BLM (Worland District).

FINDING THE TRAILHEAD

Drive east from Manderson on Wyoming 31. After 22 miles, turn left on the Alkali-Cold Springs Road. Turn right after 0.3 mile on Cold Springs Road. The pavement ends just beyond the cutoff to the Medicine Lodge Archaeological Site. Follow the main road, which climbs into the hills. Drive 0.5 mile past the Paint Rock Canyon Trailhead, and park at the spot where the road swings east of a low hilltop. GPS: 44.287560° N, 107.520264° W.

The Paint Rock Badlands.

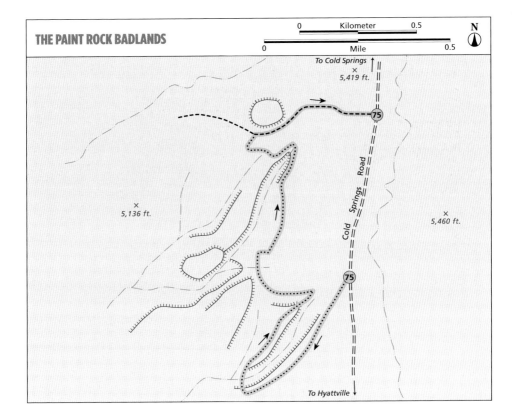

THE PAINT ROCK BADLANDS

0 Kilometer 0.5

0 Mile 0.5

N

To Cold Springs
× 5,419 ft.

75

Cold Springs Road

× 5,136 ft.

× 5,460 ft.

75

To Hyattville

THE HIKE

This wilderness route runs through the sandstone badlands north of Paint Rock Creek, visiting hoodoos, mushroom-shaped pedestal rocks, and miniature slickrock canyons of cross-bedded Tensleep sandstone. The vegetation found here is a juniper scrub accompanied by such arid-land plants as yucca, prickly pear cactus, and mountain mahogany. The soil in this area is extremely fragile. Called biological soil crust, it is infused with microscopic algae and fungi that help prevent erosion and build up soil nutrients needed by higher plants. Walk on bare rock and established game trails wherever possible.

From the starting point, follow the deer paths that run atop the south rim of a slickrock gulch. The caprock juts out over the gulch in some places, and in others it forms mushroom-shaped pedestals. Follow the gulch down to its mouth, where a sheer pouroff leads down into a deeper canyon. Cross the mouth of the original gulch and follow its north rim upward. The rims ultimately lead to a peninsula of stone where the caprock devolves into wind-carved hoodoos. Descend into the sandy, juniper-filled basin to the north, then hike westward along the base of the cliffs.

Higher walls rise on the northwest side of the basin, and the route leads to the base of these walls. It then turns northeast, bearing toward the pastel-yellow mushroom rocks that crown the ridgetop straight ahead. As the route skirts the head of a forbidding cleft, a pale butte of solid sandstone rises to the west. The route now runs east-northeast, crossing burned-over sand hills as it follows the next wash upward. This gulch can be

Sandstone buttes in the Paint Rock badlands.

crossed near its head, and the route now follows a ledge westward and soon climbs to the ridgetop that bears the yellow mushrooms.

Skirt to the west of the first yellow hoodoo as the route rises to join an ATV track near the base of a large, red-topped butte. A short jaunt westward leads to the top of a yellow formation for superb views of the surrounding badlands, the verdant pastures along Medicine Lodge Creek, and the crimson buttes to the west. To complete the trek, follow the ATV track eastward to the saddle above the red-topped butte. It then makes a sandy climb to emerge on the Cold Springs Road 0.6 mile north of the starting point.

MILES AND DIRECTIONS

0.0 Starting point. Hike southwest along south rim of gulch.

0.5 Cross mouth of gulch and hike up north rim.

0.7 Route descends from rim into sandy basin. Hike west.

0.8 Route turns northeast to cross basin.

1.3 Route crosses wash and follows ledge westward.

1.5 Trail strikes unsanctioned ATV trail. Follow it to top of ridge.

1.6 ATV track turns east. Follow it.

2.1 Track meets Cold Springs road 0.6 mile north of starting point.

76 **PAINT ROCK CANYON**

General description: A backpack through Paint Rock Canyon to FR 349, 12.8 miles one way.
Difficulty: Moderate.
Route finding: No problem.
Best season: Late June to mid-September.
Visitation: Light.
Elevation gain: 2,570 feet.

Elevation loss: 500 feet.
Maximum elevation: 7,500 feet (end of trail).
Topo maps: Hyatt Ranch, Bush Butte.
Jurisdiction: BLM (Worland District), Bighorn National Forest (Buffalo Ranger District).

FINDING THE TRAILHEAD

Drive east from Manderson on Wyoming 31. After 22 miles, turn left on the Alkali-Cold Springs Road. Turn right after 0.3 mile on Cold Springs Road. The pavement ends just beyond the cutoff to the Medicine Lodge Archaeological Site. Follow the main road, which climbs into the hills to reach the well-marked trailhead on the left side of the road, 5.8 miles from the highway. GPS: 44.282644° N, 107.517958° W.

To reach the upper trailhead, follow the Cold Springs Road all the way to the crest of the range, about 15 miles. Turn right onto FR 352 and follow it for 0.6 mile. Turn left onto FR 349. Park at the top of the hill, or (if you have four-wheel drive) make the perilous descent of 3.2 miles to reach the bridge over North Paint Rock Creek. The end of the trail joins this road 0.2 mile beyond the bridge. GPS 44.332030° N, 107.381034° W.

THE HIKE

This trail follows Paint Rock Creek through its deep chasm, then climbs into a meadowy basin where it enters the Bighorn National Forest. The canyon was once considered for wilderness status and is a critical winter range for elk and deer. It is also considered to be rich in archaeological sites. Paint Rock Creek is a blue-ribbon trout stream. The lower reaches of the trail cross part of the Hyatt Ranch, and non-motorized access is allowed from May 11 to September 30. Be considerate as you cross these private lands, staying on the designated trails and roads and leaving all gates as you found them. This way, access to Paint Rock Canyon will remain open for future travelers.

The trek begins on low, arid hills covered in juniper scrub. As the path wanders down to cross the first wash, it enters an area that burned in 1996. After a short southwestward climb, the path descends into a second draw, this one untouched by fire. After crossing it, the trail follows the watercourse downward and soon drops into the lush, pastoral bottomlands of Paint Rock Creek.

The route now enters private land owned by the Hyatt Ranch and follows a dirt road past irrigated hayfields and verdant pastures. Rocky cliffs rise on both sides of the valley, low at first and then rising to great heights. As the valley constricts to form a narrow canyon, the trail returns to BLM lands. Motor vehicles are prohibited beyond this point.

The tall cliffs of limestone now rise above sagebrush slopes, and a verdant ribbon of cottonwood shades the stream banks. The green waters of Paint Rock Creek hurry downward through an endless series of riffles and pocket water. As the trail reaches the first big bend in the canyon, watch for a small natural arch high on the north rim.

Paint Rock Creek
above the canyon.

PAINT ROCK CANYON

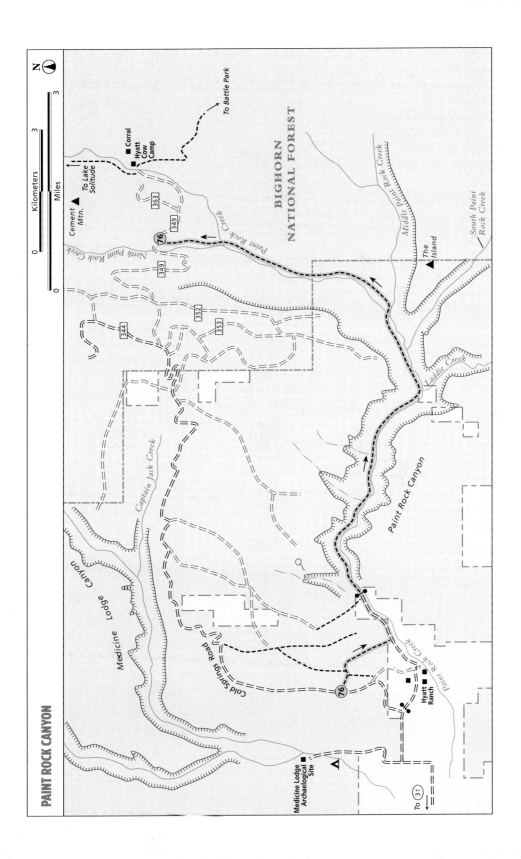

Douglas firs now stud the north-facing slopes across the creek, and soon they rise along the streamcourse as well. The canyon walls maintain an impressive height as the trail continues eastward, climbing at a modest pace. The old road crosses a small tract of private land at the mouth of Laddie Creek; here, the south walls of the canyon are robed in a climax forest of Douglas fir.

As the trail continues upward, it enters a broad, grassy basin guarded by the Island, a sphinx-like butte that rises between South and Middle Paint Rock Creeks. Upon reaching a fence, follow it downward to reach the gate at a section corner. Pass through the gate and continue eastward beside the tumultuous, boulder-choked rapids of Paint Rock Creek. A grove of mature aspen grows at the confluence of Middle Paint Rock Creek and the main fork. Here, the trail crosses a sturdy bridge over the main fork and climbs through the muddy seeps of the main fork.

The next part of the journey crosses open sage meadows, following the great northward bend of Paint Rock Creek as the canyon falls behind. Now a pack trail, the route dips into the bottoms, then rises again to cross a long flat beneath a timbered mesa. At the far edge of the clearing, the trail leaves BLM land and enters the Bighorn National Forest.

It now becomes an ATV trail, which winds gently upward across open benches. The streamside woodland now takes on a montane character, with spruce and lodgepole pine replacing the cottonwoods of the lower elevations. At the confluence of the main fork and North Paint Rock Creek, the trail crosses a bridge over the main fork and follows North Paint Rock Creek. On the far side, a sustained climb leads up to gentler country where tawny grasslands stretch eastward from the stream. The trail emerges onto FR 349 at a ragged grove of aspen, marking the end of the trek.

MILES AND DIRECTIONS

0.0   Paint Rock Canyon Trailhead.

2.0   Trail reaches Hyatt Ranch road. Turn left and follow road east.

3.2   Road enters BLM land. No motor vehicles beyond this point.

7.1   Trail passes mouth of Laddie Creek.

7.3   Head of Paint Rock Canyon.

8.5   Bridge over Paint Rock Creek. Old road ends. Follow trail north along main fork of Paint Rock Creek.

9.9   Trail enters Bighorn National Forest.

11.5   Bridge over main fork of Paint Rock Creek. Trail now parallels North Paint Rock Creek.

12.8   Trail joins FR 349.

77 THE SALT TROUGH-CENTER CANYON LOOP

General description: A wilderness loop route through the canyons of upper Brokenback Creek, 7.4 miles overall. **Difficulty:** Moderate. **Route finding:** Map and compass. **Best season:** Mid-June to early October. **Visitation:** Light.	**Elevation gain:** 1,440 feet. **Elevation loss:** 1,440 feet. **Maximum elevation:** 6,300 feet (starting point). **Topo map:** Pierce Draw. **Jurisdiction:** Wyoming Department of Game and Fish; BLM (Worland District).

FINDING THE TRAILHEAD

From Hyattville, drive south on Old Hyattville Road. After 0.8 mile, bear left onto the Hyattville Logging Road (BLM 1117). Follow this fair-weather trunk road 13 miles to reach a road marked "Renner Habitat Management Unit" at the lower edge of the trees. Turn right and follow this jeep track, staying with the lower road. After 1.3 miles, bear left, following the arrows around a parcel of private land. Some 1.4 miles farther the road dips into a draw and then ascends into a grassy saddle. Park here to begin the loop. GPS: 44.146506° N, 107.438960° W.

THE HIKE

This loop route begins in the high meadows of the Renner Wildlife Management Unit, and it follows a series of minor canyons into the arid scrub at the foot of the mountains. The upper reaches of Salt Trough are winter range for elk and deer, but these animals migrate to higher elevations during the summer. The area is popular with hunters and is best avoided during rifle season.

From the grassy saddle that marks the start of the hike, walk westward along the jeep trail that wanders down across grassy slopes. As the road nears a side gulch of Salt Trough, watch for the more direct livestock trail that will carry you to the floor of the canyon. The route now turns south, following Salt Trough down amid grassy canyon bottoms guarded by the cross-bedded walls of the Tensleep formation. It soon reaches the ruins of an old cabin beside a reliable spring. This spring is the source of the North Fork of Brokenback Creek. After crossing a rail fence, follow game trails for easy traveling along the sagebrush slopes to the east of the stream.

Salt Trough is a pleasant canyon that descends moderately through juniper hill country and is guarded to the west by Tensleep rimrock. At the confluence with Center Canyon, the stock trails cross to the western side of the stream. As the canyon devolves into arid hills, the trail returns to the east bank and soon climbs steadily to reach a gap in the hills. Wander westward to the rims for a superb view down the newly deepened canyon, now guarded by impressive walls of sculpted stone. A good cattle-drive trail leads through a gate to cross a tributary draw, then climbs again to stay above the eastern rim of the canyon.

After a short distance, the path descends into the bottoms once more. Although the trail is well-beaten here, expect brushy traveling in spots as the bottomlands are choked with cottonwood, brush, and vines. Before long, the brush gives way to sage-clad benches

In the heart of Salt Trough.

that flank either side of the streamcourse, and the traveling is easy as the canyon walls begin to dwindle away. The stream ultimately enters a basin flanked with gentle, arid hills, and a fence marks the end of public land. Turn around here and retrace your steps to the confluence of Salt Trough and Center Canyon.

Back at the confluence, hike up the more easterly cleft, which is Center Canyon. At first there is a good livestock trail that ascends vigorously through the canyon. Steep hills surround the watercourse, and the path climbs to avoid a bedrock sill that is transformed into a picturesque waterfall when it rains. As a side gulch enters from the east, the stock trail climbs away to the right. Stay with the main course of Center Canyon, following game trails through rugged country. Eventually it will be advantageous to ascend onto the slopes to the east, and soon the route enters a burn that dates from 1996. As two rocky buttes rise on either side of the canyon, descend to the grassy bottoms and follow them to the fence that marks the south boundary of the Renner Wildlife Management Unit. The rock strata soon submerge beneath grassy hills, and the route strikes the original road just east of the starting point.

MILES AND DIRECTIONS

0.0 Saddle between Salt Trough and Center Canyon drainages. Hike west on road.

0.3 Cattle trail leaves road. Follow it to floor of Salt Trough.

1.0 Spring and cabin ruins. Route leaves Renner Wildlife Management Unit.

2.1 Mouth of Center Canyon. Continue down Salt Trough.

2.4 Trail climbs away to left (east). Follow it upward.

THE SALT TROUGH–CENTER CANYON LOOP

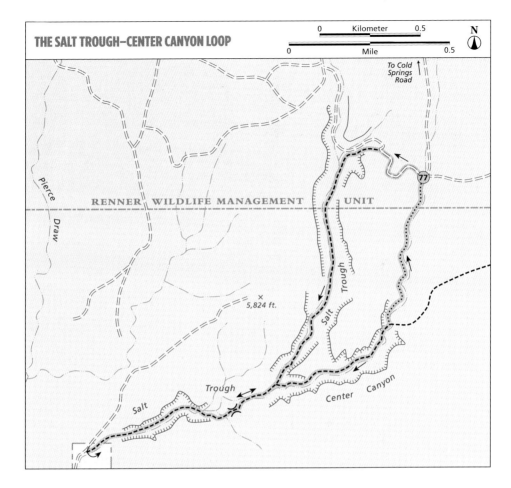

2.8   Trail returns to bottoms of Salt Trough.

3.6   End of route. Turn around and return to Center Canyon.

5.1   Confluence of Center Canyon and Salt Trough. Hike up Center Canyon.

6.1   Confluence of draws. Trail climbs away. Continue up Center Canyon.

7.0   Route returns to Renner Wildlife Management Unit.

7.2   Route returns to original road 0.2 mile east of starting point.

78 RED BUTTES

General description: A wilderness route through the foothills country of the Double-H Ranch, 7.2 miles overall.	**Elevation gain:** 1,130 feet.
	Elevation loss: 1,130 feet.
	Maximum elevation: 5,250 feet.
	Topo map: Big Trails.
Difficulty: Moderate.	**Jurisdiction:** Double-H Ranch
Route finding: Map and compass.	Coordinated Management
Best season: Late March to mid-June; early September to early October.	Area (private and public lands administered by the BLM, Worland District).
Visitation: Light.	

FINDING THE TRAILHEAD

From Tensleep, drive south on Wyoming 434 for 21 miles. As the pavement ends, turn left on the Big Trails Stock Drive Road (Dry Farm Road). Take an immediate left on the Spring Creek Road, and follow it 3.7 miles to a road junction in a low pass. Park on the road to the right to begin the hike. GPS: 43.820676° N, 107.300015° W.

THE HIKE

This route follows abandoned roads and natural landmarks to make a nice day loop through the Double-H Ranch, a foothills landscape dominated by red buttes of the Chugwater sandstone. This ranch is part of an area in which the BLM manages access to a combination of public and private land to allow public recreation. If you plan to stay overnight, we recommend that you study the land ownership maps and camp exclusively on BLM lands. Leave all gates as you found them, and do not disturb the cattle that sometimes graze here. Perhaps if we can all make public access to these private lands a pleasant experience for the landowner, the BLM's coordinated management program will get a boost of good publicity, and other lands may open to public access.

The trek begins on a dirt road that runs northwest from the high saddle that marks the divide between Red Gulch and the Crooked Creek watershed. The road dips down to cross the sagebrush basin of Red Gulch, then rises toward the base of an imposing butte of crimson sandstone. Rusting, antiquated farming equipment marks the ruins of an old ranch. Here, the main road swings north and descends along Red Gulch, while our route follows the abandoned jeep trail that starts on the south side of the ruins and glides up into a saddle.

After cresting the divide, the track descends along the valley beyond, which is guarded by a juniper-clad scarp to the west and by sagebrush slopes to the east. The track passes a redrock knob and crosses the floor of the valley. It then makes its way along slopes covered in juniper scrub. Eroded hills of red clay stretch northward to Otter Creek and beyond. The jeep trail ultimately rises to the top of the escarpment, and from the heights views stretch northward to the lofty summits of the Cloud Peak Wilderness. The road now descends along the ridgeline, and a gate marks the spot where it leaves the Double-H Ranch and enters BLM land.

The road splits at the base of the next high point; from this junction, follow a stock trail southwest as it descends a finger ridge to reach the floor of a broad basin. Once on

Slickrock country along
the Red Buttes route.

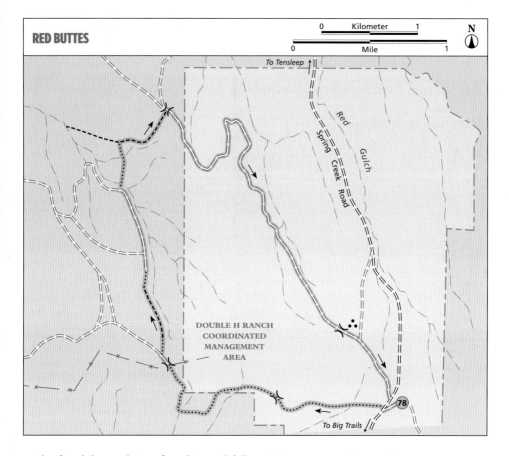

the flats, hike south to a fenceline and follow it to a gate near the marshy streamcourse that drains this rather drab little valley. After passing through, cross the gulch and climb to meet a jeep track on the far side. Follow this road southward as it ascends gradually through the grasses and sagebrush. The jeep road ultimately turns west; continue straight ahead on a lesser track that soon becomes an old stock trail. It heads for the low gap at the head of the drainage, meeting another primitive road along the way. Follow this road to a gate that leads to the pass; beyond this point, it is safe to assume that you are crossing Double-H property.

Beyond the divide, a steep ravine leads down through eroded badlands of pink and red. Stick to the ridge to the right (west) of this ravine, descending below its crest at first and then atop the ridgeline. At the bottom of the grade, turn east to ascend a grassy draw, which leads to a saddle beneath a crimson knob. After passing through, you will find yourself above a beautiful canyon where grassy bottoms are guarded by wind-sculpted walls of red slickrock. Traverse northward along game trails, staying above the rim until a side draw offers a safe route to the bottoms. Next, hike up the canyon, passing gracefully curved walls of stone.

A stock path soon leads to a sliding-rail gate atop a windswept gap. After passing through, follow the trail to reach the next wash, then hike cross-country on an eastward heading. The final leg of the trek traverses grassy hills beneath a massive butte of red

Among the Red Buttes.

stone. Look back for final views of the badlands as the route crosses the sage-juniper steppe, ascending to reach the Spring Creek Road close to the starting point.

MILES AND DIRECTIONS

0.0 Starting point on Spring Creek Road. Hike northwest on dirt road.

0.4 Old homestead. Turn left onto jeep trail.

0.5 Track crosses ridgetop saddle.

2.3 Track reaches top of escarpment.

2.9 Road leaves Double-H Ranch and enters BLM land.

3.2 Road junction in low saddle. Turn left (southwest) onto stock trail.

4.0 Route crosses streamcourse. Follow jeep track southward.

5.3 Saddle at head of valley. Route returns to Double-H Ranch. Follow ridgetop downward.

5.6 Route crosses streamcourse and turns east up draw.

5.8 Route crosses saddle. Traverse north above canyon rim.

6.1 Route reaches floor of canyon.

6.3 Trail crosses saddle and leaves canyon behind. Continue east.

7.2 Route returns to starting point.

ADDITIONAL TRAILS

A nature trail makes a short loop hike to a pretty waterfall just above **Five Springs Campground**.

White Canyon is reputed to be a good hiking destination for off-trail exploration, but the direct access is blocked by private land and the indirect route is virtually impassable, even to four-wheel-drive vehicles.

Brokenback Canyon is extremely rough and brushy in its upper reaches, and this hike is strictly for the hard-core masochist.

EXTENDED TRIPS

Although most of the backcountry of the Bighorn Mountains can be accessed in a single day of hiking, there are several spots where one can hike for long distances without ever encountering a road. The routes described here combine several featured trails from the main body of this book. Refer to individual trail descriptions for more detailed information on each trail segment. Do not forget that any trek that passes through any part of the Cloud Peak Wilderness will require a permit, which is available free of charge at ranger stations as well as self-registration boxes.

THE SOLITUDE TRAIL   ALLOW 8-14 DAYS

The granddaddy of trails in the Bighorn Mountains, this long loop was constructed in the 1920s. It can be reached from most trailheads surrounding the Cloud Peak Wilderness, but the shortest and most direct access is via the Hunter Trailhead. To begin, follow the routing for Florence Pass (Hike 8) to reach the scenic meadows of Trail Park beside North Clear Creek. Then follow the Ant Hill routing (Hike 9) northward across several divides to reach spectacular Elk Lake. From this point there are two options. The original Solitude Trail follows an ATV road down to Willow Park Reservoir and then on to Kearny Creek where it picks up a pack trail to Kearny Lakes Reservoir (see The Reservoirs, Hike 43). Hikers who are confident in their navigational skills will prefer the wilder and more scenic route via Flatiron Lake (Hike 42).

From the dam at the foot of Kearny Lake Reservoir, follow the road northeast for 0.2 mile to pick up the second trail that ascends to Highland Park (see The Lake Winnie Loop, Hike 39). A steady climb leads to the vast wet meadow of Highland Park, which enjoys a stunning backdrop of high peaks. Follow the Highland Park routing (Hike 38) along the east edge of the park, then across the heads of several valleys before the trail descends toward the head of Bighorn Reservoir. Just above the head of the reservoir, turn left onto a connecting trail that runs west to ford Cross Creek and then climbs over a low ridge to meet the Geneva Pass Trail (Hike 36) beside the East Fork of Big Goose Creek. The route follows this valley upward, passing Geneva Lake en route to a pass of the same name.

Entering the Paint Rock watershed, the trail descends along North Paint Rock Creek to meet the Cliff Lake Trail (Hike 26). Take extra time to explore the upper lake basin before proceeding down North Paint Rock Creek to Teepee Pole Flats. Here, the route follows the Poacher Lake segment (Hike 24) southward across wooded uplands and open fens to reach Paint Rock Creek. Turn east, following the Lake Solitude Trail (Hike 21) past the vast waters of Lake Solitude and into the alpine country at the head of the valley. A tundra-clad pass leads to Mistymoon Lake, which is often thronged with campers. Hike around the south shore of the lake to strike the Florence Pass Trail. Follow this trail past alpine lakes and over a high and rocky saddle to return to the North Clear Creek drainage. You can now follow North Clear Creek down through its spectacular valley to reach Soldier Park and Hunter Corrals.

THE GENEVA-EDELMAN LOOP   ALLOW 3-6 DAYS

This convenient loop follows good trails through the northern part of the Cloud Peak Wilderness, taking in two of the three high passes in the Bighorns as well as an assortment of high lakes. Start at Lower Paint Rock Lake, where the Cliff Lake Trail (Hike 26) runs eastward across the uplands. It soon seeks out North Paint Rock Creek and follows its grassy meadows up into the high country. At the head of the valley, choose to do some extra exploring in the alpine lake basin or proceed directly up the Geneva Pass Trail (Hike 36). After surmounting Geneva Pass, this trail leads into the Big Goose watershed. It passes tiny Crystal Lake and the fjord-like arm of Lake Geneva, then follows the East Fork of Big Goose Creek downward through a timbered valley where prospectors once tunneled for gold.

Just beyond the spur trail to Duncan Lake, turn left onto the Edelman Pass Trail (Hike 28). This trail runs up the valley of Edelman Creek, then crosses through Edelman Pass to reach the Lakes of the Rough. Hike across the outlet of Emerald Lake, then continue along the Edelman Trail as it climbs over a higher and tundra-clad saddle. The trail then leads down the valley of Medicine Lodge Creek. The valley soon opens out into broad grasslands, and the trail descends gradually to reach its end on FR 17. Hike south on this road for 1 mile, bearing left at major intersections, to return to the starting point at Lower Paint Rock Lake.

THE BATTLE PARK LOOP   ALLOW 3-5 DAYS

This route follows some of the more obscure trails through the rolling hills and grassy meadows along the western edge of the Cloud Peak Wilderness. Some of the trails are rather faint, putting a premium on cross-country navigation skills. This loop also makes a superb long day ride for horsemen.

To begin the loop, follow the Lake Solitude Trail (Hike 21) north from the Battle Park Trailhead. It crosses through Long Park and then climbs over the ridgetop to reach Grace Lake. The loop then enters the Cloud Peak Wilderness as it descends to Paint Rock Creek. Turn left to cross the creek, then take a right at the next junction as the loop follows the Poacher Lake Trail (Hike 24). This trail crosses wooded uplands and swamps, descending to North Paint Rock Creek at Teepee Pole Flats. Cross the creek and follow the Cliff Lake Trail (Hike 26) north and then west. It crosses timbered high country, then crosses vast meadows before reaching the eastern shore of Lower Paint Rock Lake.

Automobiles can be seen across the lake, but the loop turns left onto the Kinky White Trail (Hike 25). This path descends to cross Anthony Park, then rises to the edge of a scarp for sweeping views. It then descends to cross the valley of North Paint Rock Creek before seeking out a low gap that leads down to Paint Rock Creek. Turn right and follow the Paint Rock Creek Trail (Hike 23) for a short distance to reach the road. Ford the creek to Hyatt Cow Camp, then follow the Battle Park Trail (Hike 22) southward. This trail is rather faint in places as it makes its way across the valley of Long Park Creek and then up to the elevated grasslands of Battle Park. From here, it is only a short climb through the forest to reach the Battle Park Trailhead.

THE BIGHORN MOUNTAIN PASSAGE   ALLOW 6-10 DAYS

This point-to-point hike allows travelers to hike from the western edge of the Bighorn Mountains up and over the divide and down to the High Plains, almost entirely by trail. It is a strenuous journey, involving extremes of altitude and often temperature. Pick up permits for the Cloud Peak Wilderness at a ranger station before you set out.

Start out from the Cold Springs Road, where the Paint Rock Canyon Trail (Hike 76) runs eastward into the arid foothills. It soon seeks out Paint Rock Canyon and follows it (with fine angling opportunities) through the outer wall of the Bighorns. Above the canyon's head, the route enters a broad basin, where it continues to follow Paint Rock Creek upward. The trail ultimately plays out onto FR 349; turn right and follow the road for 0.5 mile to reach its end near the Hyatt Cow Camp. The route now follows the Paint Rock Creek Trail (Hike 23) into the higher, cooler country of the Cloud Peak Wilderness.

Follow the trail up the valley as it turns east, then continue up Paint Rock Creek on the Lake Solitude Trail (Hike 21). After passing Lake Solitude, this trail ascends into the upper reaches of the valley, where alpine tundra accompanies the hiker all the way to a high pass above Mistymoon Lake. Descend to the lake and hike around its south shore to strike the Florence Pass Trail (Hike 8). This trail leads eastward, climbing along a narrow vale that bears the Fortress Lakes en route to Florence Pass. The cold, deep waters of Florence Lake lie on the far side of the divide, and a rocky passage through barren country leads down the valley toward the lush meadows of North Clear Creek.

At Trail Park, turn left onto the Ant Hill Trail (Hike 9), which leads up across two lofty divides, crossing the subalpine basin of South Rock Creek en route to Elk Lake. There is a bit of a tricky spot here. Hike east from the lake toward the top of a scarp, watching for the faint path that will lead north to Gem Lake. This lake is the endpoint of the Middle Rock Creek Trail (Hike 47). Follow it eastward as it descends into the lodgepole pine forest, then follows Middle Rock Creek down to its confluence with the south fork.

Here, the route adopts the South Rock Creek Trail (Hike 46), which stays in the timbered bottoms for 1.5 miles, then climbs into the high grasslands of Firebox Park. From a signpost in the midst of the park, hike southeast across a grassy saddle to reach the Firebox Park Trail (Hike 45), which descends along North Sayles Creek and then travels through a brief but stunning gorge. The trail breaks out onto the High Plains in the Bud Love Wildlife Management Unit, where the hike reaches its terminus at a trailhead beside an old homestead.

THE MOUNTAIN PRAIRIE TREK   ALLOW 3-5 DAYS

This route runs along the open grasslands behind the range of sedimentary reefs that guards the eastern front of the Bighorn Mountains. To begin the trek, follow the Walker Prairie routing (Hike 48), which descends down the timbered valley of the East Fork of Big Goose Creek. There are several significant fords along the way, and adventurous souls can make a cross-country side trip to visit a major waterfall 0.7 mile downstream from the point where the trail leaves the East Fork. A jaunt over meadowy hilltops leads to an old jeep road that descends to the West Fork of Big Goose Creek.

After crossing a bridge, the trail climbs over a hilltop, then follows Prairie Creek down to Walker Prairie. The route leads north along the entire length of this great grassland, finally crossing a divide and descending to Wolf Creek. Follow the Wolf Creek Trail

(Hike 49) north and then east. Along the way, the Wolf Falls Trail (Hike 50) offers another fine side trip. Upon reaching Sibley Creek, follow the Horseshoe Mountain Trail (Hike 51) north as it crosses a number of grassy divides and runs through open vales guarded by massive reefs. Elephant Foot is visible early on, and later Horseshoe Mountain guards the protected grasslands. The hike ends at the Little Tongue River, where a two-rut road descends from US Highway 14.

THE LITTLE BIGHORN CIRCUIT ALLOW 3-6 DAYS

This route requires a 2-car shuttle and good trail-finding skills. It features the lost Palouse Prairie grasslands of Bull Elk Park, the scenic grandeur of the Little Bighorn Canyon, and the geological oddity known as Leaky Mountain, where a major stream cascades full-blown from the face of a blank cliff.

To begin, follow the Bull Elk Park Trail (Hike 63) down the wooded ridgetop to the vast meadow at its toe. Hike across the trackless expanse of Bull Elk Park, then follow the primitive track that runs northeast, ultimately making a steep descent to the Dry Fork of the Little Bighorn. One ford is required as the faint trail follows the river upward. After 9.3 miles, you will strike the Lake Creek Ridge Trail at the first tributary that enters from the north. Follow this trail up to an old cabin to reach the east end of the Dry Fork Ridge Trail (Hike 62).

Follow this trail westward across high benches, timbered on western exposures and sporting sagebrush meadows on slopes that face southeast. At the far end of the ridge, there are fine mountain views as the path descends northward through rolling uplands to reach the Little Bighorn River. After crossing the bridge, turn southwest on the Little Horn Trail (Hike 60), which passes scenic rapids beneath the towering walls of Little Bighorn Canyon. After passing through an inner gorge of granite, the trail wanders through the forest and ultimately breaks out into pocket meadows opposite the mouth of Taylor Creek.

Here, you have two choices: You can ford the Little Bighorn and follow the Little Big-horn Bench route (Hike 61) across elevated meadows, or continue along the Little Horn Trail, which crosses the more arid slopes to the west of the river. There are fine views of Leaky Mountain from both trails. Broad meadows await in the upper reaches of the valley, where the Little Bighorn heads south and the trails follow Baby Wagon Creek. The two trails converge again to follow Duncum Creek into a narrow, high valley full of pocket meadows. The route soon turns up a southern tributary and passes through a burn below Burnt Mountain, known for its unusual limestone formations. The hike ends up at the end of FR 135, beside the boundless meadows at the crest of the range.

APPENDIX: DIRECTORY OF LAND MANAGEMENT AGENCIES

Bighorn National Forest
2013 Eastside 2nd Street
Sheridan, WY 82801
(307) 674-2600

Powder River Ranger District
1415 Fort Street
Buffalo, WY 82834
(307) 684-7806

Medicine Wheel Ranger District
95 US Highway 16/20
Greybull, WY 82426
(307) 765-4435

Tongue Ranger District
2013 Eastside 2nd Street
Sheridan, WY 82801
(307) 674-2600

Bureau of Land Management
Worland District
101 S. 23rd Street
Worland, WY 82401
(307) 347-5100

Cody Field Office
1002 Blackburn
P.O. Box 518
Cody, WY 82414
(307) 578-5900

Wyoming Game and Fish Department
5400 Bishop Boulevard
Cheyenne, WY 82009
(800) 777-4600

955 Road 18
Lovell, WY 83431
(307) 548-7310

HIKE INDEX

ABOUT THE AUTHOR

Erik Molvar spends half of each year exploring wildlands in the West. He has hiked over 10,000 miles of trails, from the Arctic Ocean to the Mexican border including all of the trails and routes in this book. Erik has a Master's degree in wildlife management from the University of Alaska-Fairbanks, where he performed groundbreaking research on moose in Denali National Park. He currently serves as executive director for Western Watersheds Project, a nonprofit conservation group working to protect and restore watersheds and wildlife on public lands throughout the West.

Also by the Author:

Hiking Glacier and Waterton Lakes National Parks

Hiking Montana's Bob Marshall Wilderness

Hiking the North Cascades

Hiking Olympic National Park

Hiking Arizona's Cactus Country

Hiking Zion and Bryce Canyon National Parks

Alaska on Foot: Wilderness Techniques for the Far North

Hiking Colorado's Maroon Bells – Snowmass Wilderness